A PURELY AGRICULTUR

A PURELY AGRICULTURAL PARISH?

NAZEING BEFORE AND DURING THE GREAT WAR

DAVID PRACY

STATISTICS BY JACKY COOPER

David Pracy.

NAZEING HISTORY WORKSHOP

PUBLICATION NO. 6

2018

PREVIOUS PUBLICATIONS BY MEMBERS OF
NAZEING HISTORY WORKSHOP

Not a Better Set in the Country: the Story of Nazeing Wood or Park 1778-1950;
David Pracy, Nazeing Conservation Society, 1995.

Nazeing Bury: the Story of a House and Its People;
John H. Gervis, Nazeing Books, 1997.

Nonconformity in Nazeing: a History of the Congregational Church 1795-1995;
Norman Bonnett and Paddy Hutchings, the Authors, 1999.

Five Miles from Everywhere: the Story of Nazeing Part 1, from Earliest Times to 1914;
David Pracy and others, Nazeing History Workshop, 2000.

Seventeen Miles from Town: the Story of Nazeing Part 2, the Twentieth Century;
David Pracy and others, Nazeing History Workshop, 2002.

Copyright © Nazeing History Workshop 2018
The Authors assert the moral right to be identified as the authors of this work.

ISBN 978-1-911175-88-9
Printed and bound in Great Britain.
Published by YouCaxton Publications 2018

YouCaxton Publications
enquiries@youcaxton.co.uk

Foreword

David Pracy, supported by the team from Nazeing History Workshop, has given us a book which is invaluable for anybody wishing to reconstruct the story of this Essex village as it negotiated the years leading up to and during the Great War. By drawing on a wide range of sources a light is shone on the families who called Nazeing home, as well as on the physical and social fabric of the village in which they lived. Great use is made of the extensive detail found in the Lloyd George Domesday Survey, bringing into focus the homes, pubs, churches and schools of the village in a way that cannot be gleaned from photos alone, of which there are a generous number. Supplementing the archival sources, we have the reminiscences of those who lived through the early part of the 20th century, bringing to the story colour and texture which would otherwise be lost to us. What emerges is in some ways what we might expect from this 'purely agricultural parish', with generations from the same families following their forebears onto the land. The team have done a sterling job in untangling the various family trees and chronicling the rise and fall of fortunes across the generations, especially given the level of intermarriage and attachment to sticking with the same few forenames. The building of a new bridge and road, and the development of former farmland, saw the arrival of new families whose economic well-being was not dependent on the fortunes of agriculture. By 1918 representatives of both new and old families would be amongst those recalled in the final chapters of this book and on the war memorials of the village.

Julie Moore
University of Hertfordshire 'Everyday Lives in War'
Engagement Centre

Frontispiece

This photo was taken around 1900 when Nazeing Parish Council described the village as 'a purely agricultural parish'. The council made exactly the same claim in 1912, but by then Nazeing was beginning to change.

Left to right: Edward Perry (farm labourer), Alfred Pegrum (carpenter), Samuel Pegrum (Alfred's son, farmer), Emma Thornton née Pegrum (Edward's grand-daughter), Alfred James Pegrum (Edward's son-in-law, farmer), unknown lady. Emma's daughter Marjorie, born in 1901, later became Marjorie Sykes and wrote a fascinating account of Nazeing in this period. Emma's husband, William, was a keen photographer who took this and other fine photos which are used in this book.

Contents

Part IV
A Changing Village

Part V
The Great War (1914-1918)

Introduction

In his book *Lays and Legends of the Forest of Essex*, published in 1907, Edward Hardingham wrote that 'Nazing lies high, and dry and five miles from everywhere'. That last phrase was so striking that we chose it as the title for volume 1 of our village history, published in 2000. Since then, a wide range of sources have become easily accessible through online family history sites, and the censuses for 1901 and 1911 have been released. We have therefore decided to revisit the period and produce a new book which complements rather than duplicates *Five Miles from Everywhere*.

Our original intention was to start this new book with the death of Queen Victoria in 1901, and the main emphasis is still on the first two decades of the twentieth century. We found, however, that in some cases it was impossible to make sense of the period without going back very much further. In particular, several leading families arrived in Nazeing between 1770 and 1800, so where necessary we have started then.

In 1911, almost half of Nazeing people were born in the village, and almost half of the working population were farmers or labourers on the land. In 1900 and again in 1912, the parish council described Nazeing as 'a purely agricultural parish'. Yet it was at this time that Nazeing saw two major developments that were to transform it in the twentieth century. A new bridge and road to Broxbourne station gave Nazeing people more convenient access across the River Lea to Hertfordshire and, via the station, to London. And Keysers Farm next to the River Lea was sold for development, so by 1914 there were at least thirty dwellings there. Nazeing became an easier place to reach but also to leave, so the net population remained almost static between 1851 and 1914. The neighbouring village of Roydon experienced a similar plateau, but the population of Essex as a whole almost quadrupled, mostly thanks to the growth of south-western suburbs such as West Ham and Walthamstow.

In 1912 the parish council's statement was already less true than it had been in 1900, but then came the Great War. We cannot know how Nazeing would have developed if the war had never happened, but certainly it was a catalyst for the changes that were to come to the village in the twentieth century.

Part I

Before the Great War

Chapter 1

The National Picture
and its Effect on Nazeing

The period from 1900 to 1914 was one of the most volatile in British history. Even at the time, many felt that the death of Queen Victoria on 22 January 1901 marked the end of an era. In the Second South African (Boer) War of 1899-1902, initial defeats and the brutal methods that eventually brought it to an end shocked public opinion and left Britain internationally isolated. A weak and divided Conservative government staggered on until 1906 when the 'Liberal landslide' brought in a government with a majority of 125 seats over all other parties, and they began to implement a radical reform programme. Five major national issues affected Nazeing to a greater or lesser extent.

Lords v Commons
The fiery Welsh politician David Lloyd George declared that the government needed 'a war budget... to wage implacable warfare against poverty and squalidness'. His appointment as Chancellor of the Exchequer gave him a chance to do something about it, and in 1909 he brought in his 'People's Budget'. When the inbuilt Conservative majority in the House of Lords opposed his plans for a tax on the development value of land, the government needed a new mandate to take on the Lords. They called an election but lost over a hundred seats and were equally matched with the Conservatives. The result of a second election was almost identical and matters came to a head in the long hot summer of 1911. With the thermometer in London touching 100°F, the political temperature became equally heated and finally on 10 August the Lords voted narrowly to limit their own powers. These controversies did not bypass Nazeing and a leading

Nazeing Conservative, Ralph Bury, told a public meeting that 'Mr Lloyd George had never employed an agricultural labourer, and knew nothing about the land... The Radical programme was leading the country to civil war, and the Conservative policy would bring reduced taxes to the rural districts.'

Crisis in Ireland

The Liberals could only govern with the help of the Irish Nationalists so brought forward a Home Rule Bill, but the Conservative opposition supported the Ulster Unionists and by July 1914, civil war was a real possibility. Ralph Bury told his meeting that 'he knew something of the Irish question because he had relations in Ireland... The men of Ulster were right in resisting, because no government had the power to sell the people of Ulster to the Nationalists, without appealing to the people and deciding by an election if England was in favour of this... The Liberal government... had brought the country to the verge of civil war...' Some would have argued that it was not the government who brought the country to the verge of civil war but the opposition.

Industrial Unrest

In the first decade of the twentieth century industrial unrest simmered, but in the second it boiled over. In 1913 over eleven million strike days were lost, and there were more individual strikes than in any other year in British history. Nazeing was an essentially conservative society so was never going to be a hotbed of revolution, but in the last weeks of the Great War there was an attempt to form a local branch of the National Agricultural Labourers' & Rural Workers' Union. At a crowded meeting at the Crooked Billet, a large number of people gave in their names for membership but nothing came of it, perhaps because of pressure applied by landowners. It may be significant that the elected secretary was Fred Livings, the landlord of the Green Man at neighbouring Roydon Hamlet, rather than a Nazeing man.

Votes for Women

Before 1918 property restrictions meant that millions of men did not have the vote, including many who died in the Great War. A few women had voted in local elections since 1867 but in 1897 various local groups formed the National Union of Women's Suffrage Societies to campaign for the vote in parliamentary elections. Known as suffragists, they were led by Millicent Fawcett. Impatient with the rate of progress, Emmeline Pankhurst in 1903 founded the Women's Social and Political Union, whose supporters the *Daily Mail* dubbed suffragettes. The government opposed votes for women and in 1914 there was no sign of any resolution to the argument, but during the war women took on traditional male roles and in 1918 over eight million aged thirty and over won the vote, although it was not until 1928 that they achieved full equality. In 1910, just seven Nazeing women were registered to vote in local elections and by 1915 there were five new names on the list, all local women and four of them recently widowed. But the great change came after the war, when no fewer than 174 Nazeing women had the vote in national as well as local elections.

The Threat from Germany

The fear of Germany and its navy began to grow in the 1890s, as Kaiser Wilhelm II pursued increasingly belligerent policies. One of the reasons why Lloyd George had to raise taxes was because his proposal to reduce the number of new Dreadnought battleships was defeated by a Conservative-led public campaign on the slogan 'We want eight and we won't wait'.

This fear was fed by popular novels which warned of the need to prepare for war with Germany, of which Erskine Childers' *Riddle of the Sands* (1903) was the best-known. Of less literary merit but more relevant to Nazeing was William Le Queux's *The Invasion of 1910,* because the German invasion route passed through west Essex.

It was commissioned and serialised in 1906 by the *Daily Mail*, which advised its readers: 'Refuse to be served by a German waiter. If your waiter says he is Swiss, ask to see his passport.' One such was Emil Schade who was the only live-in waiter at the Crown Hotel, while unlimited opportunities for spying must surely have opened up to William Feltmann, a commercial traveller boarding with Mrs Ann Head at Ninnings. Nothing more is known of Schade or Feltmann, but if they had not returned to Germany by 1914 they would probably have been interned.

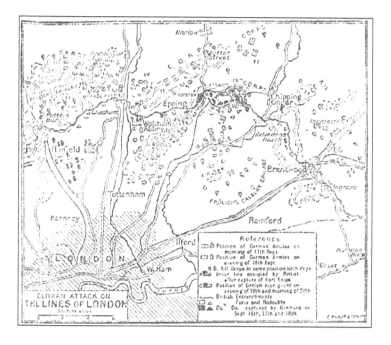

In William Le Queux's novel *The Invasion of 1910*, the Germans capture the east coast of England. The London stop line passes through Nazeing – exactly as it did for real in both world wars – but the Germans establish their headquarters at Copped Hall and take the capital after a mighty battle at Epping. Eventually, the 'League of Defenders' organises resistance and a newly-formed British Army marches to liberate London.

The Great War, 1914-1918

In addition to these political issues, three events in 1912 helped undermine the British sense of self-confidence: the sinking of the 'unsinkable' Titanic, the heroic but futile deaths of Captain Scott and his party in the Antarctic and, at home, a wretchedly wet summer that resulted in a largely failed harvest.

This helps to explain why some people greeted the outbreak of war in August 1914 as a relief from the tensions at home. When Edward Hardingham described Nazeing as five miles from everywhere, he might have thought that the village would be largely immune to such outside influences. We only have a few hints about how they affected Nazeing, but people would certainly have had an idea of what was happening. The rise of popular newspapers like the *Daily Mail* disseminated news much more widely, and by 1914 the Hoddesdon Picture Palace and other cinemas were showing newsreels. There were several cases when London youths were convicted of poaching in Nazeing, and on three occasions airmen made unscheduled landings on the Common. The influx of Londoners could have brought new ideas.

But then over 150 Nazeing men went away to war, and thirty-three did not return. Some of them were farm labourers, perhaps with a sense of adventure or seeking better pay. People left at home suffered a different kind of hardship, and women learned new skills in taking over from the men. The Great War brought Nazeing people into contact with the outside world in a way that could never be reversed.

Chapter 2

How Do We Know About Nazeing?

A variety of sources tell us about Nazeing in those years. Information about how to find them is given in the list of sources at the end of the book.

Censuses are taken every ten years and have been released for the years from 1841 to 1911. The one for 1911 was taken on the night of Sunday 2 April and aimed to record information about households and the people in them. The details noted for each person were:

- Name and surname

- Relationship to head of family

- Age

- Marital condition (married, single, widowed)

- Number of years married

- Number of children, number that are living, number who have died

- Occupation and employment status

- Industry/service with which worker is connected

- Birthplace and nationality

- Infirmity - deaf, dumb, blind, lunatic, imbecile or feeble minded.

This is the first census where we can see the original form filled up by the householder. The Hargreaves household at Nazeing Park was the largest in the village. Reproduced by permission of the National Archive and Findmypast

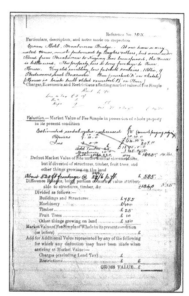

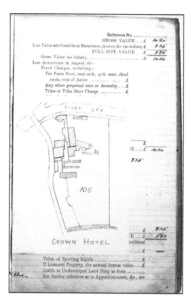

The information on the field book entry for the Crown Hotel
was exceptionally detailed but the four-page pro forma was
standard. In Nazeing, sketch-maps were provided for the pubs
but no other buildings.

Reproduced by permission of the National Archive

The Valuation Office Survey. The 1911 census is complemented by another source that tells us about property. The *Valuation Office Survey of 1910* is better known as the 'Lloyd George Domesday', after the Chancellor of the Exchequer who introduced it in his 1909 budget. (Throughout this book, it is referred to as the *Lloyd George Survey* or just the *Survey*.)

Duty of 20% was to be levied on any increase in property values resulting from building development. The survey needed to assess this was carried out over the next three years, and the country was divided into Inland Revenue Parishes (IRPs). A valuation book summarising information about each property was drawn up by a local valuation officer, and then assistant officers walked round the parish entering detailed information into field books.

IRPs did not always coincide with local government parishes, but we are very fortunate that the Nazeing IRP did, so there was just one valuation book and four field books. The main information they give us about each hereditament (portion of land) in Nazeing is:

- Occupier and owner.
- Description, including common right where appropriate.
- Situation and/or name, some very informative, others less so.
- Reference on 25-inch Ordnance Survey maps, which are in eight large sections.
- Estimated size in acres [4840 square yards or 0.4 hectares] and roods [four to an acre].
- Detailed figures, on which tax liability was to be calculated.

The tax proved unworkable and in 1920 Lloyd George's own Coalition Government repealed the legislation. But although the survey failed in its original purpose, it has provided us with the largest land database in British history and is therefore of the greatest historical importance.

Electoral registers were published annually and list all those eligible to vote. They give addresses and are therefore invaluable for tracing when people came to Nazeing and how they moved around. Under successive Acts of Parliament the franchise was gradually widened but it was not until 1928 that all men and women aged twenty-one and over were able to vote.

The 1939 Register was compiled at the outbreak of the Second World War to assess the needs of the civilian population and gives information not always to be found elsewhere.

Trade Directories listed businesses and tradespeople in a county or town and gave a general directory of postal addresses of local landowners, charities, and other facilities. Those for Essex were published irregularly from 1845 to 1937. They give a detailed gazetteer and description of each parish, with a listing of the most prominent residents and businesses.

The entry for Nazeing in the 1914 edition gives hints of a village on the cusp of change. The old is still very much in evidence. About two-thirds of those in the commercial section were in farming and related trades. Six of them were members of the Pegrum family, long-established and still prominent in Nazeing. Nazeingbury was not the village centre it became in the 1950s but just one of several hamlets. Similarly, shops were scattered throughout the village rather than on one parade.

There are signs of change. The new Broxbourne railway bridge is mentioned in the very first sentence of the gazetteer. Ten private residents and five businesses in the developing Riverside area received their post through Broxbourne rather than through Waltham Cross, because it was nearer. Among the traders were two nurserymen, the first of many in Nazeing.

NAZEING (or Nasing), in Domesday "Nasinga," is a village and parish, bounded on the west by the river Lee, over which, near the Broxbourne station of the Great Eastern Railway Co. distant 3¾ miles, is a bridge of one arch, connecting the parish with Hertfordshire; it is 6 miles north-west from Epping, 5 north-east from Waltham Abbey and 19 from London, in the Western division of the county, Waltham hundred, Epping union and petty sessional division, Waltham Abbey county court district, rural deanery of Harlow, archdeaconry of Essex and Chelmsford diocese; it was given by King Harold II. to Waltham Abbey. The church of All Saints is an edifice of brick, flint and rubble, in the Early English style, standing on a hill, and consists of chancel, nave of four bays, north aisle, south porch of wood and an embattled western tower of brick dating from the 13th century, and containing 5 bells, all dated 1779: there was formerly a spire, but this was removed in 1899: at the south-east angle of the tower is a hexagonal stair turret, on which is a sun dial, dated 1765, and bearing the inscription "Meridies, Solarius, lat. 51° 32'''," the rood-loft staircase remains, and the terminals of the rood-loft beams are still embedded in the walls of the nave: the chancel has a memorial window to William Palmer esq. d. 24 April, 1858, and is fitted with choir stalls: in the nave is a memorial window to Henry Crowther, d. 21 Dec. 1852, and there are two other stained windows, mural monuments to the Palmer and Bury families, and various inscribed floor slabs; the carved oak pulpit is a memorial to Mrs. Alice Mary Fane, daughter of the present vicar, who died 1 Feb. 1899: the church was restored in 1874 at a cost of £600, when a new organ was erected: the restoration was continued in 1891 at a cost of £400, when a new organ chamber and vestry were built and the open timber roof repaired: there are about 250 sittings.

The register dates from the year 1559. The living is a vicarage, net yearly value £201, with 39 acres of glebe and residence, in the gift of the Lord Chancellor, and held since 1890 by the Rev. Thomas Ward Goddard M.A. of Pembroke College, Cambridge. The vicarage house has been improved and enlarged. Alfred Manser esq. of Lampits, Hoddesdon, Herts, who died 27 Oct. 1902, bequeathed £300 upon trust for the maintenance of the bells in Nazeing church and the surplus income, if any, for the ringers. The Congregational chapel and school room were built in 1876, on the site of an older structure, dating from 1816: the chapel affords about 200 sittings. There are golf links of 18 holes, extending over nearly 3 miles of ground on Nazeing Common; there is also a club house. Sir Herewald Wake bart. of Courteenhall, Northants, is lord of the manor, in a part of which, called "Upper Town," the custom of Borough English prevails, by which the youngest son inherits. Nazeing Park is the property of Ralph Charlton Palmer esq: the mansion, rebuilt c. 1814, and now occupied by Walter E. Hargreaves esq stands in a well-wooded park and grounds of 67 acres, facing Nazeing Common, with a fine kitchen garden containing a number of glass houses and choice fruit trees; it is a commodious house, faced with stucco, and has a balustraded balcony, carried on five Ionic columns, and wings with balustraded parapets. St. Leonards House, the residence of Ralph Frederic Bury esq. D.L., J.P. is pleasantly situated in park-like grounds of 43 acres. Harold's Park, an estate of about 500 acres, belonged to that king, and was given by him to his monastery at Waltham; it lies chiefly in this parish, but partly in Waltham Holy Cross and Epping, and is now occupied by Mr. William Graham. The Nether Hall estate, partly in this parish, is referred to under Roydon. Sir Herewald Wake bart. Ralph Frederic Bury esq. Ralph Charlton Palmer esq. J.P. and the trustees of the late E. J. Williams esq. are the chief landowners. Nazeing or Nazeing Wood Common consists of 475 acres, over which certain ancient houses in the parish have rights of pasturage. The soil is chiefly heavy; subsoil, clay. The chief crops are wheat, barley and roots, and a great quantity is grass land. The area is 3,928 acres of land and 24 of water; rateable value, £6,331. About 450 acres of the extensive commons and waste grounds of the parish have been inclosed. The population in 1911 was 847. There are hamlets at Nazeing Common Lower Gate, Middle Street, Greenleaves, and near Nazingbury.

Parish Clerk and Sexton, Arthur Reynolds.

Post, M. O. & T. Office.—Frederick Cook, sub-postmaster. Letters from Waltham Cross arrive at 7.35 & 10.15 a.m.; sundays, 7.35 a.m.; dispatched at 10.45 a.m & 6.20 p.m.; sundays at 11 a.m
Post Office, Nazeing Upper Town.—Mrs. Matilda Ann Starling, sub-postmistress. Letters through Waltham Cross arrive at 8.15 & 10 30 a.m.; sundays, 8.15 a.m.; dispatched at 10.45 a.m & 6 p.m.; sundays, 10.45 a.m Nazeing, 1 mile distant, is the nearest money order & telegraph office
Pillar Letter Box, Greenleaves, cleared at 9.30 a.m. & 5.50 p.m.; sundays at 10.45 a.m
County Police Station, Middle street, Harry George Tilbrook, sergeant

Public Elementary Schools.

These schools are under the control of the Essex Education (Epping District) Sub-Committee; Herbert J. Goodwin, High road, Loughton, clerk
Public Elementary School (mixed), built in 1878, for 120 children; average attendance, 104; Noah William Bevan, master
Public Elementary School, Upper Town, erected in 1856 but closed in 1878, & re-opened in 1891; it will hold 90 children; average attendance, 60; Alfred Gwynn Phillips, master

Marked thus * receive letters through Broxbourne, Herts.	*Walker George Perry, Springdale	*Maynard Victor, tomato grower
	*Whitton Wm.Frederick, Marion villa	Middlemiss James W. King Harold's
PRIVATE RESIDENTS.	*Wood Leonard, Tally Ho	Head P.H
		Mugridge Edward, Red Lion P.H
Adams Ernest, Sunnyholme	COMMERCIAL.	Nicholls John, farmer, Parker's farm
*Armes George William, Lulworth	Ashby John, shopkeeper	Nicholls Sarah (Mrs.),frmr.Camps fm
Berg Alfred George, Jacks Hatch (letters via Epping)	Bridgman Chas. farmer, Curringtons	Pegrum Alfd. carpenter, The Poplars
	*Button Arthur Joseph, carpenter	Pegrum Alfred, shopkpr.Nazeing gate
Burr Ralph Frederic D.L., J.P. St Leonards house	Carvl John, Coach & Horses P.H	Pegrum Alfd. Jas. farmer, Stutsbury
	Cattermole Walt. frmr. Perryhill fm	Pegrum James, farmer, Curtis' farm
Charge Alexander, Greenleaves	*Collins John, shopkeeper	Pegrum Joseph, farmer, Bury farm
*Eastwood Frederick, Kingsmead	Cook Fredk. shoe ma. & sub-postmstr	Pegrum Samuel, farmer
Fowler Edward, Mamelons	Crowe George, farmer, Maple croft	Nazeing Bury
*Giffen James, Fairlawn	*Crowley Frank R. Crown P.H. Brox bourne Bridge	Perry Jas. (Mrs.), frmr. Allmains frm
Goddard Rev. Thomas Ward M.A. Vicarage	Dellar George, farmer	Power Richard, farmer, Church farm
	Dellar John, wheelwright	*Rich Sidney, nurseryman
Green Frederick William, Collyers, Nazeing Common	Golf Club (Capt. E. J. Christie, sec)	Savage James, general dealer, Mill ho
	Graham Wm. farmer, Harolds park	Selway James (Mrs.), blacksmith
Green George P. Wheelers	Hale Isaac, farmer, Shadwalkers frm	Sinclair Geo. frmr.Mansion House fm
Hargreaves Walter E. Nazeing park	Head Ann (Mrs.),farmer,Ninnetts fm	Smith Arthur, farmer, Cutlands
*Hughes Herbert, The Bungalow	Hollow John, farmer, Brewitts farm	Smith Jn. jun. frmr. Nether Kidders
*Jackson Ernest, The Hut	Horne Charles, Sun P.H	Smith William, farmer, Paynes farm
*La Riviere Alfd. Edwin,Meadowbank	Judd & Coleman, plumbers	Starling M.A.(Mrs.),shpkpr.& post off
Midwood Lieut.-Col. Harrison, Snows	Judd George, farmer, Shays farm	Taylor John C. farmer, Langridge
Palmer Archdale, Rockwood	Judd Jane (Miss), shopkeeper	Weare Henry, Crooked Billet P.H
Palmer Ralph Charlton J.P. Hubbards	King Langham, builder, North street	Webb Ernest, farmer
Rufus John Alfred, Old house	Lawrence William, farmer, Belchers	Webb Oscar, farmer, Goodalls farm
*Steed Thomas Dyer, Leebank	Lipson Geo. assist.overseer,Sunnyside	Webb William, farmer, Byners farm

Kelly's Directory of Essex, 1914

Newspapers provide a patchy but informative picture of village life. Reports of tragic deaths spared no detail but petty crime was the most reported activity. Newspapers are now being put on line at a great rate, which makes researching them much easier than in the past.

Birth, marriage and death records are essential for establishing family relationships. Often these can be worked out with online indexes but sometimes we have to see original certificates. For example, we knew that in 1919 David Pegrum married Dorothy Vernon Savage, who had worked for him as a land girl during the war, but we could not trace anyone with that exact name. The marriage certificate showed that her father was a farmer and so she had a background that suited her for farm work. As was often the case in the early twentieth century, she was given only one forename at birth but adopted a second one later.

Landpage is an extensive and invaluable Excel database compiled by Nazeing History Workshop member John Garbutt from many sources. The main ones are:

- Manorial records
- Baptisms, marriages and burials at All Saints' church
- Churchwardens and Overseers of the Poor accounts, 1680-1859
- Land tax, 1780-1832
- Tithe Award, 1847
- Supplemental Valuation List for the Parish of Nazeing, 1873
- Censuses

Reminiscences

Several people recorded their memories of this period. Often they add colourful detail about people and places that can never be gleaned from more formal sources. For example, we knew that Noah Bevan and his wife Clarice were head and assistant teachers at the Board School, but without Nance Colman we would not have known that she was 'a big woman' or that when the children were singing he 'used to get really cross if we were going too full blast when it should be soft and sweet'.

Nance Colman née Mead

Nance Colman lived in Nazeing all her life. She was born in Bumbles Green on 25 April 1899 and named Annie Ada Mead, but became known as 'Nance' because there was an Annie living at the Post Office next door. Her parents and their eight children all lived in a 'two-up, two-down' house. When she married Bertie Colman in 1926, Nance went to live in Ivy Cottages next to the King Harold's Head, overlooking Nazeing Common. In 1975, the schoolmaster Russell Haynes recorded conversations with her about her early life in the village. Nance was a born story-teller and ended by telling him:

> Nazeing, it used to be a wonderful little place. I can't describe it. It was unspoilt. In the Copy Wood, there were nightingales; and in Back Lane they were very common. That's what I remember. It was wonderful!

You can read her recollections of schooldays, life as a servant and her father's work at the Royal Gunpowder Mills later in this book.

Dennis Mead (1924-2012) was the nephew of Nance Colman and only son of Harry and Emily. He grew up in the Post Office at Bumbles Green, where his mother became post mistress after her father, Fred Cook, died in 1930. This was a close knit community since his other grandparents lived next door. Young Dennis often delivered telegrams while his elder cousin Rhoda Johnson managed the telephone switch board which hung in the living room. He won a scholarship to Newport Grammar School and later worked in the City as a marine insurance broker. He joined the RAF to train as a Spitfire pilot in the Second World War and became a founder member of the village association on his return. He never forgot the stories he heard growing up in the village post office.

Nita Turner (1921-2014) was Dennis's cousin and the eldest child of Arthur Mead and his wife Hettie, who was in service in Hoddesdon when they met. Arthur was a gardener in Leicestershire in 1911 and later at Collyers. Nita lived her whole life in Nazeing in and around the Common and met her husband Frank Turner when he manned the dummy airfield in the Second World War. She recorded her memories as her aunt Nance had done, in Nita's case while chatting over a cup of tea with her first cousin once removed, Jacky Cooper.

William Thornton's wonderful photo of his daughter Marjorie

Marjorie Sykes (1901-1995) was the daughter of William Thornton and Emma Pegrum, and niece of Alfred James Pegrum and Amy Perry. Her family lived in East Dulwich, but they often visited and stayed with 'uncle Alf and aunt Amy' at Sturtsbury Farm in Nazeing. Her beautifully observed and written memoir *Confident Morning* paints a vivid picture of the joys and deprivations of working country life before the Great War: no gas or electricity, all milking done by hand, all deliveries carried by cart but, on the other hand, long winter evenings spent playing games and singing, home cooked food, harvest teas and blackberrying in the fields. The full quotation from Robert Browning is 'Never glad confident morning again' and Marjorie may also have been thinking of the changes brought about by the Great War. The children she was brought up with and often mentioned included her sister Ethel and cousins May Pegrum and Winnie Perry.

Bernard Pegrum (1901-1968) was a cousin of A.J. Pegrum. He was a controversial figure in some ways but a gifted teacher who gave unstintingly of his time to the Sunday School. His vivid memoirs of the chapel life extend to the whole village and, where they can be checked, seem accurate and reliable. For instance, his reference to a monkey puzzle tree in the garden of his grandparents' home at White House Farm enabled us to identify a previously unrecognised photograph of a house that was demolished in 1911.

White House Farm with monkey puzzle tree

John William Payne (1897-1994) was seven years old when his father was appointed head gardener at Nazeing Park. He wrote his *Memories of Nazeing 1904-1914* in 1987, when he was ninety years old. After serving in the London Electrical Engineers and the Royal Tank Regiment, he graduated in chemistry and moved away from Nazeing, so his memories are largely unaffected by later developments and therefore particularly valuable.

Enid Brent (1921-2000) lived at the Red House on Nazeing Common all her life, and her husband Peter Brent (1920-2007) lived there after they were married in 1942. Their interview with David Pracy in 1994 covered a wide range of Nazeing life.

Chapter 3

Who Ran Nazeing?

Towards the end of the nineteenth century, a series of reforms began to change the way in which rural districts were administered. In 1884 the vote was extended to heads of households so in Nazeing the electorate grew from 58 to 137, an increase of 236% that was almost as large a percentage as the much better known increase in 1918. In 1888 county councils took on the administrative responsibilities of JPs such as Ralph Charlton Palmer and Charles James Bury of Nazeing, although their judicial role as magistrates remained intact. Then in 1894 the Local Government Act created powerful rural district councils, which opened up possibilities of election to a modest level of political power to a much wider range of people and left the new secular parish councils with very limited responsibilities.

The troubles of the years before the Great War did affect Nazeing, but less than many other places. It remained a conservative, traditional society led mostly by long-established local families. Nazeing responded to the Local Government Act by choosing members of the two families who had been most influential in the village since the late eighteenth century. Charles James Bury was elected unopposed as the first Epping rural district councillor, and Ralph Palmer became the first chairman of the parish council. In 1914 Palmer was still chairman and Bury's son Ralph was district councillor.

Other men (no women yet) were also village leaders. The Lord of the Manor, Sir Herewald Wake, lived in Northamptonshire but owned more land in Nazeing than anyone other than Palmer. In the decade before the war, two businessmen, Walter Hargreaves and Frederick

William Green, came to Nazeing and began to play an important part in its affairs. Joseph Pegrum (usually known as Joe), whose family had been in Nazeing since the sixteenth century, was the leading tenant-farmer and a deacon (leader) of the Congregational Church. There is more about these men and their families in Part II.

They exercised their influence through several institutions.

The Parish Council
The procedure for parish councils was to elect councillors by a show of hands. At Nazeing's inaugural meeting in 1894 there were nine candidates for seven places, so Ralph Palmer and Charles James Bury withdrew their candidatures in order to avoid a poll. Of the seven elected unopposed, only the vicar, the Reverend Thomas Goddard, could be regarded as a traditional establishment figure: Joe Pegrum was joined by four other farmers (two of whom belonged to the Chapel) and John Banks, barrister's clerk. The new parish councils were allowed to co-opt as chairman anyone qualified to be a councillor, and so the seven elected members chose Ralph Palmer, who in his usual business-like manner closed the first Annual Parish Meeting after five minutes with the laconic note 'nothing done'[1].

Under Palmer's leadership, the council pursued a cautious policy of opposing change and keeping down expenditure unless there was a good reason to do otherwise. They successfully fought a proposal to site a new sewage works in the Stoneshot area. In 1907, the new Liberal government brought in the Small Holdings and Allotments Act, so the parish council issued notices inviting applications for allotments; they investigated four enquiries and issued a public

---

1   For reasons of space, we have omitted photos of Charles James Bury, Ralph Palmer, Thomas Goddard and other leading figures that can be seen in *The Story of Nazeing* Parts I and II.

notice explaining their reasons for disallowing them all. Even though Joe Pegrum admitted that he had nowhere to house his labourers, he and other parish councillors consistently opposed plans for new housing, on the grounds that it was not needed.

The one major exception was their support for the new road to Broxbourne. The idea was first suggested in 1895, when Goddard proposed that the parish should 'memorialize' the district and county councils to 'promote free access by road between the counties of Essex & Herts at Broxbourne Station'. When the Great Eastern Railway tried to pull out of the scheme, the parish council successfully urged the district and county councils to keep the company to its word. Then they contributed an additional £70 so that the road could go directly to the river rather than via present-day Green Lane.

Nazeing Congregational Church (the Chapel)
Following the Reformation in the reign of Henry VIII, Essex became a particularly active area of dissent and by the seventeenth century Nazeing figured prominently in the dissenting movement. A plaque in All Saints' Church commemorates the departure to New England of many Nazeing families from 1630 onwards. Among them was John Eliot, who became renowned as a missionary and gave his name to John Eliot Close.

In the late eighteenth century the 'spiritual bankruptcy' of the Church of England helped stimulate the rise of nonconformity. In 1768 the Countess of Huntingdon leased a building in Breconshire to provide a college for students to study scripture for three years, after which they were free to enter the ministry of any Protestant denomination. In 1792 the college moved to Cheshunt. John James and other students from this college visited Nazeing and neighbouring villages to preach the gospel, and there are still Countess of Huntingdon chapels at Wormley and Epping Green.

Tradition has it that John James used the trunk of an old tree at the crossroads as his pulpit. The Congregational church in Nazeing was founded in 1797 when the house of James Ford at 42 North Street was registered for independent worship. By 1816, the shed they used was too small and the students encouraged the congregation to raise funds for a building on the site now occupied by the present Chapel. This early Chapel was a wooden construction with a brick front and cost around £450. It was built by Charles Hollingsworth and an indenture of 1817 suggests that the parcel of freehold meadow land, called Netherdown, was owned by Hollingsworth who sold it to the trustees of Cheshunt College for £20. The shed at 42 North Street was probably still in use as a stable in 1911.

The first Congregational Chapel

The Pegrum, Welch and Nicholls families figured prominently in these events and men from each of these families were the first deacons. In the front of the oldest minute book, dated 4 February 1822, is a list of fifteen committed members who formed the first proper church – William Collins, Samuel Pegrum, William Pegrum, John Nicholls, Josh Wilshire, James Matthews, Elizabeth Pegrum, Susannah Pegrum, Elizabeth Nicholls, John Smith, Samuel Dews, Rebecca Banks, George Standingford, Elizabeth Standingford, Ann King.

As the congregation increased, the first Chapel became too small. In 1876 the present Chapel was erected at a cost of about £900, and by 1895 a gallery had been added to accommodate a total of 150 people. An early decision of the new parish council was that its notices should be posted on the door of the Chapel as well as of the church - a small but significant pointer to its growing importance in the Nazeing community. Between 1890 and 1914, ninety-nine people became members. There were two services on a Sunday and several week-night activities, including a men's brass band which played at events such as anniversaries.

Congregation outside the Chapel, c1892. We can only name John Davies Welch (with heavy beard, back row but one, second from right) and Thomas Nicholls junior (same row, fifth from left, with hat).

Over a hundred children attended the Sunday school and the existing Chapel school room was filled to overflowing. Some Sunday school teachers were in despair about anything being done. By 1906, a building fund for new school rooms stood at only £80 and George Lipson, the Chapel secretary, who was also the Sunday School Superintendent, threatened to resign if nothing was done.

A scheme was agreed and money was raised. Thomas Nicholls of Parvills gave land for a separate Sunday School hall which was built by Charles Judd and Ted Coleman, Chapel members who went on to establish a successful building business in the village. The stone-laying ceremony for the new hall raised £41-10-0 and they obtained £100 loan from the Sunday School Union. It was more or less finished by May 1909 and the brass band played at the opening ceremony. Until the building of St Giles in 1964, it was the largest hall in the village and hosted a variety of meetings and events.

Nonconformist churches were often radical in politics, but that was not the case in Nazeing; the names of the donors displayed most prominently on the commemorative stones in the wall of the new hall are Ralph Palmer, Walter Hargreaves and John Banks, a former churchwarden but by then a member of the Congregational Church.

The Chapel gave unqualified support to British involvement in the Great War and took the lead in village events afterwards. It hosted the Welcome Home celebrations and organised the raising of funds for the first Nazeing war memorial, which was placed on the front wall of the Chapel building.

The Church of England

During the nineteenth century the Church of England made vigorous attempts to reform itself, but in Nazeing it did not grow as rapidly as the Chapel. The vicars were usually resident and apparently conscientious enough, but they were mostly in their fifties when appointed and were perhaps given a quiet rural parish for the autumn of their careers.

The Vicar of Nazeing during the Great War was the Reverend Thomas Goddard, who had arrived in 1890. In 1894 he was elected to the newly-created parish council but when he stood for election again two years later he tied with the chapel deacon, John Davies Welch, for the last place and withdrew, perhaps because relations with the Chapel were rather strained. He was a somewhat prickly character but he and his wife, Ellen, were conscientious about visiting people in the parish, so it seems certain that they helped to comfort the families whose sons had been killed. He retired in 1922 and died a year later.

Nazeingwood Common

The area called Nazeing Common is not strictly a common in the usual sense. This is because it is the property of the owners of ninety-eight houses on mediaeval sites and not of the Lord of the Manor. During the Civil War the royalist lord of the manor, James Hay Earl of Carlisle, had a dispute with the parliamentarian commoners. It was resolved in 1651 by his taking 140 acres for his own use and granting the other 414 acres to the villagers for their animals to graze. The land was not well managed and in 1778 a new Act was promoted by William Palmer, who was building up his holdings in Nazeing. The rightholders (owners) in a general meeting were to elect five Trustees to manage the land, and Palmer recorded in their minute book the names of the owners and tenants of dwellings who were entitled to graze sheep and cattle on the Common. The Trustees appointed a pindar (shepherd) to manage the Common and collect fees from tenants putting stock on it. It may well have been the increased stability provided by these reforms that attracted several experienced farmers to the village in the 1780s.

Taking over as Treasurer in 1877, Ralph Palmer found the Trust's finances at a low ebb. He did much to restore the situation but then an error of judgment left it with a great financial burden. On behalf of the Trustees, Palmer sued the owner of Harold's Park Farm and his tenant, William Graham, for carting timber on four routes across the Common to Nazeing Gate. The case of Palmer v Guadagni came before Mr Justice Swinfen Eady at the High Court on 17-20 July 1907. The two sides sought to demonstrate whether or not there was a custom of carting on the Common and called witnesses whose evidence gives us a valuable picture of daily life in Nazeing in the previous fifty years. The judge rejected most of the defendants' claims and the Trustees won £3 13s 8d in damages but it was a pyrrhic victory, because each side was to bear its own costs. The Trust's totalled £439 16s - a debt which took twenty years to clear. It only ever had a small surplus at best, so Palmer and the Trustees probably paid the costs out of their own pockets.

In 1890, when golf was gaining in popularity among the more affluent in society, Thomas Goddard and Ralph Palmer established a course on the Common. Although it encountered considerable opposition at first, by 1902 the course was well-established and *Kelly's Directory* described it as 'probably one of the best of the links within 20 miles of London'.

In 1905 the golf course was the venue for a challenge match between two of the then three best players in the world. John Henry Taylor won comfortably.

The Common was still being used for grazing sheep and cattle in 1940, but then it was ploughed up for crops so the stock and the golfers disappeared.

'The waste' and enclosure

Throughout England it had long been the right of cottagers to graze stock on riverside meadows and roadside verges[2] - an untidy custom which was seen by the early Victorian official mind as 'waste' in every sense of the word. Enclosure awards enabled landowners to take small parcels of land next to their existing property, while the poorer commoners received little or no compensation for losses which, given their subsistence economy, could be of vital importance. Middle Street, for example, was formerly up to a hundred yards wide in parts; the former line of the road can be seen at older houses such as Goodalls and Ninnings, and the enclosed waste area was so great that new houses such as Rose Cottage and Little Dormers could be built on it.

Under the Enclosure Award of 1861, all the remaining common land in the parish except Nazeingwood Common was gobbled up by the leading landowners. The 450 acres of common – arable, meadow and waste – comprised 12% of Nazeing land and its loss had a devastating effect on the villagers. In the 1880s William Westall, a former foreign correspondent and author of many books, reported in *The Spectator* the assertion of an old resident that 'before the poor were despoiled by the lords of the manor' the cottagers had pastured their geese on the greens and 'they were so well-off that, in order to levy a rate, the rate-payers had to "make a pauper"'. 'Now,' he added bitterly, 'there are paupers in plenty.' Even allowing for the effects of the agricultural depression and

---

2   A custom known in Suffolk as 'feeding the long meadow'. George Ewart EVANS, *The days we have seen*, 1975, pp80-1. Cited, THOMPSON, p148.

the human propensity to locate a lost golden age twenty years in the past, there seems to be some truth in this statement. As a famous folk poem put it:

The law locks up the man or woman
Who steals the goose from off the common
But leaves the greater villain loose
Who steals the common from the goose.

Naming of Houses

Before the Great War, Nazeing was still a close-knit, fairly isolated community, and many dwellings did not have names. As the village grew they could no longer remain anonymous, and their owners or occupiers gave them names such as 'Rose Cottage' or 'the White House'. In order to make identification easier, we have sometimes used these names in periods before they came into use. A map and key on pages 146-7 shows the locations of all buildings mentioned in the text.

Part II

Nazeing People

Chapter 4

The Palmer and Wellesley Families

The Palmer Family

The Palmers were leading figures in Nazeing from the late eighteenth century when William Palmer (1737-1821), a wealthy merchant, moved into the village and built Nazeing Park. His son George (1772-1853) was a great campaigner for safety at sea and sat as MP for South Essex from 1836 to 1847. George's son, 'George junior' (1799-1883), played an important part in saving Epping Forest but was swindled out of a large sum of money and had to let Nazeing Park out to tenants.

It was a family tradition to become members of the Mercers' Company, which is the premier Livery Company of the City of London, and some of them were elected its Master. Before the coming of the welfare state, several Nazeing people received pensions from the Mercers, presumably arranged by the Palmers.

Ralph Charlton Palmer (1839-1923) was the youngest son of George junior. He was educated at Winchester College, Balliol College Oxford, and Lincoln's Inn, following in the footsteps of his older cousin, Roundell Palmer. At Winchester Ralph became a prefect and his 'affectionate cousin' wrote a long and earnest letter, urging him: 'If you tell a junior to do anything, remember that you and he are both gentlemen's sons, and speak in the tone of a gentleman'. Ralph was to be a leading figure in Nazeing for fifty years from 1874 and conducted himself in this spirit of *noblesse oblige*.

Ralph became a barrister and worked in the chambers of his cousin Roundell, who later, as Lord Selborne, became Lord Chancellor. From 1885 to 1910 Ralph was a Lord Chancellor's Visitor in Lunacy, travelling the country inspecting asylums and private premises. There were three Visitors, two of them medical men and one a barrister, so his legal training was essential for the post. Meetings of the Visitors were held monthly and each Visitor supplied about fifteen to twenty reports. What was said of another Visitor might equally well have applied to Palmer: the post 'was perfectly fitted to his love of enquiry, of travel, of public activity, and of public pronouncements'[3].

From 1876 to 1880 Palmer was secretary to the Public Schools Commissioners, which gave him experience of and an interest in education. In 1892 he was one of twelve men appointed to the Cowper Commission which was instructed to investigate the possibility of establishing a teaching university for London. He later became Deputy Chairman of the City and Guilds Institute, and a member of the Senate of London University.

Ralph Palmer was elected Master of the Mercers' Company in 1891 and again in 1914, when he succeeded Robert Baden Powell of scouting fame.

From 1893 Ralph lived at Hubbards, where he remained for the rest of his life. On the 1901 census he is listed as 'Magistrate. Visitor in Lunacy. Farmer'. Although he employed a bailiff, he personally ran the estate. When in 1890 he recruited Thomas Hollow from Cornwall to Brewitts Farm, the tenancy agreement went into great

---

3   Medical History, 1995, 39: 399-432. *What the Doctor Thought and Did: Sir James Crichton-Browne (1840-1938).* MICHAEL NEVE and TREVOR TURNER. There is a fuller account of Palmer's career in the Nazeing History Workshop archive.

detail including a requirement to 'manure annually one fourth of the pasture land at least with eight good cart-loads of well-made farm manure per acre'.

In 1910 Ralph and his nephew Archdale owned a total of 817 acres, more than one-fifth of Nazeing and the largest estate in the village. The *Lloyd George Survey* gives an idea of how Ralph might have managed their fifty-eight properties. The largest of the working farms by acreage was Lodge Farm, where he installed Walter Brown as bailiff. Five others were described as farms – Belchers, Teys, Brewitts, Mansion House and Whitehall. All had the description of 'house, buildings, common right and agricultural land' and all had resident farmers. Another five dwellings, also described as 'houses', were occupied by farm workers and had their own agricultural land but no outbuildings. Two dwellings were called 'cottage and garden' and the remaining forty-five were 'tenements', twenty-seven of them with common rights. Although we think of tenements as overcrowded city slums, the word originally referred to any rented property. The Palmer tenements were usually smaller than the farmhouses, mostly rented by farm labourers. The farm labourers would probably have worked directly for the Palmers, who would then have made them available to the farmers as needed.

Most of the properties were on a three-month tenure starting on Michaelmas Day, 29 September. As would be expected with a conscientious and rather paternalistic landlord, most were in fair condition or better but there were a few exceptions. Profits Hill Cottages, King Harold Cottage and 42 North Street were poor; Keepers Cottage, Vine/Clematis/Heather Cottage and the Nook were very poor. Unsurprisingly, all were described as old. By contrast with the village as a whole, the majority of Palmer dwellings were timber, perhaps because they tended to be older. The Palmers owned eighteen brick dwellings, some of which were replacements built by

Ralph Palmer. Certainly in Back Lane, Northside and Southside were built on the site of a demolished farmhouse called Shepherds. Other possibilities are Rose Cottage and Park Cottage in Back Lane, and Bentons in Middle Street. Although Ralph was a wealthy man, he did not have infinite amounts of money and could not afford to replace all of the dwellings.

Kate Henty of Nazeing Park painted the old Queens farmhouse in the 1870s. By 1881 the farm had been merged with Belchers Farm and the house had been replaced by a pair of farm workers' cottages. Rose Cottage is on the right.

Archdale Palmer (1865-1950) was the son of Ralph's older brother, Archdale Villiers Palmer, who also had four daughters. Like Ralph, he attended Winchester College. There he was a younger contemporary of his cousin William Waldegrave Palmer, later the second Lord Selborne, and of Sir Edward Grey, the Foreign Secretary who in August 1914 famously declared: 'The lamps are going out all over Europe; we shall not see them lit again in our life-time'.

Grey and Archdale Palmer were both enthusiastic and skilful players of real tennis and Archdale also played lawn tennis at a high level. His best year was 1893 when he reached the semi-finals of Wimbledon and won a prestigious tournament at Dinard in Brittany by beating Arthur Gore, later three times Wimbledon champion.

Archdale was attracted to business and did not go on to university. He was described as 'bland but decisive in manner, of first-class business capacity, sanguine but not reckless, with many friends in the City, a man of the world with no known vices'[4]. He combined business with pleasure when in 1899 he was appointed Secretary of the ailing All-England Lawn Tennis Club at Wimbledon. He turned around the club's fortunes but in 1903 he apparently organised a round-robin of the leading players, asking that the balls of the Slazenger sports company should replace those of the longer-established Ayres Company. The Slazenger balls were slightly larger than specified, so one of the Wimbledon referees resigned in protest and reported that, to keep him quiet, Slazenger's had offered him £100 in an envelope. Then, early in 1905, Palmer was appointed to a well-paid senior post at Slazenger while retaining his job at Wimbledon. A magazine article envisaged Archdale Palmer, Secretary of the All-England Club, complaining to Archdale Palmer, manager of Slazenger's, about the oversize balls, and he finally resigned from the All-England Club in December 1906. On

---

4   HILLYARD, G.W. *Forty years of first-class tennis*. London, 1924. p43.

the 1911 census Palmer described himself as 'Manager Sporting Goods Manufactory'. Production changed from hand-made to factory-made and within three years annual profits were almost £50,000. For Nazeing people, Archdale Palmer *was* Slazenger's – and 'a real gentleman'.

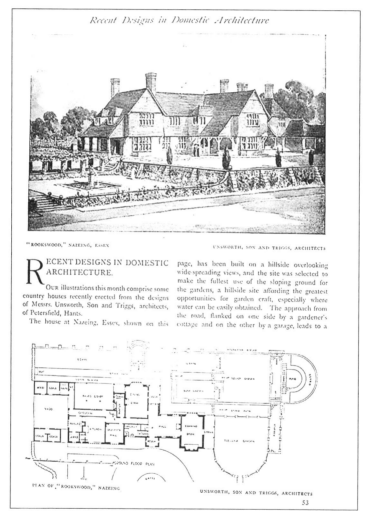

Recent Designs in Domestic Architecture

"ROOKSWOOD," NAZEING, ESSEX   UNSWORTH, SON AND TRIGGS, ARCHITECTS

RECENT DESIGNS IN DOMESTIC ARCHITECTURE.

Our illustrations this month comprise some country houses recently erected from the designs of Messrs. Unsworth, Son and Triggs, architects, of Petersfield, Hants.

The house at Nazeing, Essex, shown on this page, has been built on a hillside overlooking wide-spreading views, and the site was selected to make the fullest use of the sloping ground for the gardens, a hillside site affording the greatest opportunities for garden craft, especially where water can be easily obtained. The approach from the road, flanked on one side by a gardener's cottage and on the other by a garage, leads to a

PLAN OF "ROOKSWOOD," NAZEING   UNSWORTH, SON AND TRIGGS, ARCHITECTS

53

1914 article in *The Studio: An Illustrated Magazine of Fine and Applied Art.* It had a major influence on the development of the Art Nouveau and Arts and Crafts movements, and is still published as *Studio International.*

His work for Slazenger's made Archdale a wealthy man. He bought and demolished White House Farm, described in the *Survey* as 'a very old house much out of repair', which faced on to Back Lane. In 1913, on a site behind the old farmhouse, he built Rookswood, a substantial red-brick house in the Arts and Craft style which commanded splendid views over the Lea Valley. The house, garden and two cottages on Back Lane either side of the entrance to Rookswood (now Homefield and Windrush Lodge) were designed by Henry Inigo Triggs, then well-known as an author, country-house architect and designer of formal gardens. A nostalgic link between the old and new houses was provided by the staircase at Rookswood, which is a replica of the one in White House Farm. Archdale's phone number, Nazeing 2, shows that his was the first telephone to be installed after the exchange was set up at the Bumbles Green Post Office and numbered Nazeing 1. Rookswood became the home of Cliff Richard and his family in the 1960s, when he was making many chart-topping records.

The Wellesley Family

In 1892 Archdale Palmer's sister Charlotte Elizabeth (Lotta) married Herbert Arthur Wellesley, the great-nephew of the Duke of Wellington and a member of the London Stock Exchange. They had three children, Ronald (1894-1914), Eric (1896-1915) and Violet (1897-1971), and lived at Collyers. Both parents were drowned in 1905 when the S.S. *Hilda* was wrecked on rocks outside St. Malo harbour with the loss of 132 lives.

The three children were looked after by their uncle, Archdale Palmer, who became their guardian. Ronald and Eric both followed in their uncle's footsteps to Winchester College. He intended them to have Windrush Lodge and Homefield, but both died in the Great War.

In 1913 Ronald emigrated to Vancouver to pursue a career as a surveyor. When war broke out he enlisted in the Canadian Seaforth Highlanders and a detachment from the regiment was incorporated into the 16th Battalion (Canadian Scottish) of the Canadian Expeditionary Force. They proceeded from Vancouver to the Valcartier camp in Quebec, where contemporary reports describe persistent heavy rain, which may be why Ronald and several others contracted pneumonia. On 19 September 1914, before he could leave for Europe, Ronald died in the Quebec Military Hospital.

Eric died in action on the Western Front a year later. A fellow-officer in the 8th Battalion, Captain Francis Dodgson, wrote to his fiancée a few days after Eric's death on 21 December 1915, explaining what happened:

> We had one very unfortunate incident [during] our last spell in the trenches, which resulted in the loss of Wellesley. He was sent out on a reconnoitring patrol to inspect the enemy's wire and, having done this quite successfully without being spotted by the Hun at all, he needs must go and start throwing bombs into their trench, after which they had, of course, to make a hasty retreat, at the beginning of which he must have been hit... Personally I shall miss him very much, as I used to see a lot of him and we had many a cheery game of cards together. And the Battalion can ill afford to lose officers such as he.

Thus Violet lost both parents and both brothers in barely ten years. Because Eric was reported missing rather than killed in action, she was convinced that he was still alive. Eventually the War Office concluded that Eric was dead and in March 1917 it proposed that the money in his account should go to his sister. Archdale asked that it should be paid to him and a Wellesley uncle as trustees because sending the money to her would involve explaining that the authorities had given up hope for Eric.

Perhaps when the war ended Violet came to terms with Eric's death, for in 1920 she was granted administration of his will.

Eric George Wellesley,
Second Lieutenant in the Yorkshire Regiment

Chapter 5

The Green Family[5]

In 1911 Archdale Palmer was still the owner-occupier of Collyers. When he built Rookswood, he leased Collyers to Frederick William Green. Green (1857-1937) and his wife Elizabeth Louisa, née Poole, (1860-1950) were born in Shoreditch although later, on censuses, they both gave their birthplaces as Islington. His father, Robert, was a ticket porter who wore a badge or ticket licensed by the City of London to carry goods and documents in the Court of Probate at Doctors' Commons, described by Charles Dickens as 'a lazy old nook near St. Paul's Churchyard'. His mother, Elizabeth Evershed, came from a Surrey nonconformist family. Elizabeth Poole's father was a house painter and she was probably the ten-year-old girl of that name who, on the 1871 census, was listed as a servant in St Pancras. In 1881, Frederick was a commercial clerk in the fur trade and Elizabeth was a flower maker. His family was clearly higher than hers in the Victorian pecking order.

They were married in 1884 at New Court Congregational Chapel, Tollington Park, Islington. Both of their sons were baptised there, although later the family had little involvement with the Nazeing chapel. In 1911 they were living in College Road Cheshunt, where they had been since 1898. With them were their unmarried sons and four servants - a cook, parlour maid, housemaid and house boy. There were sixteen rooms in the house.

---

5   Much of the information in this chapter comes from Jennifer Andrews, whose detailed research can be seen in the Nazeing History Workshop archive.

No doubt the opening of Nazeing New Road in 1909 played a part in their decision to move, because Broxbourne station was now more accessible and all three men of the family worked in the City. The Greens took part in social life as soon as they arrived in Nazeing and were generous in supporting village activities. Mrs Green donated a prize for a ladies golf tournament in December 1912. She also hosted work parties in aid of the Red Cross during the Great War, when the local women made garments, bandages and other items that were needed for hospitals.

Diamond Merchant and Director of Mining Companies

Censuses show the career path that made Green such a wealthy man. At the time of his marriage in 1884 and in 1891 he was a 'mercantile clerk'; by 1901 he was a self-employed 'merchant on own account'; it was not until 1911 that he identified himself as a diamond merchant and an employer. Green was a partner in the Dunkelsbuhler Company and would have been responsible for buying and selling uncut diamonds imported from South Africa. The company was one of several that were owned by German-Jewish merchants who were interconnected by marriage, so it was quite an achievement for a gentile from a fairly humble background to reach such an important position. By 1914, Green was listed as a London director, or on the London committee, of six South African companies that mined gold and/or coal. From about 1897 Green was also a director on the board of the Consolidated Mines Selection Company (CMS), which had a large number of German shareholders and directors and so became unpopular during the Great War. Like many people who had close personal links with Germany, he would probably have found the war particularly distressing although he was on the London committee of the Anglo-American Corporation of South Africa Limited, which in 1917 was formed to buy up that part of the CMS owned by German interests.

Frederick Mason Green (1885-1950) and
Henry Edwin Green (1888-1916)

Frederick was born at Barnet and Henry at Stroud Green. Both boys attended Repton, the public school in Derbyshire. Frederick became a stockbroker at the firm of Woolley and Day, and Henry an insurance broker for James Hartley, Cooper & Company Ltd, Lloyd's brokers.

Both Frederick and Henry were given the Freedom of the City of London at the end of 1911. As young men working in the City, they were members of the Inns of Court Officer Training Corps, which was initiated in 1906 to address the shortage of officers in the country and incorporated into the new Territorial Force in 1908. Both joined the London Regiment with the rank of Second Lieutenant and were promoted to Lieutenant, Frederick in 1911 and Henry in 1913. Frederick was made a Captain in April 1912.

The 22nd (The Queen's) Battalion, the London Regiment, was a Territorial unit with its headquarters in Bermondsey, serving as part of 6th London Brigade, 2nd London Division. The Division had just arrived for their annual summer camp on Salisbury Plain when war was declared in August 1914, and they were at once recalled to their home base and mobilised for war service. The Green brothers' active service in the war began when they entrained for France on 15 March 1915. Ernest J. Woolley, Frederick's business partner, was promoted to Captain in the same regiment on the same day as Henry, 25 May 1915.

Henry returned to England on leave on 14 December 1915. He had a spell of illness but returned to the front in July 1916. He is mentioned several times in *A Yankee in the Trenches*, a book by Robert Derby Holmes that is available online. Holmes was an American Corporal assigned to the 22nd London Battalion, and served under Green. His highly regarded book was written in

1918, to give the public an American view of the trenches and life on the Western Front.

Henry Edwin and Frederick Mason Green in France

With the Green brothers went Harry and Arthur Mead as batmen. Harry was the family butler and Arthur a gardener. Frederick sent this photo home to his parents or to Arthur, who was convalescing in Boulogne at the time. The reverse of the photo states that they were going on their first leave from France, in July 1915, and mentions the Regimental Sergeant Major, who is the man on the right. The captain in the centre is Frederick and, since he did not identify the captain on the left, we can assume that he is Henry, who would need no introduction to the recipient. It is signed FMG. Little is known about Frederick's time in France, except that his son-in-law, James Pottinger, said he was gassed and invalided out.

In September 1916 in the Somme District, after two months of fighting with huge losses on both sides, the British were seeking to gain control of a strategic hill called High Wood, seventy-five wooded acres that become known as 'The rottenest place on the Western Front'. They were amazed to see British tanks arriving to join the fight: 'The tanks were an absolutely new thing to us. Their secret had been guarded so carefully, even in our own army, that our battalion had heard nothing of them'. Captain Green and Corporal Holmes survived that battle, which was the first to use tanks, although several hundred men did not. High Wood was taken.

Holmes's recollection gives an idea of Henry Green's character and how he led his men:

> Around nine o'clock Captain Green gave us a little talk that confirmed our suspicions that the day was to be a hard one. He said, as nearly as I can remember: 'Lads, I want to tell you there is to be a most important battle – one of the most important in the whole war. High Wood out there commands a view of the whole of this part of the Somme and is most valuable. There are estimated to be about ten thousand Germans in that wood and in the surrounding supports. The positions are mostly of concrete with hundreds of machine guns and field artillery. Our heavies have for some reason made no impression on them, and regiment after regiment has attempted to take the woods and failed with heavy losses. Now it is up to the 47th division to do the seemingly impossible. Zero is at eleven. We go over then. The best of luck and God bless you.'
>
> Captain Green had me up along with Lieutenant May and as nearly as I can remember these were his instructions: 'Just beyond High Wood and to the left there is a sap and small trench leading to a sunken road that lies between the towns of Albert and Bapaume. That position commands a military point that we find necessary to hold before we can make another attack. The Germans are in the trench. They have two machine guns and will raise the devil

with us unless we get them out. It will cost a good many lives if we attempt to take the position by attack, but we are under the impression that a bombing party in the night on a surprise attack will be able to take it with little loss of life. Take your twelve men out there at ten o'clock and take that trench. You will take only bombs with you. You and Mr May will have revolvers. After taking the trench, consolidate it, and before morning there will be relief sent out to you, best of luck.'

On 9 October 1916 the battalion made an unsuccessful night attack on Snag Trench. They established forward posts on the Eaucourt l'Abbaye-Wancourt Road and were relieved on 10 October. Holmes described what happened next:

We were waiting for the order to advance as shells began to burst over and around us. Captain Green and the Sergeant Major, with whom he had been talking, went down. Captain Green was fatally wounded and died a few days later, and the Sergeant Major lost an arm.

Henry Green was evacuated to the 1/1st South Midland Divisional Casualty Clearing Station, where he died of his wounds on 13 October 1916.

Chapter 6

Other Leading Residents

John Banks (1834-1909) and the Banks Family[6]
From their arrival in the 1650s the Banks family played an
important role in Nazeing life. Most of them were called John,
Thomas or George, and it is not always easy to disentangle them.
In the early 1700s, Thomas Banks owned Brewitts Farm and
inset his initials in the front of the house where they can still be
seen. His son John (1703?-1781) farmed at Paynes and left it to
his nephew Thomas (1754-1825), who in 1781 bought it and
was elected a Trustee of the Common. Thomas's son George
(1786-1864) succeeded him as a Trustee and at Paynes, where
in 1847 he farmed his own seventy-three acres and a further
fifty-seven acres on the Marsh, owned by Sir Charles Wake. By
1861 George was the owner and his son George Thomas (1833-
1897) the occupier of Paynes, and they were respectively overseer
of the poor and churchwarden at All Saints'. George senior had
bought Wheelers and was living and working there. George was a
Trustee of the Common from 1845 until his death in 1864, when
he was succeeded by his son George Thomas. In 1856 George
Thomas Banks married Clara Susannah Gray from neighbouring
Langridge Farm, and they had four children. He stayed at Paynes
until 1878 when he sold the farm that his family had owned for
a hundred years and moved away to Chingford, although he was
buried at All Saints'.

---

6   Most of this section is based on research into the King and Banks families
     by Derek Armes.

One of the most successful of the family was John (1834-1909). He was the youngest child of the less successful John Banks senior (1787-1855), who in 1813 married Susannah King (1790-1868), the daughter of Robert King who owned the King Harold's Head. Robert gave her a generous dowry of 'Motts' (Walnut Tree Cottages), which was to remain in the family for a century. John senior inherited Burnt Hall from his father and farmed there until the 1840s, but he ran through his money so had to sell up and take a job as George Palmer's bailiff, while Susannah became an indoor dairymaid.

John junior married his second cousin Mary King (1834-1892) in 1856 at St Giles Cripplegate. In the 1860s they had rooms in Shoreditch but by 1871 they were living at Grove Road Tottenham. In 1877 John bought Wheelers from his cousin George Thomas Banks for £649 7s 6d, and moved in there. In 1886 they left Nazeing, but three years later returned to live in Coburg (now Warwick) House, where they remained for the rest of their lives. John and Mary had no children and they more or less adopted Mary's nephew Lewis King, son of Thomas and Mary King who were witnesses at their wedding. Lewis lived with John and Mary in Tottenham and then at Wheelers. In 1888 he married Clara Pedder and moved to Islington and later to south London, but in 1901 his five-year-old son Lewis Claude King was staying at Coburg House with John Banks, by then widowed.

Banks was probably educated with the Palmer family at Nazeing Park and was encouraged by them to become a barrister's clerk in London. He and Ralph Palmer worked for neighbouring chambers at New Court in Lincoln's Inn and the two young men were among the first of Nazeing's commuters. By 1881 the fourteen-year-old Lewis King was also a barrister's clerk, a job doubtless obtained for him by his uncle.

Over the years John became the most prosperous of the Banks family. He was astute in his property purchases:

- 1867. He paid his second cousin, William Robert King, £136 for two cottages, now Yew Tree Cottage, built on former waste ground that had been enclosed.

- 1874. He purchased Byners from his brother-in-law Richard Benton junior whose father had bought it for £859 in 1860. Banks, knowing full well that Benton was in financial trouble, was only prepared to offer him £790 for the property.

- 1881. He bought Coburg House from his second cousin Thomas King, a builder, for £375.

- 1881. He paid £90 for three acres of agricultural land in the Marsh.

- 1891. He purchased six cottages built at the King Harold's Head by Thomas Chaplin from Chaplin's widow Elizabeth.

- 1892. He bought Motts and several nearby fields.

- 1898. He sold Wheelers to Joe Pegrum for £750, making a modest profit over a period of twenty years.

- 1902. He bought Camps Cottages (now Little End) from the executors of George Nicholls.

These were all copyhold but he also bought Goodalls, Ivy Cottage and Yew Tree Cottage, which were freehold so the transactions were not recorded at the manorial court.

Banks's treatment of relatives who had financial problems suggests that he had a hard streak and was not slow in making the most of their misfortunes. His purchases of Coburg House and, to a lesser

---

Freehold and Copyhold

By 1911 most Nazeing properties were freehold but some were still copyhold, a form of land tenure conducted through the court of the Lord of the Manor. A fee was payable for transactions which were recorded in a book and a copy given to the tenants, who were therefore called copyholders. It was possible to convert copyhold to freehold by a process called 'enfranchisement', a one-off payment to the Lord. Copyhold was finally abolished under the 1922 Law of Property Act.

---

degree, Byners, were real bargains, tending to confirm allegations in the family that he was a rogue and a cheat.

As a parish councillor and in various other capacities, John Banks was a major figure in the village. In 1875 he was a member of the board formed to found the Bumbles Green School. Chairman of the School Board at the time of the South African (Boer) War, he explained the meaning of 'relief' and impressed on the children the duties and lessons of patriotism. In his later years he was a great supporter of the Congregational Sunday School and, in 1908, laid one of the cornerstones outside its new hall.

In 1877, the year he bought and moved into Wheelers, he was elected a Trustee of Nazeing Wood or Park and, until he moved away in 1886, he was joint Treasurer with Ralph Palmer. In 1891, after his return to Nazeing, he won a vote that 'there should be no games on the common without the consent of the majority of Common Right owners' although permission for golf was granted two years later, 'Mr Banks alone dissenting'. Banks was not re-elected as a Trustee until 1904, but soon made his presence felt as a kind of self-appointed policeman. During the Palmer v Guadagni court case, he carried out a perambulation of the Common with Joe Pegrum and also 'warned off would-be poachers & London bird catchers'. The case was heard in the High Court and the Trust paid for the witnesses' attendance and railway expenses: the labouring men got £1 and £1 4s 0d respectively, but 'Mr J. Banks gentleman' received four guineas and £2 10s 0d. It was a sign of good breeding to think in guineas rather than pounds and to travel first class rather than third on the railway.

John Banks died in November 1909, six months after the operative date of the *Lloyd George Survey*. On the *Survey* Coburg House had already been sold, but Banks was listed as owning Camps Cottages, Goodalls, Byners and eight dwellings in Belchers Lane and Common Road. Perhaps because he had recently died, the information provided on the *Survey* is unusually sparse. He left a long will in which he left an estate valued at £1775 3s 7d. Lewis King held Motts in trust for his son Lewis Claude and in 1917, when the young man was twenty-one, the cottages were sold off for a total of £120 although Lewis Claude later purchased four of the six cottages at the King Harold's Head. John's other beneficiaries were mainly his sixteen nephews and nieces, each receiving between £40 and £150.

Ralph Bury (1876-1954) and Family[7]

The Bury family had lived at Bulphan in Essex for many generations. The family fortune in Nazeing was founded by an ensign who fought under Clive in India and found soldiering to be quite profitable; his son bought property in Nazeing and gave Leonard's Green House to his son, James, who moved there in 1797, when he married.

James Bury rebuilt Leonard's Green House, incorporating some of the existing building, and renamed it 'St Leonards'. He bought many of the properties nearby and had built up an estate of 336 acres by 1824. The Burys became Nazeing's second family after the Palmers. James engaged in financial transactions in the City of

---

7   This section based on research by Colin Dauris.

London where he was closely associated with the banking partners who were the founders of the banking firm of Prescott, Grote. George Grote was a political philosopher and author of a twelve-volume history of Greece and he was for many years the trustee of his friend James Bury's Essex property.

The estate was inherited by James Frederick Bury (1798-1860) in 1825. The family suffered sadness when James's nineteen-year-old daughter, Augusta, died in 1854 and her fourteen-year-old sister, Selina, died six months later. In 1860 the estate passed to James's son Charles James (1831-1897). In 1869 Charles James married Anna Loftus Tottenham (1840-1933), who was quite a catch: her family owned Glenfarne Hall and estate at Enniskillen, over 14,000 acres which amounted to the fourth largest estate in Britain and Ireland. Their cousins were the Marquesses of Ely and owned Loftus Hall, a large mansion in County Wexford that is said to have been haunted. However sadness continued for the Bury family because their eldest son died aged eight days and their second son at the age of thirteen.

For many years Charles James was on the Board of Guardians of the Poor. During the 1870s he set up a charity that distributed hundreds of pounds in cash and kind to the needy. In 1894 he was elected unopposed as Nazeing's first Epping Rural District councillor. When he died suddenly three years later the chairman of the board commented: 'He was a man who never spared himself and I cannot help feeling he has shortened his life by his devotion to his work'. The parish council paid tribute to 'the energy and ability displayed by the late Mr Bury in the discharge of his parochial duties'.

Ralph Frederic Bury, the only surviving child of Charles James and Anna, inherited the St Leonards estate on 13 December 1897, nine days before his 21st birthday. He read law at Trinity College, Cambridge. He was a young man of great energy and by the age of twenty-five was a barrister at Lincoln's Inn, a JP and a district councillor. He became a member of the board of management of the Bumbles Green School and then chairman, a post he held until 1950. He was a district councillor in Nazeing and a churchwarden. He was always a keen supporter of the Conservative Party and was closely involved in the two general elections of 1910. He became a Deputy Lieutenant when he was about thirty years old and in 1910 was appointed as High Sheriff of Essex. One of his duties during his year in office was to proclaim the accession of George V at various centres in the county.

Ralph Bury: article in the Chelmsford Chronicle 18 March 1910, at the time of his appointment as High Sheriff of Essex

Ralph's connection with the Army began in 1900 at the time of the South African War, when he became an officer in a voluntary company at Waltham Abbey. In 1904 his keenness on motoring was recognised and he was asked to transfer to the Army Motor Reserve, in which he held a commission until 1907. When war broke out, he joined the Essex Regiment and raised half a company which went to France in 1915, when he was thirty-nine years old. He remained there over three years, was mentioned in dispatches and received the *Croix de Guerre*. He was wounded and contracted trench foot, which gave him difficulty for the rest of his life. On his return from the war and always afterwards he was known in Nazeing as 'Major Bury'.

Edward James Fowler (1867-1948)

Edward Fowler was born at Elmton near Bolsover in Derbyshire, the son of George who, on the certificate of his marriage to Ellen Piggin, described himself as a gentleman. In 1871 George was listed as a farmer at Oxcroft near Bolsover, where he took over a 215-acre farm from his own father, Edward's grandfather. Evidently the venture did not work out and the family moved to London. In 1881 young Edward was attending Christ's Hospital School in London, and in 1891 he was a veterinary assistant at Etwall in his native Derbyshire.

Although Edward's father was still alive, he and his sisters Constance and Elizabeth owed much to their uncle, Edward James Smith Piggin (1848-1935). Edward Piggin had been born in Braintree, the son of a draper employing twelve persons and later became a hosier with his own shop. He never married but was like a father to his nieces and his nephew, who may have been named after him. Constance and Elizabeth went to live with him while their own father was still alive. In 1896 Edward Fowler married nineteen-year-old Amy Beatrice Howard Wasnidge Weedon and they eventually had children Constance, Beatrice, Edward (Teddy) and Dora Margaret. By 1901 Edward and Amy had moved with their growing family to 126 Dalston Lane Hackney, where he had his own veterinary practice.

In 1905 Edward Fowler bought Mamelons Farm and Mamelons Cottages [Campions] for £1,400 (see page 168-9). The *Lloyd George Survey* shows that by 1912 he had built a new house, which may have been partly funded by a substantial legacy from his father. His speciality was horses and, since there was not quite the same demand for this service in Hackney, he settled full time in Nazeing and turned to farming.

Amy Fowler died early in 1915 and in 1920 Edward married the widowed Victoria Adrina Louie Norton née Groves. They had two children together – Edna and Stanley – but there is a tragic aspect to this story. In 1911 Victoria and her first husband, William Charles Norton, were living further along Dalston Lane, at no. 164. He volunteered for the army but took his own life (see page 356).

Walter Ernest Hargreaves (1865-1954)

Walter Hargreaves was brought up in Cheshunt. He was educated at Merchant Taylors School and, like his father before him, became a Lloyd's underwriter. By the age of forty he was one of the leaders of the profession, having been largely responsible for establishing the market for Lloyd's insurance in the United States. In 1892 he married Lydia Dixon and they had five children.

In 1907 he began to lease Nazeing Park from the Palmers, and a year later made a donation towards the new Chapel Hall. He built the Princess Louise Convalescent Home in Middle Street, reportedly in thanks for having missed the maiden voyage of the Titanic when his chauffeur, James Sadler, lost his way to the docks.

The Hargreaves family at Nazeing Park

Opening of the Convalescent Home in 1913. Walter Hargreaves is seated third from left and Lydia Hargreaves is the tall lady in front of the tent.

Walter was renowned in Nazeing for his generosity and in October 1914 sent £10 to the *Daily Telegraph* Fund for Belgian refugees.

Chapter 7

Absentee Landlords

According to the *Lloyd George Survey*, around half of the agricultural land of Nazeing was owned by just three families. Of these, Ralph Palmer and Ralph Bury lived in the village and played an active part in the management of their farm land, but the land of the Lord of the Manor, Sir Herewald Wake, was managed by local farmers. The next largest holding was the Common, owned by the Trustees. But none of the land owners with between fifty and five hundred acres lived in the village, although between them they owned just over 30% of the total acreage. More than half of the agricultural land in the parish was thus owned by absentee landlords, some of it managed by the executors of estates.

Owner and place of residence	Acreage	% of all land
Sir Herewald Wake (Northamptonshire)	816	18
Ralph and Archdale Palmer, Nazeing	811	18
Ralph Bury, Nazeing	596	13
Trustees of Nazeing Wood or Park	483	11
Williams family (Worcestershire and Brighton)	243	5
Harold Smith (Coventry)	186	4
Guitto Guadagni (Florence, Italy)	178	4
Executors of Barnard Acres (Birmingham)	124	3
Mrs Charlotte Bugg (Enfield)	114	2.5
Col Archer Houblon (Berkshire)	67	1.5

Thirty-four owners with between five and fifty acres held 13% of the total acreage of agricultural land (562 acres) and only twelve of those owners occupied their land. Small parcels of land under five acres were scattered around the village and owned by sixteen landlords. This group accounted for twenty-eight acres.

In total, there were at least fifteen landowners who did not live in Nazeing but owned properties in the village, ranging in size from 816 acres to less than one. Some had inherited properties that had been in their families for a century or more and some had acquired properties by marriage.

There are no general sources giving details of ownership between 1873 and 1911, a period in which many properties changed hands. We can seldom trace exactly when or why the transactions took place and can only assume that – when the change was not through inheritance – people bought property as a small-scale investment. Most of the transactions are dealt with in Part III under the property they owned but three families with more widespread holdings are described here.

Lords of the Manor: The Wakes
The Wake family had been lords of the manor of Nazeing since the 1680s. They had lived at Courteenhall in Northamptonshire since the 1740s, but still had an interest in Nazeing. Sir Herewald Wake (1852-1916) had a steward to manage his affairs in Waltham Abbey and in Nazeing, where he owned 816 acres – almost exactly the same as the Palmers and far more than anyone else. His Nazeing estate included the 330-acre Nazeingbury Farm, occupied by Joe Pegrum, and 320 acres in Upper Town, farmed from Church House Farm by Alexander Frogley and then Richard Power.

Although Courteenhall is seventy miles from Nazeing and Waltham Abbey, a report in the *Northamptonshire Mercury* suggests that there was a good relationship between the Wakes and their tenants. In 1897 Sir Herewald's son Hereward celebrated his twenty-first birthday and several of the tenants from Waltham Abbey and Nazeing were invited to the official celebrations. Arthur Chapman of Abbey Farm proposed a toast and said: 'The tenants at Nazeing and Waltham had already had the pleasure of showing their high opinion of Mr Hereward Wake by a small present of a gun and he was sure that none of his friends wished him with more sincerity every prosperity and happiness than did the tenants he (Mr Chapman) represented'. Joe Pegrum 'heartily endorsed the remarks of the previous speaker'. When Sir Herewald died in 1916, his Nazeing tenants were represented at the graveside by Joe Pegrum and his son David, and John Argent Nicholls who farmed ninety-two acres for him.

Sir Herewald Wake, 12th baronet (1852-1916). He was called Herewald because an older brother named Hereward died young.

Barnard and Other Acres[8]

The Acres family were, appropriately, farmers of hundreds of acres. They farmed mostly in Hertfordshire, where most of the villages and farms mentioned in this section were situated, but also in Roydon and Nazeing. The family history is extraordinarily complicated, not least because five of them were called Barnard Acres, commemorated in 1979 with the naming of a new road in one of the areas of Nazeing where they owned land.

The condition of their Nazeing properties as recorded on the *Lloyd George Survey* illustrates the difficulties faced by an absentee owner of limited means. The Valuation Book of 1910 listed Ernest Acres as the owner but, in the 1912 Field Book, Sworder and Longmore, solicitors in Hertford, were the owners as 'mortgagees for E. Acres'. Most of the farms and cottages had been neglected for several decades and even the tenants themselves had seldom lived on the properties, subletting them to farm labourers. Ham Farm was already in ruins and Shottentons, Porters and Little Dormers were later demolished. Upper Gatehouse Cottages were 'very old and in poor repair and condition' although they survived and were refurbished. The only exception was Parkers which was 'old but in fair repair and condition', perhaps because the tenant from about 1890, John Argent Nicholls, lived there.

Despite owning three small farms and the cottages in Nazeing, the Acres family rented the farms they themselves lived in. The Nazeing properties were scattered throughout the village and none was large enough to sustain a farmer and his family in the lifestyle to which the Acres were accustomed. They seem to have lacked

---

8   This section is based on extensive research by Jennifer Andrews and Samantha Sillitoe, which can be found in the Nazeing History Workshop archive. Only the briefest summary is possible here.

the resources to maintain their properties or employ someone else to do it. Then a dispute between two cousins both called Barnard coincided with the agricultural depression in the last quarter of the nineteenth century. The following account shows how the family acquired and then lost an estate of over a hundred acres in Nazeing.

The Acres first came to the village in 1697, when Joseph and Mary Acres moved into Haywards, now Mansion House Farm. After Joseph's death, Mary took over the farm[9] and, in 1743, an ownership dispute caused the family to move away. Between 1775 and 1791 Joseph and Mary's grandson *Randall Acres (1728-1791)*, the tenant of Holyfield Hall in Waltham Abbey, bought Ninnings, Shottentons, Ham Farm and Parkers. Randall's properties passed to his cousin *Barnard Acres I (1738-1810)*, who was born in Nazeing shortly before the family left. Barnard's only surviving child, Mary (1783-1818), inherited the Nazeing farms.

In 1802 Mary Acres married her cousin *Barnard Acres II (1777-1862)*. After her death he managed the farms on behalf of her heir *Barnard Acres III (1804-1867)*, their only child. He also bought three further properties in his own right – Porters in Cemetery Lane; a pair of cottages on the site of Little Dormers, which he may have built himself; and seven cottages at Upper Gate near the Broadley Common boundary. Ninnings, Shottentons, Ham Farm and Parkers were formally transferred to *Barnard III* in 1828.

In 1830 *Barnard III* married his cousin Martha Acres (1801-1862), daughter of his father's brother Jeremiah. They had already baptised four children in Nazeing and the delay in marriage may have been the result of opposition from their parents, because this was the second marriage of first cousins in their family. They probably lived

---

9   She became one of the few women elected as an Overseer of the Poor.

at Ninnings until 1831, and then sold it to Edward Williams when they moved away to Clothall, near Baldock. In 1847 *Barnard III* sold Parkers, The Ham and Shottentons to his father and bought a large farm at Bridgenorth in Shropshire but within ten years it became the sixth farm he had sold or given up. In 1861 he was a 'retired farmer' staying with his half-brother, John Joseph Acres, at Weston in Hertfordshire, where he drowned in a water hole on the way back from the Three Horseshoes pub. The *Herts Guardian* reported that he was 'unfortunately much addicted to drink' and that the surprising sum of £16 10s was found on his person.

When *Barnard II* died in 1862, he left his Nazeing and Welwyn properties to his youngest son, *Thomas Randall Acres (1835-1878)*, who was living at home with him and helping to run his farm at Codicote Bottom. Thomas had no children, so he named his two sisters and his deceased brother's children as his heirs and divided his properties between the three family groups. The Nazeing properties were left to his sister Mary Acres (1824-1882) and her husband John Acres (1822-1884) – yet another marriage of Acres first cousins. But two features of Thomas's will may have hastened the family's decline. First, the properties were entailed, which meant that John and Mary Acres had to pass them on to their heirs rather than sell them. Secondly, a badly-worded phrase led to a dispute between two of his nephews.

The will stated:

> And after the decease of the survivor of them, the said John Acres and Mary his Wife, I give and devise the same unto my *said* nephew Barnard Acres for his life and after his decease I give and devise the said hereditaments and premises at Nazeing unto the eldest son of the said Barnard Acres that shall live to attain the age of Twenty one years his heirs and assigns for ever.

The problem was that Thomas had two nephews named Barnard, who were cousins. John and Mary's eldest son, who we will name *Barnard IV*, was ten years older than John Joseph's Barnard. Thomas probably intended to leave a lifetime interest in the property to John and Mary's son and not their nephew, thus providing an inheritance to the heirs of all his three siblings. Because, however, the will had already mentioned *Barnard V*, the 'said' nephew Barnard Acres would have been John Joseph's son, and not John and Mary's.

Both Barnards were young, prosperous Hertfordshire farmers, who received inheritances and loans from family members to help them build on a century of farm acquisitions by their ancestors. But within a few years, their fortunes declined irretrievably.

In 1871, aged twenty-three, *Barnard Acres IV (1847-1899)* was a farmer of four hundred acres employing eight men and three boys at Olives Farm, Hunsdon. In 1872 he married Emma Sullins of Sheering, and they had seven children. He had fallen on hard times by 1882, when he appeared before the Ware Board of Health for refusal to pay a rate. He argued that he paid his other rates but objected to paying the special sanitary rate for improvements to Stanstead Abbotts which was some two miles from him, saying 'it is a great injustice on the poor farmers: they have ruined nineteen farmers out of twenty, and now they want to ruin the last'. He lost the case and in 1886 there was an auction of livestock and agricultural implements at Olives Farm, 'with instructions from Mr. Barnard Acres who is quitting the farm'. In 1888, a bankruptcy order was filed against him. His debts were nearly £1,000 and he was being supported by his father-in-law, Peter Sullins. He spent his remaining years in Much Hadham working as a labourer.

Barnard Acres IV (1847-99) and family at Olives Farm,
Hunsdon, c 1878

Barnard Acres V (1858-1922) was born in Weston where his father, John Joseph Acres, farmed 529 acres. John died in 1867, when Barnard was only nine years old, and named his brother Thomas Randall Acres as one of the executors of his will. Thomas was almost certainly involved in Barnard's upbringing, particularly since he had no children of his own. The other executor was John Joseph's solicitor, Matthew Longmore, and they were in charge of the estate until the children married or attained the age of twenty-one years. In 1881, aged only twenty-two, Barnard was renting the 839-acre Cumberlow Green Farm in Rushden, employing twenty-one men and eight boys. He also owned a number of his deceased father's farms that had been held in trust and had 'very substantial resources'.

Barnard V was like an adopted son to Thomas and would have had a good case for being regarded as his heir but, as the son of John and Mary, Barnard IV believed that he should have inherited the properties, and he contested the will. He declared at his bankruptcy trial in 1888 that he had 'an interest in some property in Nazeing for which Messrs. Sworder and Longmore were acting but he never expected to get anything out of it'. Barnard V, perhaps suspecting he was about to lose a portion of his wealth, appears to have transferred half the Nazeing properties to his son John Joseph (1884-1916), who was still a minor at the time.

It was not until 1897 that the case was finally resolved in favour of Barnard IV, who then wrote his will. He stated that he had recently mortgaged his interest in the Nazeing properties to the Norwich Union Life Insurance Company for £1,000 and to Sworder and Longmore for £200. His was rather a hollow victory because he died two years later in the Bishops Stortford Workhouse. The loss of the Nazeing properties that Barnard V 'believed to be rightfully his' could have been the major factor in his financial problems, which began around this time. In 1891 he was still a farmer but by 1901 was a farm labourer. He apparently lost all his wealth, not even leaving a will. Further sadness came when his son John Joseph died in December 1916 of wounds received in the Battle of the Somme.

When Barnard IV died in 1899, half the Nazeing properties passed to his eldest son, *Ernest Acres (1874-1949)*. The other half was transferred to him by Barnard V's son John Joseph a few years later. Ernest married Ella Marian Lake and they had nine children. He served an apprenticeship as a jockey at Newmarket and by 1895 had his National Hunt license. According to newspaper reports Ernest (known as Snowy) was a well-known and popular steeplechase jockey. In 1904 he was admitted to hospital with a dislocated ankle after his horse fell and rolled on him and this may have brought about a change in his circumstances. He moved to Epsom in Surrey and became licensee of the Organ Inn in Ewell. A newspaper report of 1909, which recorded his conviction for receiving stolen wines and spirits and his subsequent imprisonment for three months, described him as an 'ex-jockey'.

One of his daughters told how he not only enjoyed riding horses, he also enjoyed backing them. They lived in hotels for months whilst Snowy competed in races, then over a period of time he lost all his winnings and they ended up destitute in Birmingham, where he worked as a stable lad. He might not have been the best landlord, but in trying to manage his Nazeing properties he was fighting a losing battle.

The Williams Family of Enfield, Worcestershire and Bournemouth
On the *Lloyd George Survey*, Greenleaves, Darmers, 'Ninnetts' [Ninnings], Perry Hill Farm and Little Profits were listed as being owned by the executors of E.J. Williams Esq. The family never lived in Nazeing but were among the leading landowners for over a century.

Edward Williams (c1775-1859) was a magistrate and landed proprietor whose family had a substantial property in the centre of Enfield. In 1809 he married Elizabeth Sarah Jones, who as an infant had inherited Perry Hill Farm and Little Profits. Under the property laws of the day, Edward became the owner. Between 1832 and 1847 he bought Greenleaves, Darmers and Ninnings. On his death, aged eighty-four in 1859, his son Edward Jones Williams inherited the properties. He also was a magistrate, who in 1864 aged fifty-two married Emily Ann Austin, twenty-eight years his junior.

Around 1866 they moved to Rochford House at Rochford in Worcestershire, and had at least six children. He died in 1886, leaving an estate worth almost £110,000. Edward senior was born in Worcester, so there may have been some family connection there. In 1901 some of the family were staying in Bournemouth and by 1911 they had moved there, still living on private means and with several servants.

In 1906-10 Kelly's directories listed E.J. Williams' eldest son Edward Francis (1869-1919) as the owner of the Nazeing properties, and the *Lloyd George Survey* initially gave a younger daughter, Elizabeth Jessie (1867-1962) as owner. Kelly's in 1912 and 1914 and later alterations to the *Survey* list 'the Trustees of the late E.J. Williams' as the owners although it is not clear whether these changes are significant. On the survey, the executors were represented by Braikenridge & Edwards, solicitors of 16 Bartlett's Buildings, Holborn E.C.

Having prospered for over a century, the family seems suddenly to have fallen on hard times. The *Survey* shows that on 8 July 1918 they sold Ninnetts and Perry Hill for £1,605 and Little Profits for £460 to Edward Piggin, uncle of Edward Fowler of Mamelons. On 4 October 1918 they sold Greenleaves and Darmers for £2,275 to David Pegrum. Despite this income, a few months later Edward Francis Williams left barely £1,200 and in 1931 his mother left only double that – small sums indeed, compared with Edward Jones Williams' fortune.

Chapter 8

The Pegrum Family[10]

One of the earliest baptisms recorded in the Nazeing parish registers is that of a John Pigrim in 1559, so the name Pegrum is one of the oldest in Nazeing. Most nineteenth-century Pegrums were descended from *Abraham Pegrum (1744-1824)* and Susannah Forster (1745-1828) and their three sons, **William, Thomas and Samuel**. Their heyday came in 1881 when they were leading members of the Chapel and tenant farmers at five of the largest farms in the village – Nazeingbury, Greenleaves, Darmers, Ninnings and Perry Hill. The owners were absentees so day-to-day responsibility for running the farms would have fallen entirely to the Pegrums, who were mostly comfortably off and reasonably well educated. Their influence was strengthened by intermarriage with the Nicholls and Standingford families, similarly prominent in the farming community and the Chapel. Several members of these families became Trustees of the Common and, after 1894, members of the parish council.

William Pegrum (1777-1874)
In 1805 William married Jane Tizley and they had a daughter, Ann, but Jane died in 1812. William then married Sarah Argent at St Leonard's Shoreditch, where the register described him as a widow and her as a widower. William lived at Darmers and in 1847 was farming thirty-five acres there and sixty-nine for Sir Charles Wake. Aged over seventy, he left the village where he had lived all

---

10 This chapter is based on research by Paddy Hutchings and David Pracy. You can see a fuller version in the Nazeing History Workshop archive.

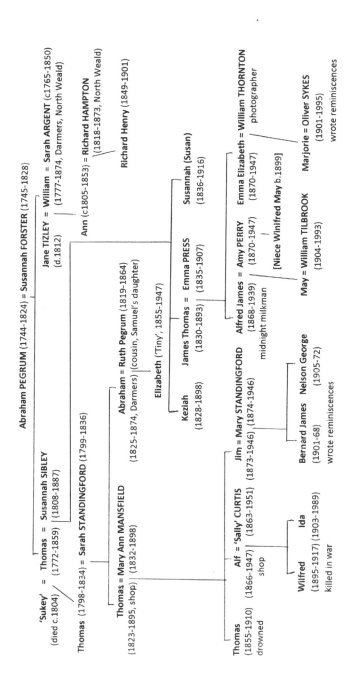

Descendants of Thomas Pegrum (1772-1859) and William Pegrum (1777-1874): selective family tree

his life and moved with Ann and his son-in-law Richard Hampton to North Weald, where they farmed 150 acres and employed five men. He died a month short of his ninety-eighth birthday and was buried in Nazeing, as were Ann and her son Richard Henry Hampton, who lived at Broadley Common.

William Pegrum

Portrait of Thomas Pegrum aged 84

Thomas Pegrum (1772-1859), His First Wife and their Descendants

Thomas's first wife, who is known only as 'Sukie', died young and her sole surviving son was *Thomas Pegrum II (1798-1834)*. He married Sarah Standingford (1799-1836), and their two eldest sons, Thomas III and Abraham, lived in Nazeing.

Thomas Pegrum III (1823-1895) married Mary Ann Mansfield (1832-1898) and they had eleven children, of whom sons **Thomas IV, Alf and Jim** stayed in Nazeing. Around 1860 Thomas III opened a shop at Nazeing Gate, and after he died it was taken over by his son Alf.

Alf (1866-1947) described himself in 1911 as 'General dealer, coal & corn & general shop'. He married Sarah Ann 'Sally' Curtis of Waltham Abbey: Marjorie Sykes recalled 'little Alf Pegrum and his wife Sarah, [...who] was certainly a character and very definite of speech'. They had Wilfred (1895-1917) and Ida. In 1911 Wilfred was a telegraph messenger working for the Post Office over the road. He became the only Nazeing Pegrum to die in the war.

Thomas Pegrum IV (1855-1910) was an unmarried farm labourer rather than a farmer or tradesman with a family, and did not live up to the Pegrums' respectable chapel-going image. He had a drink problem and seems to have found condemnation rather than support from the Chapel. He lodged with his cousin Ann Head on-and-off for seven years until she had had enough of his behaviour and told him to leave. This was apparently the final straw for him, and he carried out his threat to drown himself in his brother Alf's pond.

Jim Pegrum (1873-1946) worked at the gunpowder factory. He married Mary Standingford in 1899, and they had sons Bernard James and Nelson George. Bernard recalled a journey from his grandfather George Church Standingford's White House Farm along the old road to the doctor at Broxbourne:

> I remember the high step between the living room and the kitchen and the great fall I had there. How my head bled. I well remember a great bandage, I think it must have been a sheet, it seemed so huge, being wrapped round my head and the drive to the doctor's. Quite well I remember going down Back Lane on that journey, round through Keyser's Estate – the new road was not made then – over the level crossing, past the Mill and the Church at Broxbourne, and so to old Dr. Hoskins' surgery. Frequently now when I pass that house [Lansdowne House in Broxbourne], I remember that visit and the stitches with which he closed the wound while (I think it was my mother) held

me; also, I recall the sweets which he gave me afterwards. They were
very large for my baby mouth – I think they were known as 'almond
cushions'. Perhaps I should have mentioned that that journey was
made in a horse-drawn light cart – I think they were known as dog
carts; made to hold four people comfortably, two facing forward and
two facing backward. Motor cars were almost unknown in those days.

After his uncle William moved away, *Abraham (1825-1874)* became
the farmer at Darmers, where he employed two men. In 1849 he
married his cousin Ruth, daughter of Samuel of Greenleaves. They
had Elizabeth ('Tiny', 1855-1947) who was a domestic servant,
initially in Nazeing and later as a cook in the London suburbs. She
and Joseph Pegrum senior were the only two people commemorated
with a plaque at the Chapel. Abraham was the enumerator for the
1861 and 1871 censuses. His death coincided with the start of the
great agricultural depression. Joseph Pegrum took on the farming
of Darmers, and the Coleman family became tenants of the house.

Thomas Pegrum (1772-1859),
His Second Wife Susannah Sibley and their Descendants[11]
Thomas was fifty-six and Susannah Sibley from Broadley Common
was only twenty when they married. They had three children, Kezia,
James Thomas and Susannah, known as Susan. After Thomas's
death, the family moved to Hubbards in Betts Lane, where Susannah
was listed in Kelly's as a farmer.

Around 1860 *James Thomas Pegrum (1830-1893)* fell in love with a
girl from Great Parndon called Emma Press. Susan was teaching in
the Nazeing church school, Kezia was in the house, and James was
helping run the farm, so there was nowhere for the couple to live.
In 1866, by which time they were both in their thirties and getting

11   Most of the information in this section comes from Marjorie Sykes.

desperate, they eloped and married at St Leonard's Shoreditch. They settled at Parkers Farm and Alfred James was born in 1868, followed by Emma in 1870 and then four more boys. Their mother could not cope, so Alfred James went to live with his grandmother and aunts Kezia and Susan at Hubbards. Meanwhile, James and Emma fell on hard times, because James stood surety for a friend who let him down, leaving him liable for his debts. This ruined him so he lost Parkers, and eventually the family moved to Cheshunt, where he became landlord of The Rose and Crown. In 1893 James's daughter Emma contracted typhoid and recovered but then she gave it to her father, who died.

| James Thomas Pegrum | Emma Press His wife |

Susannah Pegrum ('Susan', 1836-1916)

After the family moved to Hubbards, Susan became a teacher at the Upper Town Church School and in 1871 was given a leaving present of a large Bible. On the census of that year, she was listed as a servant in the grand Kensington household of William Taylor, grandfather of the then five-year-old Archdale Palmer, who was also there. Soon after that, she and her sister Kezia began supplementing their income by boarding children whose parents had died or were living abroad.

The first of the boarders were Edgar Sykes and his siblings (no relation to Marjorie), who were born in India where their parents still lived. Edgar 'could not be described as a man of few words, for he was a man of practically no words at all', but Marjorie liked him because he was kind and friendly. One of his hobbies was making fireworks and on several occasions he put on a display in the back field at Sturtsbury[12]. He was an electrical engineer working in London but returned to Nazeing for weekends and holidays, and was staying with Susan on the night of the 1911 census.

In 1881 the family were living at Byners, where Susannah was described as a farmer and Susan as a dressmaker. The sisters had just taken in Amabel Catherine Alexander ('Kate', 1877-1919) and her brother George Osbert ('Ozzie', 1879-1899). Their father, William, had died in Hastings only seven weeks earlier, just eleven days after his wife, Elizabeth, leaving an estate valued at £369. Administration was granted to the children's official guardian, William's brother George, an unmarried foreman tailor. He probably felt unable to look after them himself, and perhaps used the interest from the money to board them with the Pegrums.

Sadly, both children had what would now be called learning difficulties. Ozzie, in the more forthright language of the time, was described in 1891 as 'idiot since childhood', and when he grew to adolescence the sisters could not keep him. The Pegrum family blamed cousin marriage which, ironically, was not unknown among them; there is no evidence for this suggestion, but it indicates the thinking of the time.

---

12 In 1890, aged only seventeen, he wrote a book called *Firework Notes*, of which the only known surviving copy is in Brown University Library, Rhode Island.

Kate continued to live with Susan and although 'she was queer and getting worse' was asked to look after the children, which pleased her and them. 'She was as much a child as we were… but certainly had a way with children, and she could play the piano with great panache and a jingle of bracelets and chains'. On the 1911 census Kate was described by Susan as a 'companion' but in another hand as 'feeble-minded'. After Susan's death there was nobody to take care of Kate and in 1919 she died in the Brentwood Mental Hospital[13], where her brother had also died. She left £395, just a little more than her parents had left forty years earlier, and administration was granted to her mother's sister, Emily Eunice Pearson. When Susan died Marjorie found that she had less than £1 in her Post Office savings account, so presumably at some point she ceased to receive money for boarding Kate, and in effect adopted her.

After Susannah Pegrum's death in 1887, Susan and Kezia moved with their nephew Alfred James Pegrum to Mamelons, where in 1891 all three were listed as farmers. Marjorie Sykes recalled:

> Mother was specially insistent that we should visit Aunt Susan, our great-aunt … I must have visited her at Mamelons Farm, but I can't remember it. I do remember, however, the great news being discussed everywhere when she moved, after years of family occupation there, to a nice old house in Hoe Lane[14], next door to Parkers Farm. It later became too expensive and she moved to a cottage on Long Green, next door to a very big family, the Palletts.

Marjorie 'regarded her [Great-Aunt Susan] with reverence and affection for she had great age and wisdom, and she was very kind and understanding… She did not condescend to us and with her

---

13   Later the Warley Hospital.
14   To the White House in 1907.

we felt dignified and important.' It was a great occasion when Susan decided that Marjorie – then aged about eight – was old enough to be given Aunt Kezia's treasured workbox, and solemnly handed it over.

At Mamelons in the 1890s (clockwise): Kate Alexander, A.J. Pegrum, Kezia Pegrum, Susan Pegrum

Alfred James (A.J.) Pegrum (1868-1939) married Amy Gertrude Perry in 1901. Her family had lived for at least sixty years at a cottage always referred to as 'uphome', which could be seen from Sturtsbury across Carter's Mead (A.J.'s field). Its real name was Allmains South, one of a pair of old cottages where Amy's father, Edward, created a wonderful garden of cottage flowers. The other cottage, occupied by Edward's widowed sister-in-law, Eliza, was Allmains.

When he married Amy, A.J. moved from Mamelons a few doors along Long Green to Salem, a then modern semi-detached red-brick house with an acre of land. He farmed the Riddens, across the parish boundary in Waltham Abbey. Salem and next-door Riddens View were rebuilt in 1900 by Ralph Bury, who had the date and his initials inscribed on the front. The *Lloyd George Survey* describes them as '…a pair of substantially built freehold brick and tile cottages… 3 bedrooms, 2 living rooms & scullery'.

Bury persuaded him to move again and run a dairy farm at Sturtsbury where there was more land but a less convenient house. A.J. and Amy's daughter May told her cousin Marjorie that Bury had promised them a new farmhouse: 'This promise was never fulfilled and Aunt was most disappointed, which was natural as she ran the place and encountered the difficulties involved. However, Uncle would never hear a word against Major Bury despite this.'

When Marjorie Sykes came to Nazeing, she stayed initially in Waltham Cross with her Uncle Bert Pegrum, his wife Kate and their children Ronald and Hettie. Then her Uncle Alf called for her in the trap:

> I always enjoyed sitting in the trap if I could sit in the front. It was good to sit high up, to see the harness and the mare's mane dancing for us to a merry rhythm as we made our way along the Waltham Road, through avenues of great elms, past outspread fields, cottages and farms.

The extended Pegrum family outside the gates of Sturtsbury. Adults: Kate and Bert Pegrum, Emma Thornton née Pegrum, Amy and A.J. Pegrum. Children: Ethel Thornton, May Pegrum, Marjorie, Ronald, Hettie in pushcart.

Formal portrait: Kate, Bert, Emma, A.J, Amy;
Ronald, Marjorie, Ethel, May

On the farm: Amy, May, Marjorie, Emma, Ethel

Picnic: May, Marjorie, Kate, Ronald, Emma, Hetty, A.J., Ethel

Emma Thornton née
Pegrum as a young woman:

A.J. Pegrum
outside Sturtsbury

A.J. was known as 'the Midnight Milkman', and Nance Colman explained why:

> In the summer he didn't bother to take the cow in, he would milk it in the field. He would fall asleep and then suddenly wake up, look down at the pail and the cow had walked off. He brought the milk to the house in the can at around 12 o'clock at night. Our milk cans were on hooks by the door.

Marjorie Sykes commented:

> ...it was universally agreed they were a wonderful pair; there was no end to their hospitality ... I can still hear their accents. Aunt's gay and cheerful, Uncle's with a slight Essex drawl, his phrases ending on a higher note.

A.J. Pegrum with wife Amy, daughter May and friend

When A.J. died in 1939, he was the last of the Pegrums farming in Nazeing, and a family tradition of at least 170 years came to an end.

Samuel Pegrum (1779-1842) and His Descendants

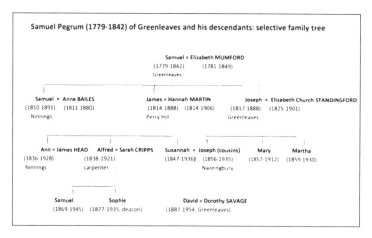

Family Tree of Samuel Pegrum (1779-1842)

Samuel lived at Greenleaves, which was occupied and farmed by the Pegrum family from the 1770s, and married Elizabeth Mumford. They had six surviving children, who all stayed in and around Nazeing and the farming business. Mary (1811-1878) married William Welch the shoemaker of Smalldrinks. Ruth (1819-1864) married her cousin Abraham Pegrum of Darmers. Susannah (1821-1869) married Thomas Nicholls who farmed Parvills at Epping Upland. Their sons were **Samuel**, **James** and **Joseph**.

Samuel Pegrum (1810-1891)

Samuel lived at Ninnings, where he farmed seventy-five acres and employed three men. He married Ann Bailes and they had ten children but only three stayed in Nazeing.

Mrs Ann Head née Pegrum (1836-1928) married James Head and moved to Cheshunt, but when he died she returned to Ninnings. At first she was her father's housekeeper but after his death she took over the farm. In 1888 the chapel was authorised for the registration of marriages and the first bride was her daughter Elizabeth, who married George Lipson. For many years George produced minutes in a beautifully clear copperplate hand for the chapel and the parish council. In her eighties, Ann Head was on the wartime Parcels Committee which was renamed the Welcome Home Committee and instructed to organise a meat tea for servicemen returning from the war (see pages 362-363).

Alfred (1838-1921) became a self-employed carpenter, active at the Chapel. It was said that he made the wooden forms for the Sunday School which are still in use at badminton matches in the Hall. He was also the tenant of School Meads, ten acres of 'very good pasture [with] high agricultural value' behind the Bumbles Green School. He married Sarah Cripps in 1863 and they had six children, living successively at Wheelers, Meadgate, Curtis Farm and the Poplars. Their three eldest daughters were all unmarried and all worked as servants in Broxbourne and Hoddesdon. Emily, the eldest, went to Buenos Aires as a missionary. Their only son Samuel (1869-1945) married Mary Ann Moss in 1893 at Clapham where she lived, and they had seven children; he was employed as a carpenter on a farm but around 1907 became the farmer at Meadgate Farm when David Standingford had to give it up (see page 102). Sophia (1877-1935), the youngest, was a dressmaker and the first deaconess at the chapel.

Susannah (Suey, 1847-1936) married her cousin Joe Pegrum (see below).

Samuel's seven children who moved away are typical of how the next generation in Nazeing found employment further afield. *William (1831-1904)* worked at the gunpowder factory but finished up as a labourer in Poplar. *Rebekah (1840-1921)* married David Snaith in 1870 and they moved to Walthamstow, where he was a tailor and they also ran a post office. *Ruth (1844-1922)* married William Lawrence, a baker from Roydon, and took on the business after he died. *Samuel*

(1845-1920) went to Bishops Stortford and became a railway guard. *George (1849-1936)* married Charlotte Nicholls of Camps Farm and moved to the 150-acre Shaftesbury Farm in Epping, where his descendants still farm, and also farmed eighty acres in Nazeing. *Caleb (1852-1934)* became a baker and confectioner who moved around before settling at Sudbury in Suffolk. *Joshua (1854-1940)* was a baker and confectioner in Walthamstow. Rebekah and Joshua were among those who in 1908 donated foundation stones for the Chapel Hall.

Joshua Pegrum's jubilee celebration, 21 September 1904. Back row: Suey and Joe, Ruth, Caleb and Elizabeth, Sam and Sarah, Joshua and Laura, Alfred and Sarah. Front row: George and Charlotte, Becky, Ann. The nine underlined were siblings; their eldest brother William had died earlier in the year. Names provided by one of George and Charlotte's children.

James Pegrum (1814-1888) was known as 'Peg-leg' because he only had one leg. He lived at Perry Hill, where in 1881 he farmed fifty-four acres and employed 'two men & boys'. He married Hannah Martin but they had no children. After his death she moved to the White House in Hoe Lane and her widowed sister

Eliza Stainton came to live with her. On the 1901 census Eliza said she was 'living on own means' and grumbled that Hannah was 'living on sister's means'.

Joseph Pegrum (1817-1888) continued to live at Greenleaves Farm after his father's death. By 1851 he was managing its 160 acres, and he added a further sixty acres at Darmers when his cousin Abraham died in 1874. Joseph became the first treasurer of the Chapel and one of its first three deacons. When he died suddenly in 1888, within a week of his brother James, the members were devastated and an elaborate memorial plaque was placed on the Chapel wall.

Joseph (1856-1935) was usually referred to familiarly as 'Joe'. In 1881 he married his cousin Susannah (Suey), daughter of Samuel Pegrum of Ninnings. Joe took his father's place as deacon and treasurer and was very active in Chapel affairs for the rest of his life. A man of great drive and ability, he was at various times an Overseer of the Poor, a district and parish councillor and a Trustee of the Common.

Aged only twenty-five, Joe became the tenant at the 300-acre Nazeingbury, the largest farm in Nazeing. In 1911, he was farming a total of 680 acres which, in addition to Nazeingbury, included: 150 acres at Greenleaves and Darmers, managed by his son David (1887-1954) who was described on the census as 'father's foreman'; Manor Lands, 152 acres either side of Hoe Lane; thirty-four acres in the Marsh and the Mead. With Joe and David on the 1911 census were Joe's wife Suey (who in 1901 had declared she was a 'woman of all work') and their three unmarried daughters, all described as 'mother's help' although Agnes was also 'father's clerk'.

After Joseph Pegrum senior's death, his unmarried daughters Mary (1857-1912) and Martha (1859-1930) lived at Greenleaves, partly on income from properties elsewhere in Nazeing. During the war Martha moved to Warwick House where Marjorie Sykes recalled having tea: 'Very posh and you had to be careful of what you said. Martha was a difficult lady to please and there were frequent changes of companions and dogs.' David moved into Greenleaves and made enough profit from wartime farming to buy it and Darmers in 1918 for £2,275 but sold them a few years later, thus ending a five-generation occupation of over 150 years.

Opposite

Pegrum family gathering at Nazeingbury on the occasion of Suey Pegrum's 50th birthday, 1897

1. George Golding. 2. George Lipson. 3. William Lawrence. 4. George Pegrum. 5. Alfred Pegrum. 6. William Pegrum. 7. Caleb Pegrum. 8. John D Welch. 9. Thomas Nicholls. 10. Joshua Pegrum. 11. Frederick Lawrence. 12. William Pegrum. 13. Samuel Pegrum. 14. Frederick Pegrum. 15. Maurice Pegrum. 16. Annie Pegrum. 17. Sophie Pegrum. 18. Elizabeth Pegrum. 19. Sarah Pegrum (Sam's wife). 20. Sarah Pegrum (Alfred's wife). 21. Sophie Pegrum. 22. Nellie Head (James Head junior's wife). 23. James Head. 24. Ann Head. 25. Suey Pegrum. 26. Joe Pegrum. 27. Ruth Lawrence. 28. Rebekah Snaith. 29. Lottie Pegrum. 30 Sophie Golding. 31. Connie Pegrum. 32. Laura Pegrum. 33. May Pegrum. 34. May Lawrence. 35. Alice Pegrum. 36. Agnes Pegrum. 37. Edie Pegrum. 38. Mary Standingford. 39. Maurice Lipson. 40. Leslie Lipson. 41. Hilda Pegrum. 42. Hannah Pegrum. 43. Betsey Pegrum. 44. Winnie Pegrum. 45. Norah Lipson. 46. Lizzie Lipson. 47. Annie Pegrum. 48. Clara Lawrence. 49. Willie Lawrence. 50. Sidney Pegrum. 51. John Pegrum. 52. Frank Pegrum. 53. Winnie Pegrum. 54. Ethel Pegrum. 55. Eric Lipson. 56 Evie Lipson. 57. Maggie Pegrum. 58. Ruth Pegrum. 59. Ralph Lawrence. 60. David Pegrum. 61. Hugh Pegrum. 62. Percy Pegrum. 63. Charlie Pegrum. 64. Dulcie Lawrence.

Chapter 9

The Coleman Family

A Nazeing family

Alfred Coleman (1847-1922) was born into a family that had been in Nazeing since about 1800. In 1869 he married Sarah Burling (1847-1929), who was born at Bobbingworth and in 1861 was living in High Ongar, both in Essex. After the death of Abraham Pegrum in 1874, they moved to Darmers and became the sub-tenants of the Pegrums. They had six boys and four girls, who all grew to adulthood. They were: Mary Jane (born 1870), Sarah (Tot, 1871), Alfred (Sammy, 1875), Ada Rachel (1878), Edward (Ted, 1879), John Daniel (Jack, 1881), Arthur (Arch, 1884), Percy (Wick, 1885), Annie Elizabeth (Nance, 1888) and Ernest George (1891). The girls went away to find work as domestic servants but the boys stayed in Nazeing, and the family became well known and respected in the village.

The Coleman family at Darmers in 1915. Left to right: Ernest (in uniform), Edward, Sarah, Arthur, Ada, Percy, John Daniel, Mary Jane, Annie, Alfred. Seated: parents Sarah and Alfred.

In 1891 Mary Jane was a domestic servant in the Cattermole family, who lived in Islington but bought property at Bumbles Green and became tenants at Perry Hill Farm (see page 213-5). While in Wandsworth in 1898, she married a railway porter called Edward Barker and they had three children. Edward died in 1914 and Mary Jane returned to Nazeing with her children. In 1918 she married Eric Mansfield, a widower with two boys (see page 113) and they set up home in St Leonards Road. Mary Jane died in 1953 and Eric in 1964. In 1901 Sarah (Tot) and Ada Rachel were unmarried domestic servants, Tot to the manager of the Xylonite factory in Highams Park, Walthamstow, and Ada to a metals merchant in Islington. In 1911 Tot was still in Highams Park as housemaid to a bank clerk and his sister, while Ada was cook in the family of Harry Ernest Ketchley, vicar and historian of Barton-le-Street in Yorkshire. Tot was not in Nazeing in 1918 but probably returned soon after to look after her elderly parents.

In 1901 the boys were all still living at home. The four eldest were employed at the gunpowder factory, with one of their workmates as a lodger at Darmers. Ten years later, only Percy was working there, and three of them had married and moved to other parts of Nazeing.

In 1902 Alfred junior (Sammy) married Selina Woodley (see page 296). In 1911 they were living at Belchers Lane with their five-year-old daughter Dorothy and Selina's widowed mother. Sammy was a domestic gardener, probably at nearby Nazeing Park. He died in 1953 aged eighty-two and Selina in 1966 aged ninety-three.

In 1908 John Daniel married Florence Marie London, known simply as Marie. In 1901 she was a housemaid for the Raincock family, who had lived in Nazeing in the late 1890s, and probably met him then. Their children were Maurice, Vera and Molly. They moved to Park View Cottage on Nazeing Common and he continued to work at the gunpowder factory where he lost an eye in an explosion.

Arthur (Arch) was listed in 1911 as an agent for the Wesleyan & General Assurance Company, so he was the only one of the boys to get a clerical job and work away from Nazeing although he continued to live in the village. He served in the Royal Air Corps as an observer on barrage balloons because from them it was possible to see over the enemy lines - but the balloons needed to be pulled down pretty quickly when German planes came near!

In 1911, Percy was still at Darmers, working as a cowman on a farm. He never married and died in 1950 aged sixty-four. In 1911 Annie Elizabeth (Nance) also was still at Darmers with no recorded occupation.

In 1911, Ernest George was a cowman on a farm but his smart appearance contrasts with the image of his father as a typical agricultural labourer. The youngest of the siblings, tragically he was the first to die when he was killed in action on 30 December 1915 aged twenty-four (see page 343).

Coleman Family Business

In 1905 at Nazeing Chapel, Ted Coleman married Alice Ashby, who lived at Mayflower in Middle Street. The photo of their wedding was probably taken in the 'Chapel Field', on the left of where the Hall was built in 1908. After their marriage, Ted and Alice lived in one half of the White House in Hoe Lane, but in 1911 they moved to Camps Cottages (now Little End). They had three children: Edward Frederick Frank born 1910, Lewis John born 1912 and Ena born 1920. Ted joined up at the Recruiting Office in Epping on 13 June 1916 and served in the Norfolk Regiment. He was stationed in India and Mesopotamia. When he came home after the war, recurring attacks of malaria prevented him from working for a whole year.

Ted Coleman in India and the photo of his wife and sons on his desk

According to Ted's son Frank, Ted left the Nazeing Board School somewhat unconventionally, by climbing out of the window to go bird scaring on Joe Pegrum's farm. During his teens, Ted had various jobs and apparently attended night school. When he married Alice Ashby he was a painter and decorator with Langham King at 60 North Street (see page 279). Shortly after his marriage, he started working with Charles Judd and they became Judd & Coleman, Builders. A few years after forming the partnership, they tendered for the building of the new Congregational Sunday School and put in the lowest quote (£438 + stoves), which was accepted. Most of the Colemans and Ashbys joined the Chapel during the early 1900s, and Charles Judd was also a member.[15]

---

15 Thanks to Brian Coleman (Ted's grandson) and John, Richard and Susan (John Coleman's grandchildren) for help in preparing this profile.

Marriage of Ted Coleman and Alice Ashby, 1905

3. Ernest Coleman. 4. Fred Ashby (Alice's brother). 7. Charlie Judd. 8. Sophie Pegrum. 10. Ted Coleman. 11. Alice Ashby. 12. Ada Coleman. 13. Annie Coleman. 14. John Ashby. 15. Ann Head née Pegrum. 22. Eliza Ashby 'Shop Gran'. 23. Sarah Coleman. 24. Alfred Coleman. 27. John Daniel Coleman. 30. Alfred Coleman junior. 32. Percy Coleman. 33. Sarah Coleman. 34. Marie London who married J D Coleman.

Chapter 10

The Nicholls Family

In 1780 two cousins from Epping became neighbours and farmers at two properties in Hoe Lane that had been unoccupied for at least two years. Abraham Nicholls was John Blake's tenant at the White House, and Thomas Nicholls was Thomas Brewitt's at Parkers. Their descendants continued to farm in Nazeing for well over a hundred years.

Abraham Nicholls (1743-1811) and Descendants

In 1803 Abraham bought Camps Farm from Blake, and his son John inherited it when Abraham died. John (1777-1858) married Elizabeth Boreham (c1774-1820) at St Leonard's Shoreditch in 1797. Their six children were baptised at All Saints' between 1798 and 1810 and their only surviving son was called Bryant or Brian (1808-1839).

Bryant Nicholls married Elizabeth Pegrum at St Leonard's Shoreditch in 1833 but he died in 1839. In 1841 Elizabeth was listed as a farmer but she did not appear on the 1847 Tithe Award and in 1851 was described as a 'holder of land'. She lived at Belchers Farm where her father-in-law John was farming and her son William was a labourer. After John's death, William married Mary Ann Bridgeman (1836-1893) and became a farmer of thirty-two acres, employing three labourers and a boy. When William died in 1887, Mary Ann carried on farming for another three years but they had no children and, when she gave up farming, the family connection with Belchers ended.

John Nicholls was among those who officially formed the Chapel on 4 February 1822. Also on the list of founders was Rebecca Banks of

Paynes Farm (c1790-1865) who married John Nicholls in 1830. In 1847 John owned thirty-one acres at Camps and farmed a further seventy-seven acres, including thirty-four acres at Belchers for George Palmer. In 1851 he said he farmed a total of 150 acres, employing four labourers and a milk-maid. When he died on 4 November 1858, he left effects valued at 'under £800' so he was comfortably off. He fully justified the sturdy, even then rather old-fashioned description of him in his will as a yeoman, defined as 'a freeholder holding and cultivating a small landed estate'.

The only child of John and Rebecca, George (c1832-1901) inherited Camps when John died. John had been elected a Trustee of Nazeing Wood or Park in 1826 and George succeeded him in 1859, remaining in office until his own death. He was also elected to the first Nazeing Parish Council in 1894. In 1853 he married Sarah Argent (1829-1914), daughter of Thomas who had Nazeing's first shop, in Middle Street, and also farmed at Parkers. For a while George farmed only fifty acres but by 1881 had 145 acres, so may well have taken on Parkers from his father-in-law. George and Sarah had nine children of whom four had died by 1911.

Of the children who survived, only John Argent Nicholls (1861-1950) is known to have married and had children. He grew up at Camps and probably moved next-door-but-one to Parkers when he married Edith Sarah Webb (1865-1934) in 1890.

On the *Lloyd George Survey* John was listed as the tenant for four small farms with common rights – Parkers, White House, Porters and Ham. He was working 190 acres, including about eighty-five acres on the Mead and the Marsh, for four owners: his mother, the lord of the manor, Samuel Smiley and Ernest Acres. White House and Porters were occupied by other people, and some of John's holdings may also have been sub-let.

John Argent Nicholls outside a cottage on the site of present-day Little Dormers, where he moved in 1930

No	Owner	Description	Place	Acres
127	Acres, Ernest	House, CR, ag land	Ham Farm,	10.4
128	Acres, Ernest	Cottage, CR, ag land	Porters,	9.7
129	Acres, Ernest	House, CR, ag land	Parkers	15.1
217	Nicholls, Mrs Sarah	House, buildings, CR, ag land	Camps	35.6
285	Nicholls, Mrs Sarah	Agricultural land	Nazeing Mead	3.5
290	Smiley, Samuel	Agricultural land	Nazeing Mead	2.1
237	Smiley, Samuel	House, buildings, CR, ag land	White House	22.3
114	Wake, Herewald Sir	Agricultural land	Horsenails	5.4
116	Wake, Herewald Sir	New Grounds	Foxfields, near Camps	7.5
116	Wake, Herewald Sir	New Grounds	Nazeing Marsh	78.9
				190.5

Another William (1774-1861) was the eldest son of Abraham who bought Camps in 1803. In 1806 William married Ann Mumford (1784-1861) and they had ten children. Five of them moved away from Nazeing after marrying, and none of those who stayed had children. William was a farmer all his life. When in 1818 he transgressed by turning a stallion on to the Common it was 'pounded and 10s laid thereon', with a further 40s fine for any second offence unless the animal was immediately removed. In 1841 William was farming near Camps and by 1851 was managing twenty-eight acres at Queens Farm in Back Lane. After his death in 1861 Queens was probably farmed by his son Ephraim (1824-1891), but by 1871 it had been combined with Belchers and was being farmed by William's namesake and great-nephew.

Thomas Nicholls (c1754-1812) and Descendants

Thomas Nicholls married Elizabeth Green in 1780, the year he moved into Parkers. After Thomas died in 1812, Elizabeth took on the farm until 1824, which was probably the year of her death although she was not buried at All Saints'. She is probably the Elizabeth Nicholls who was one of the founders of the Chapel in 1822. From 1825 Parkers was farmed by her son *Abraham (1792-1836)*. In 1806 an older son, *John (1785-1839)*, married Sarah Argent (1783-1869). She was the sister of Thomas the shopkeeper, who was farming Parkers in 1847 and may have taken over after Abraham Nicholls' death in 1836.

By 1824 John Nicholls was the tenant farmer of Barnard Acres II at Shottentons and his will gives an insight into the management of the farm at the time. His lease expired in 1844. He wished to extend it to his wife Sarah, so she could carry on the farm for the benefit of herself and their youngest son, Abraham (1818-1886), provided he remained with his mother and helped her with the farm. At her decease, or if she remarried, all the farm stock, personal property etc, should be for the use and benefit of Abraham. John appointed his wife Sarah, his cousin John Nicholls of Camps Farm and his friend William Pegrum as executors.

After John's death, Sarah was listed on censuses as a farmer of thirty-two acres at Shottentons, and in 1861 Abraham was farming a further thirty-five acres. When she died, he combined the two holdings and by 1881 had the luxury of retiring to Parkers. He married Elizabeth Thompson (1823-1911) in 1848 and their only child was Sarah (1849-1927). Aged forty, Sarah married Alfred Cook, a wheelwright in Epping, and they had daughter Edith (Edie, 1891-1974). By 1901 Elizabeth was living with them 'on own means'.

William Nicholls (1807-1885) was Sarah and John's eldest son, and the black sheep of the family. When John died in 1839, William was omitted from the will except for a payment of £5 from his brother Thomas for 'giving and providing him with mourning', probably because a lifestyle that later led him to become a publican was already in evidence. Whereas Thomas became a prosperous farmer, William was a farm labourer. In 1831 at Waltham Abbey he married Rosetta Rand, who died in 1839. Their daughter Esther (1832-1877) married William Dean and they lived at Burnt Hall. In 1840 at Waltham Abbey, William married widow Phoebe Holt, and in 1841 they were living 'near Camps' but she died in 1847. His third known marriage, to widowed laundress Mary Ann Ives in 1865, may have prompted a late change of career. In 1871 he was a 'keeper of ale and spirits house' at The Woodman in Wormley West End, and in 1881 a beer-house keeper in Cheshunt.

John William Nicholls (1834-1908) was the only son of William and Rosetta. He stayed in Nazeing and remained a farm labourer all his life. In 1851 he was living with his grandmother Sarah Nicholls at Shottentons, described as a servant. He is probably the John Nicholls who in 1904, on the instructions of William Graham, broke down a fence erected by the Trustees of the Common to block carting from Harold's Park Farm. He married Jane Withers (1842-1921) in 1864 and they lived at King Harold Cottage. They had nine children but their six boys all moved away except Joseph, who was the only Nazeing Nicholls to die in the Great War.

Thomas Nicholls (1809-1889) was the second son of John and Sarah. Again John's will gives some interesting information. He said Parvills Farm at Epping Green belonged to Edward Williams, owner of Greenleaves, Darmers, Ninnings and Perry Hill. John jointly held it with his friend William Pegrum, farmer and co-founder of the Chapel. He had placed his son Thomas to manage that farm and his daughter Esther to assist him in the house. John had borrowed about eighty pounds from Thomas to enable him to carry on the farm where Thomas had laboured, so he bequeathed to Thomas his part-share right and interest in the farm and hoped William Pegrum and Edward Williams would accept him as joint tenant. He wished Thomas to make payment of forty pounds to Esther in annual instalments over six years.

In 1841 Thomas senior married William Pegrum's niece Susannah (1811-1869, daughter of Samuel of Greenleaves), and they had son Thomas (1845-1923). Esther (1813-1900, sometimes called Hester) married George Thompson (1824-1882), who worked as a labourer and haybinder at Parvills. Thomas's wife and his niece Ann Head's husband both died in 1869 and for a while Ann stayed with him, probably as a housekeeper. With eight men and a boy, he farmed 180 acres that included land at Copped Hall. He left £1,415, and it probably says more about the state of British farming than about the family finances that in 1923 his son Thomas left £638 and in 1951 his grandson John Egbert (Bert) only £187.

In 1870 Thomas junior married Emily Lawrence but she died in 1879 aged only thirty-four. In 1907 he gave evidence in the Palmer v Guadagni court case, remembering from his schooldays in the 1850s that there were three gates on to the Common and that he had seen hay and wood carted across it. Thomas junior probably bought Parvills from the Williams family in 1918, when they also sold their Nazeing properties.

Although Thomas Nicholls senior's farm was just outside Nazeing, his name headed the list of subscribers to the new chapel building in 1876. He gave £21 and his son Thomas junior £5 5s. George Nicholls of Camps and Abraham Nicholls of Shottentons each gave £10 10s. William Nicholls of Belchers donated £2 10s and four other members of the Nicholls clan gave a total of £2 10s, William the publican unsurprisingly not among them. One of the Mr Nicholls put on a magic lantern show that raised £1 2s. The influence of the Nicholls family at the chapel was second only to that of the Pegrums.

Yet when the chapel hall was built only thirty years later, none of the Nicholls family presented a donation stone. Although they had been so influential, in 1911 the only Nicholls households left in Nazeing were at Camps, Parkers and King Harold Cottage, and by 1932 just John Argent Nicholls and his son Arthur John and their families remained.[16]

---

16   Thanks for information from Jennifer Andrews and Samantha Sillitoe about Nicholls genealogy, and from Jacky Cooper about Nazeing farms and farmers.

Chapter 11

The Standingford and Frogley Families

The Standingfords were tenant farmers in Nazeing throughout the eighteenth century. In the 1770s William Standingford (d.1782) bought Gardners and Havenslea and moved to White House Farm. In 1797 his son William II (d.1828) took advantage of rising wheat prices during the war with France to sell his two cottages and buy White House Farm from Mrs Elizabeth Welch. William I was a Trustee of Nazeing Wood or Park 1780-1, and William II was a Trustee 1784-96 and 1803-10. The telling of this story would be much easier if more of the Standingfords had been called something other than William or George.

William Standingford III (1784-1833)
and Dinah Church (1793-1868)
In 1828 William II's son, William III, inherited White House Farm. He had married Dinah Church at St Leonard's Shoreditch in 1818 and they had at least six children, who were all given 'Church' as their middle name. William III died in 1833 and Dinah took over the farm. In addition to her own twenty-nine acres, she farmed 144 acres for Sir William Wake, employing seven men and three boys. In 1838 she attempted to cart dung from Betts Lane to Wake's fields at Nazeing Grove across the land of George Palmer senior, who instructed his men to block the way with planks and a ditch. She and Wake therefore prosecuted him and after a prolonged court case they won £2 damages. You get the impression that Dinah was quite a formidable woman. She died in 1868, leaving over £1,000.

After Dinah's death her youngest son, George Church Standingford (George II, 1832-1904), continued to live at White House Farm although he farmed only about a hundred acres with three men. George was elected as a Trustee of Nazeing Wood or Park in 1871, and it was to him that George Palmer junior wrote in 1877 when he resigned. In 1871 George II married Elizabeth Ann Parker at St Mary Newington. Evidently there was still money in the family because, for many years, George's unmarried brother John and widowed sister Mary Izard lived with him 'on own means'.

George Church Standingford at White House Farm

When George II died in 1904 he left £1,381. His daughter Mary married Jim Pegrum in 1899 and their son Bernard was only three when his grandfather died, yet he remembered clearly that George was 'in the last weeks of his life ... carried downstairs in a sedan chair by two stalwart henchmen from the farm'. George Church Standingford had belonged to the West Essex Yeomanry, of which Palmer was Colonel, and after his death Bernard 'used to almost worship his old military tunic... and for many years his rusty riding stirrups were a treasured plaything'.

White House Farm was described on the *Lloyd George Survey* as 'A small freehold farm with a very poor house... timber built & tiled &

much out of repair. 5 bedrooms, 3 rooms on ground floor, kitchen & brick & tiled addition of brew house at rear'. The buildings also were very poor and the land very heavy.

Bernard Pegrum painted a vivid portrait of White House Farm in its last days:

> The white paled fence separated the garden from the road, and the long path from the front gate was bordered on each side by lawn, until it reached the point near the front door where two huge drainpipes, set on end, stood sentinel…The tall 'Monkey Puzzle' tree outside the front-room window I remember well. Paths ran left and right of the front door, that to the left leading into the stack yard and farm buildings, that to the right led to a cluster of trees and shrubs known as 'the Arbour', and beyond that the orchard.
>
> The front door opened on a small, dark hall. To the right was 'the parlour', a room which does not seem to have been used a great deal. I recollect that it had a musty smell, and contained furniture which oppressed me. To the left of the entrance was a large room which extended from front to back of the house, with large windows at each end…
>
> I remember the long, low kitchen, with its large fire-place, with the 'Dairy' beyond, and I can still smell the peculiar odour of the Dairy. I remember the long kitchen table…on which Grandma used to draw and dress fowls for the table, and in doing so explain to me the mysteries of a chicken's inside…

Archdale Palmer bought it for £1,250 in 1909 and demolished it to make way for Rookswood and the neighbouring cottages.

From 1919 to 1925 George II's son George IV (1880-1965) was pindar of Nazeing Common, not an insignificant post but one that earlier generations of the family had, as Trustees of Nazeing Wood or Park, supervised rather than occupied.

William Church Standingford (1818-94) and His Descendants
Around 1820 William II's son George I (1783-1846) became the
Palmers' tenant at Mansion House Farm. In 1822 he and his wife
Elizabeth were among those who officially formed the Nazeing
Congregational Church, and it shows continuing nonconformist
influence in the family that most of their marriages took place in
London. In 1846 their daughter Lydia married Joseph Pegrum in
Nazeing, perhaps because George, who died a few weeks later, was
too unwell to travel to London. In 1852 Lydia died in childbirth
and two years later Joseph married her cousin Elizabeth Church
Standingford (1825-1901). Elizabeth became the mother of Joe,
whose strength of character may well have been inherited from his
grandmother Dinah.

In 1848 Mansion House Farm was taken on by George I's nephew
William Church Standingford (William IV), who in 1842 married
farmer's daughter Betsy Izard (1818-1900) from Roydon. Six years
later her brother William Izard married George I's sister Mary
Church Standingford, but William died within a year and she
never remarried. At first William IV farmed just thirty acres with
one man, but by 1871 he had taken on an extra 120 acres and two
more men. When the new Congregational Chapel was opened
in 1876, he subscribed £5 5s, his daughter Rachel 10s 6d, and her
prospective mother-in-law, Sarah Frogley, 15s. He retired in the late
1870s and in 1891 described himself as 'living on own means', but
they must have become fairly limited because he left only £33 12s.

William IV's son, George III (1849-1918), married Fanny Harriet
Nottage in 1879, shortly after the death of her father David. David
had farmed ninety acres at Marshgate Farm, which was taken over
by his widow Susan née Watson and son Joseph. George was then
a gardener in Edmonton but Susan and Joseph died in the 1880s
and in 1890 George bought Meadgate Farm for £1,500, probably

from the Palmers who had owned it in 1847. For reasons unknown, it was Susan Nottage and then Fanny Standingford rather than George who were listed on electoral registers.

On the 1891 and 1901 censuses George was the owner and farmer of Meadgate, but on the *Lloyd George Survey* the owner was 'J. Pegrum Nazeingbury for D.W. Standingford'. This reflects a strange and rather sad episode in 1907, when an Inquisition of Lunacy was requested by George's cousin Joe Pegrum, whose mother was the sister of George's father. It found that George's son David was 'of unsound mind and not sufficient for the government of himself or his property'.[17] In 1911 George was employed as a cowman on Harold's Park Farm, while David was a farm labourer and boarder with the Wootton family at Rose Cottage, described in the language of the time as 'feeble-minded'. Until 1915 David was listed on electoral registers as owning Meadgate Farm although it is a mystery why he should have become the owner when he was considered incapable of managing it and his father was still working.

The problems at Meadgate and the state of White House Farm symbolised the decline of the family. Other family members did prosper but had to move away from Nazeing to do so. In the 1870s Frederick Standingford moved to Oxford and in 1987 his grandson Bert was elected Lord Mayor. Bert died two days before taking office but his wife Elizabeth took his place.

The Frogleys
In 1876, at St. Botolph Bishopsgate, William Church Standingford's daughter Rachel Elizabeth married Alexander Freeborn Frogley from Broxbourne. On the marriage certificate, he was described as a seedsman and his father Joseph as a nurseryman. In 1879 Alexander

---

17   TNA C211/69/26. [See also ERO D/Djg/M37].

bought Church House Farm in Upper Town from Joseph Pegrum for £210. The house probably needed refurbishing, because on the 1881 census the family were still living at Mansion House Farm. Alexander was head of the household, a farmer of 150 acres employing four men and a boy, with William described as his father-in-law and a retired farmer.

The family moved into Church House Farm soon afterwards. It had been copyhold and in 1894 Alexander enfranchised it for £30 16s 8d, which was twenty-five times the yearly amount of the rent charge. He probably managed all or most of the Wake land that had been farmed by his father-in-law's mother, Dinah Standingford. In 1905 he gave up farming and sold his house for £700, a very healthy profit on his original outlay, even allowing for the cost of refurbishment and enfranchisement. The purchasers were the Wake family who rented it to their new tenant, Richard Power. Frogley reverted to his original trade, describing himself on the sale document as 'nurseryman and seedsman'. On the 1911 census he was a 'corn and seed merchant' at Sun Street in Waltham Abbey. His older brother Gerard James, a dairy farmer at Spitalbrook in Broxbourne, owned some fifty acres in Nazeing Mead which became the Herts & Essex Aerodrome.

Chapter 12

The Bugg and Sinclair Families[18]

The Bugg family had their origins in south-east Suffolk and came to west Essex in the 1830s. William Bugg (1808-1851) was taken on as an apprentice by William Lewis, a veterinary surgeon, and he later married William's daughter Annie. In 1841 William and Annie Bugg and their family were in Roydon Hamlet and nearby were a William and Mary Lewis, who were probably Annie's parents. Both Williams were listed as farriers, defined as a blacksmith who shoed horses and provided general veterinary care for them.

William and Annie's children were Richard (1834-1902), Eliza (born 1835), Harry (1837-1912) and Robert (1839-1915). By 1851 William and Annie were in Halls Green Roydon with their sons, while their daughter Eliza was employed as a servant at Nazeing Vicarage. William's occupation was given as veterinary surgeon but he died later in the year of phthisis (tuberculosis).

Richard Bugg
Richard took over his father's business and described himself as a farrier. In 1858 he married Charlotte Margaret Cornell, whose father was a farmer in Halls Green. In 1868 they moved with their growing family to Stanstead Lodge Farm in Hertfordshire, where he was a farmer. Richard bought Paynes Farm in 1882 and moved there later in the decade. He had owned two copyhold cottages at Broadley Common since the 1860s, and he also bought Denver

---

18   Information in this chapter from Joy Tizard, daughter of Cliff Chapman and Pat Sinclair.

Lodge and Wyndith in Nazeing. He was a Trustee of Nazeing Wood or Park from 1889 to 1898.

Richard and Charlotte had nine children who all survived childhood. Walter followed in his father and grandfather's footsteps and became a veterinary surgeon although, unlike them, he had formal training and attended the Royal Veterinary College in London for six years. Robert married Emma Elce Acres in Hoddesdon in 1891. Their son Norman Elce was killed in the Great War (see page 355). After Emma's death in 1904, Robert married Jane Barrett and they went to Canada in 1910, changing their surname to Budd. Richard and Charlotte's youngest son was Golden, a forename that comes up several times in the Bugg family. Golden married Agnes Coy and in 1911 they too emigrated to Canada.

Three of Richard's daughters, Ellen, Louisa and Agnes became members of Nazeing Congregational Church, where Ellen in particular was very active. She visited prospective members and was frequently mentioned in the church minutes, helping to organise bazaars, reading circles and mothers' groups. Richard was still at Paynes Farm with his mother Annie Bugg in July 1901, when she died. He then moved with Charlotte and Ellen to Bush Hill Park in Enfield, but died a year later.

After Richard Bugg left Paynes Farm, it was farmed by a series of tenant farmers, until it was sold much later. The first tenant was Thomas Chapman (1869-1953), a brother of George Chapman who later bought Langridge Farm. He was the eldest son of Thomas Chapman, who by this time was farming at Holyfield Hall Farm on the Waltham Abbey side of the parish boundary, not far as the crow flies from Paynes Farm. In 1901 Thomas married Alice Mary Chetwood and they had son Thomas Herbert. In 1910 Thomas moved with his family to be a farm bailiff at Fern Hill, Great Parndon.

Marriage of John Frederick Mugleston and Louisa Bugg:
photo taken at Paynes Farm

7. William Bugg. 10. George Sinclair. 12. Annie Lewis. 13. Annie
Bugg. 14. Robert or Henry Lewis. 15. Eliza Lewis née Bugg. 16.
Harry Bugg. 17. Mary Ann Bugg. 20. Richard Bugg. 21. Charlotte
Bugg. 30. John Frederick Mugleston. 31. Louisa Mugleston. 33.
Annie Sinclair. 34. Ada Sarah Sinclair. 35. Arthur Sinclair. 40.
Golden Bugg. 44. Ellen Bugg.

Harry Bugg and the Sinclairs

Richard's brother Harry became a bank clerk, working for Martins
Bank in London. In 1861 he married Mary Ann Brown in Enville,
Staffordshire, where she was born. They lived in the Westminster
area for twenty years but evidently Harry became dissatisfied with
his banking career and decided to try his hand at farming.

In 1881 George Church Standingford and his son-in-law Alexander
Frogley left Mansion House Farm, and Harry Bugg became the new
tenant. The Buggs and their younger children, George and Annie,
had just moved in when he received a letter from Martins Bank.
He had expected a pension but the bank wrote explaining their

conclusion that his leaving present was sufficient because 'as you left us to go into business on your own account, and in the prime of life, you were not entitled to a pension which is usually granted when anyone has grown old and incapable of further service'.

Harry and Mary Ann Bugg

When Harry became the farmer at Mansion House, he took responsibility for farming Damsel Mead and Rushy Mead, eighteen acres of meadow next to Paynes Farm. They were owned by Ralph Palmer but later incorporated into Paynes, almost certainly because Richard negotiated with Ralph to buy them and take over the farming.

Harry became involved in local life. In 1886 he was listed as farmer, overseer and surveyor of highways, and in 1894 he was elected to the newly formed parish council. In 1891 and 1901, he was the census enumerator for part of Nazeing. In 1897 his signature headed a petition to protest against the possible movement of Hoddesdon livestock market and three of his brother Richard's sons also signed.

By the time Harry had moved to Nazeing, his two eldest sons Arthur and William had changed their surname from Bugg to Sinclair. No one knows why they chose the name Sinclair, although apparently William did comment later that everyone assumed they were Scottish. Arthur became a headmaster and William was a merchant banker. Although they never lived permanently at Mansion House Farm, they were frequent visitors. George worked on the farm and took over from his father as Harry grew older. Annie went to a small private school in Epping for a while and later trained as a children's nurse.

Shortly before George's marriage to Winifred Constance Lee, both he and Annie also changed their name to Sinclair. According to her son-in-law Cliff Chapman, Winifred would not marry George unless he changed his name! They were married at All Saints' in 1899 by the Reverend Thomas Goddard and had Harold Norman (1901-1983), Wilfred George (1904-1969) and Winifred Patience (Pat, 1908-1991). Winifred's father Henry farmed at Fidges Farm in Roydon Hamlet and during the final years of his life went to live at Mansion House Farm, where he died in 1923. George and Winifred started their married life at Whitehall Farm but exchanged homes with his parents in about 1906.

Harold Sinclair at Mansion House c1915

The Sinclair family at Mansion House Farm: George, Pat, Winifred, Harold (front left), Wilfred

On 6 February 1911 there was a special dinner at Mansion House Farm to celebrate Harry and Mary Ann's golden wedding anniversary, but she died two months later and Harry died on 30 April 1912. They are both buried at All Saints'.

Chapter 13

The Mansfield Family[19]

One of the largest family groups in Nazeing on the 1911 census was the Mansfields, who occupied ten of the 202 dwellings in Nazeing. They demonstrate the extent to which Nazeing families intermarried, with a further thirteen households having Mansfield ancestors. All but one of these families were descended from Edward and Joseph Mansfield, two of the sons of a couple who married in All Saints' Church in 1765 – *Thomas Mansfield (1747-1817)* of Roydon and *Elizabeth Jennings (1747-1823),* who lived at Longyard Cottage Nazeing. Edward and Joseph were both agricultural labourers, as were most Mansfield men and boys living in Nazeing up to 1911. There is only room in this book to summarise the lives of those who stayed in Nazeing and a few of the more interesting ones who moved away.

Descendants of Edward Mansfield (1778-1847) and Charlotte Pegrum (1781-1869)
Thomas Mansfield (1797-1876) married Ann Derbidge (1797-1842) in 1817, and seven of their ten children survived childhood. Four of them left the village and lived in Waltham Abbey for at least part of their married lives. The other three married siblings of the Starling family, who had moved from Roydon Hamlet to Back Lane in the 1830s, and they remained in Nazeing or nearby in Broadley Common.

---

19   This chapter is based on the work of Jennifer Andrews. You can see her full account of all Thomas and Elizabeth's descendants in the Nazeing History Workshop archive.

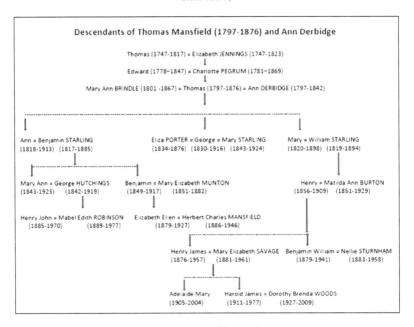

Thomas Mansfield family tree

George (1830-1916) married Mary Starling (1843-1924) in Southwark in 1880, when he rather grandly described himself as a farmer although he was in fact a farm labourer. Censuses listed a daughter called Esther Starling who at her birth registration in 1874 had the middle name Webb, which was probably her father's surname. In 1891 they moved from Shottentons to Pound House, where in 1911 George was listed as an old age pensioner.

John Mansfield (1802-1888) married Mary Hannah Smith (1808-1882) in 1828 and they had nine children.

James Mansfield (1829-1894) was a farm labourer who in 1854 married Sarah Webb (1833-1920) who was born in Nazeing, the daughter of William and Susan. They lived in one half of Longyard Cottage when it was divided into two. Their son William (1855-1938) married Ellen Campkin (1856-1922) and moved to Hoddesdon, where he was a brewer's drayman. In an arrangement similar to that of Alfred James Pegrum and his grandmother and aunts, William's eldest son James went to live with his grandparents. After her husband's death in 1894, Sarah remained there with her grandson until he married, and then on her own.

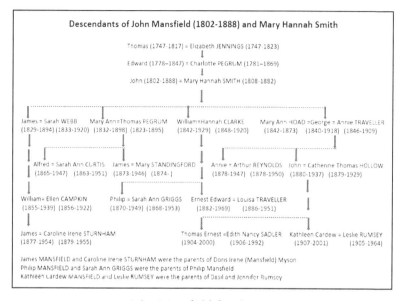

John Mansfield family tree

James (1877-1954) in 1891 was a houseboy, perhaps next door to Longyard Cottage at Hubbards, or at Nazeing Park. In 1901, single and still living with his grandmother he was a guncotton moulder at the Gunpowder Factory. In 1902, James married Caroline Irene Sturnham (1879-1955), the daughter of a retired Metropolitan policeman, James Sturnham and Martha née Guess. James and Caroline moved into Vine Cottage across Betts Lane, and had three children. Evidently Caroline's parents liked Nazeing because they settled at Heather Cottage, next door but one to her, and were later buried in All Saints' churchyard. Their daughter Nellie Sturnham married Benjamin William Starling, a Mansfield descendant, in Nazeing in 1908 and her youngest sister, Margaret, married William Cecil Mansfield (no relation to the other Nazeing Mansfields) in 1925.

George Mansfield (1840-1918) married Annie Traveller (1846-1909) in 1876. George was a farm labourer and they lived in Upper Town for some or all of the time, at Honeysuckle Cottage. Their children were:

Herbert (1876-1938), a horsekeeper, married Rebecca Ann Saville (1876-1931) in 1896. They lived at Camps Cottages in Hoe Lane, with their six children.

Annie (1878-1947) married Arthur Reynolds (1878-1950), who became parish clerk and lived at Church Cottage.

John (1880-1937) married Catherine Thomas Hollow (1879-1929) in 1901 and they had seven children. In 1911 John was a 'horsekeeper on a farm' and they were living at Gardners Farm.

Eric (1883-1964) married Henrietta Crisp (1886-1915) from Bishops Stortford. In 1911 he was a cowman, and they were living in Back Lane with his father George. They had two sons but Henrietta died in 1915, when they were living in Profits Hill, and Eric married the widowed Mary Jane Barker née Coleman.

Ernest Arthur (1886-1942) went into service and in 1911 was first footman to Reginald McKenna, First Lord of the Admiralty, in Whitehall. His army service record shows that in 1916 he was a butler at Smith Square, Westminster. Although he did not return to Nazeing, he was buried at All Saints' in 1942.

William Mansfield (1842-1929) married Hannah Clarke (1848-1920) from Bramfield, Hertfordshire, in 1869. They had ten children and lived at Profits Hill. Their children included:

Philip (1870-1949) married Sarah Ann Griggs (1868-1953) from Hatfield Broad Oak in Essex. Philip was a labourer at the Royal Gunpowder Factory, and they lived in Belchers Lane Cottages.

The 1911 census showed that six children were living at home and three had died.

Charles (1880-1914) was aged thirty in 1911, single and living with his parents, described as 'late agricultural labourer'. In the infirmity column was written 'age 24 paralysis', so evidently he was injured or taken seriously ill six years earlier.

Ernest Edward (1882-1969) married Louisa Traveller (1886-1951) from Broadley Common in 1908. He was then a labourer at the Gunpowder Factory but three years later he was a hay and straw dealer at Marshgate Farm, the first Mansfield descendant in Nazeing to become an employer.

Jemima Smith Mansfield (1844-1900) married James Neale (1837-1900) in 1868 in Waltham Cross. They settled in Back Lane but in 1891 Jemima was described as married and the head of a household that included her uncle Edward, while James Neale was lodging in Maldon, Essex. A newspaper report in the *Chelmsford Chronicle* in 1885 explained the circumstances:

> James Neale, blacksmith of Nazeing, was brought up on a warrant, charged with using threats towards his wife, Jemima Neale, whereby she went in bodily fear ... the defendant threatened to kill her; he had struck her on several occasions, and had treated her badly for a long time past ... The prisoner was bound over in his own recognizance of £10 to keep the peace for six months.

Their daughter Emily Neale (b.1871) was for many years a housemaid to Edward and Agnes Agar née Henty, the daughter of Robert Henty who leased Nazeing Park from 1872 to 1886. Living with the Agars in 1901 was their son-in-law Hugh G. Rose, whose occupation was 'manufacturer of lime juice cordial'. He was the son of Lauchlan Rose, who patented a product to preserve citrus juice without the addition of alcohol that became known as Rose's Lime Juice Cordial.

§

The only Mansfield family not descended from Thomas and Elizabeth was that of John Mansfield, a carter living at Kingswood Chase. He was born in Great Wilbraham, Cambridgeshire, in 1871, married Elizabeth Selina Ricketts in Nazeing in 1895, and was the father of Henry Charles and William Cecil Mansfield. William, known as Cecil, became a chauffeur and gardener at the Vicarage, and was the father of Dorothy (Mansfield) Wood, the parish organist.

Chapter 14

The Starling family

The Mansfields often intermarried with another well-known Nazeing family, the Starlings. In 1793 a Thomas Starling was baptised in Roydon where he had sons Benjamin, William and John with a woman called Ann, who died in 1826. In 1835 Thomas was remarried to a Mary and they had six children – James, Ann, Sarah, Elizabeth, Mary and Esther (or Hester) – who were all born in Nazeing. In 1841 the family were living in Back Lane but the parents died in the late 1840s.

A Family at the Red House
Benjamin Starling (1817-1885) married Ann Mansfield (1818-1913) at St Leonard's Shoreditch in 1842. They probably moved to the Red House straight after their marriage and certainly by 1851. Their great-great-grandson Philip Brent was living there in 2018, making Red House by some way the house with the longest continuous occupation by one family in the village.

Ann lived to the age of ninety-four and was known as 'Granny Starling'. When she married she simply signed her mark but she must have learnt to read and write later, because people brought letters for her to read and explain. She and her daughter Eliza were dressmakers, and Ann also ran a little shop in the cottage.

In 1851 it was a pretty full house. Benjamin and Ann already had three children of their own – Mary Ann, William and Ben[20] – and

---

20 To differentiate the two Benjamins, we have throughout called the father Benjamin and the son Ben.

they took in Benjamin's orphaned brother John and three of his sisters. For good measure there was also a lodger – a total of eleven in just half the house, the other half being occupied by Ann's cousin James Mansfield.

Their eldest daughter, Mary Ann (1843-1923), married George Hutchings (1842-1919), who was pindar until he was dismissed for embezzlement. They had eleven children.

Benjamin and Ann's eldest son, William (1845-1911), lived with Elizabeth Purkis from about 1874 although no marriage has been traced. Elizabeth's daughter was Fanny Maria Purkis (b.1874) who was also shown as Fanny Starling in some censuses; she was baptised in Nazeing in 1875 aged fifteen months, the daughter of 'Elizabeth, single woman, who later married William Starling'. They lived initially in North Street and from 1890 at the Rookery. Three of their nine children were still living at home in 1911, and the two sons who had married were also in Nazeing. In 1901 two of the boys were working at the Gunpowder Factory but by 1911 all were farm workers. John Victor (1887-1917) moved to Chingford but died in the Great War and is recorded on Nazeing memorials.

The next son, Ben (1849-1917), lived at the Red House until, in 1872, he married Mary Elizabeth Munton (1851-1882), a general servant at Harold's Park Farm. They moved to Betts Lane but Mary died in 1882 and old Benjamin in 1885 so young Ben moved back to the Red House. The fact that it was Ben and his young family who moved, rather than his mother, may suggest that the family had already built up a tradition at the Red House and felt comfortable there.

Ben and Mary had three children. William Henry was a farm labourer like his father but died of typhus aged nineteen. Their daughter, Eliza Annie, married Walter Grant Sissons in 1908 and they emigrated to Canada. She was pregnant and had an uncomfortable sea passage, so she was relieved to be able to send home a telegram with the single word 'Safe'. Her sister Ellen Elizabeth ('Nellie', 1879-1927) worked for the Pegrum family at Greenleaves and later as a lady's maid in London, but came home to look after her father and grandmother.

Nellie Mansfield née Starling outside the Red House

There were some shops in Nazeing, but very often tradesmen used the gravel roads to deliver their goods by horse and cart. One such was a baker from Roydon named Herbert Charles Mansfield whose round included the Red House, and before long he and Nellie fell in love. His branch of the family came from Epping Green rather than Nazeing, so it is unlikely that they were cousins.

Granny Starling was now in her nineties and upstairs bedridden, but her mind was as sharp as ever. On one occasion Herbert came to take Nellie out and brought a peace offering for the old lady. 'Here's a box of chocolates for you, Granny,' Nellie called up. 'Don't you come the old soldier with me!' she replied. She died on 22 January 1913 and under the headline 'Oldest resident's death' the local newspaper paid her the following tribute:

On Monday the funeral of Mrs Ann Starling the eldest and greatly respected resident of Nazeing took place at the parish church. Deceased had reached the age of 94 years and six months. In the evening a half-muffled peal of bells was rung at the church as a token of esteem.

Herbert and Nellie married on 24 June 1915. By now most of the family had died or gone away and it seemed sensible for Herbert to move in.

Soon he went into the army and like thousands of other wives Nellie must have wondered whether her young husband would come back. She sent him a postcard of the Red House with the message 'Just for you to have a peep at now & then & think of us inside'. But Herbert did come back, bringing the card with him. In 1917 Edwin Mansfield was born, to be followed in 1921 by Enid, who married Peter Brent.[21]

As part of a scheme to give East End children a taste of country life, a boy named Ernest Proctor visited the Starlings. They liked him and he liked Nazeing, and he became a regular visitor. His courting days were before Nazeing New Road was built in 1908, so when he and his girl-friend Lily walked from Broxbourne Station via Keysers, she thought they would never get to the Red House. He played cricket on the Common but once a ball hit him in the face and he lost the sight of one eye. Later he married Lily, and they became Enid's godparents and unofficial aunt and uncle. Perhaps because he was a Londoner unused to country ways, he seems to have noticed things that the family might have taken for granted. Enid recalled:

---

21 Much of the information in this section came from David Pracy's interview with Enid in 1994.

Uncle Ernie told me that when he first came here the fireplace was open and of course it did not give a lot of heat. They had a rail round with sheep skins hanging from it, and they all used to sit inside the sheep skins in the very cold weather to keep warm.

Enid believed that it was her mother and sister who chose the name of the Red House - an appropriate and attractive one for the brick cottage. The red brick made the building something of a landmark so that strangers seeking directions would be told 'Go to the red house...', and this may have given the family the idea.

A Scattered Family

Benjamin's brother *William* (1820-1894) married Granny Starling's younger sister Mary Mansfield (1820-1898) in 1844, again at St Leonard's Shoreditch. They had at least six children. The eldest, also William (1848-1903) married Betsy Brace in 1871 and succeeded his cousin George Hutchings as pindar in 1877. William's son Henry Starling (1856-1909) married Matilda Ann Burton (1851-1929) in 1876. Their eldest son was Henry James (1876-1957) who married Mary Elizabeth Savage, whose family had moved into Betts Lane in the late 1880s. They and then their daughter Adelaide (1905-2004) ran the Upper Town Post Office until she retired in 1972, and she lived there until her death.

In 1853 *John* (1825-1884) married Mary Ann Hunt, who lived at the Rookery. They had four sons, who all became farm labourers, and two daughters who were servants. Members of the Hunt and Starling families lived at the Rookery from 1851 until 1915, when Mary Ann's son George Starling and nephew John Hunt shared a house. In the neighbouring dwellings were John Starling's niece Mary Ann Hutchings and nephew William Starling with their families, and William's daughter Lottie as a servant to James and Emily Kimpton. Although we do not know exactly how farm tenants found their homes, it seems unlikely that branches of the extended Starling family were in adjacent dwellings by coincidence.

By 1911 there were thirty-two members of the Starling family scattered in ten households throughout the village – Ben with Granny Starling at the Red House; Matilda Ann at Upper Town Post Office; her sons Benjamin William and Henry James with their respective wives and daughters at neighbouring cottages in Back Lane; Charles with his wife, daughter and Aunt Mary Ann née Hunt at Belchers Lane; William with his wife and three of his children at the Rookery, and his brother George next door; his daughters Louisa and Lottie servants at Mulberries and the Rookery; William junior with his wife and five children at Laundry Lane; Arthur with his wife and three children at the newly built Langridge Cottages. Thus the extended Starling family was very mobile within Nazeing, which makes their continuous occupation of the Red House all the more remarkable.

Chapter 15

The Mead and Cook Families[22]

The Meads

On the first page of the first Nazeing parish church register in 1559 is written 'O Lord increase our faith, Nicholas Grave, Olem Mead, John Mead'. After that, there were no more entries for Meads until the 1820s. The ancestors of the Nazeing Mead family were Edward Mead and Judith Peagram, who were both 'of North Weald' when they married in London in 1734. They raised their family in Latton, and Edward's grandson William (1774-1842) moved to Thornwood Common. William's daughter Sarah (1801-1876) married Joseph Everett in Nazeing in 1821, and his son William (1807-1832) followed her there several years later with his wife Mary Ann.

A William Mead was buried in Epping Upland in May 1832 aged twenty-five, the parish register noting that he was from Nazeing. This was eight months before his son, William Henry Mead, was baptised in Nazeing. William the elder may have been unaware that a child was expected at the time he died but his descendants have lived in Nazeing for nearly 200 years.

William Henry Mead (1833-1870) married Emma Smith (1833-1915) in Nazeing in 1857. They lived for a short time in one of the two cottages now known as Yew Tree Cottage in Bumbles Green, where William had been raised by his uncle John Mead.

---

22 This chapter is based on research by Jennifer Andrews and Jacky Cooper, daughters of Dennis Mead.

William was employed as a carter at Gardners Farm. He seems to have had a wild streak and had several brushes with the law. In 1861 he was fined one shilling at the Cheshunt sessions for riding in a cart without reins, which lends credence to the stories that horses pulling hay carts from Nazeing knew their own way. In 1866 he was found guilty of 'furiously driving' a horse and cart on the highway and fined five shillings or fourteen days' imprisonment.

When William Henry died of pleurisy on the last day of 1870, the family had moved to Nazeing Common and his death certificate showed his occupation as 'husbandman'. His widow Emma became a laundress and moved with her family to 1 or 2 Betts Lane. William Henry and Emma had seven children.

Ellen (1858-1933) married a domestic coachman, George Palmer, in 1887 at Streatham, Surrey. Their first son, Sidney Robert Palmer, who was baptised in Nazeing in 1888, was killed in Flanders in 1918.

Julia (1859-1951) left school aged about twelve. According to Nita Turner, when she was sent for a job at Greenleaves, she was told to say 'Please, I've come! Will I do?' In 1888 she married William James Snell and they lived at Broadley Common with their three children, who were all born there. Around 1909 they moved to Harknetts Gate, into a home that was originally two cottages. In 1911 William James was a coachman, and their sons William (a steward at the Golf Club) and Frederick were also at home. Tragically, both boys were killed a few years later. William was hit by a train at the Essex Road level crossing in Hoddesdon in 1914, and Frederick died in France in 1918 (see page 351).

George Henry (1862-1945) was a farm labourer who lived with his mother for many years. In 1901 they were in Gardners Farm

Cottages, described by her great grandson Dennis Mead as 'wooden cottages with a pond in front, now the site of Common View'. In 1909 he married Jane Elizabeth Cordell, the daughter of John Cordell and Emma King Clayden, who lived at Longyard Cottage. Although he was forty-six and she was forty-five, they had probably known one another all their lives, and certainly since they were both witnesses at Julia Mead's marriage in 1888. They lived at Sibleys Row, Broadley Common.

James (1864-1949) worked as a carman in Bromley-by-Bow, where he settled after his marriage in Nazeing on Christmas Day 1895 to Lydia Mary Mansfield, daughter of George Mansfield and Mary Ann Hoad of Back Lane.

Sarah Anne (1869-1921), known as Annie, was a servant at Nazeing Vicarage for over 20 years. *Elizabeth* (1871-1960) became a housemaid in Kensington, and after retiring returned to Nazeing and lived with her sister Julia Snell at Harknetts Gate. Neither Sarah Ann nor Elizabeth married and both were buried at All Saints'.

James, George and Henry Mead

Henry Mead (1866-1953)

Henry, the fifth child of William Henry Mead and Emma Smith, was the only one of their children who lived to see children, grandchildren and great-grandchildren born in Nazeing. He was born at Keepers Cottage on Nazeing Common in 1866 and married Sarah Ann Littlechild (1865-1949) in Nazeing in 1887. She was born at Gooseberry Hall, Epping Long Green, overlooking Nazeing Common, and was the daughter of John Littlechild of Waltham Abbey and Eliza Dean of Nazeing. In 1891, Henry and Sarah Ann were living in one of the two cottages now known as Kingswood Chase, where their son Harry was born. Later in the 1890s, they moved to the cottage in Betts Lane where Henry had lived as a boy, or the one next door. Nita Turner said:

> My father, Arthur Mead, lived in Betts Lane as a very young child, in the cottages in the dip that were later occupied by Mr. Eldred (chauffeur) and Mr. Ring (head gardener), who both worked at Collyers. There was a path from the cottages directly into the garden, behind the Golf House. I am not sure whether he was born there.

By 1901 Henry and Sarah Ann were living in the cottage next door to the Bumbles Green Post Office. Their son Harry would eventually marry Emily Cook, the Postmaster's daughter.

Harry Mead and Emily Cook at school c1898.
Twenty-five years later they were married .

The Royal Gunpowder Factory

Henry was described as a 'mechanic at the powder mills' in 1889, a 'munitions foreman' in 1918, a 'charge man Royal Gunpowder Factory' in 1919, and a 'munitions worker' in 1923. By 1926 he had retired to be a gardener. He was one of the first men who walked to Waltham Abbey to work at the gunpowder factory. He eventually saved enough money to buy a bicycle, but it was stolen on the first day he rode it to work! His daughter Nance Colman recalled:

My father worked at the munitions place - the gunpowder factory. He was in the experimental place ... We don't understand the bits and things that go to make explosives ... No buttons, no shoes, anything that could cause friction. With him, you never saw his fingernails dirty. The least bit of grit could cause an explosion ... He had some terrible experiences there during the war, that's the first war. They had explosions there. They had to sink all their stuff, during the war, in the river.

He walked to work and back ... up Bumbles Green Lane, across the hill, up the old lane, right across to Aimes Green to the back of Monkhams; down what used to be a golf course there ... along the road by the gates ... in the back of the church, through the gates into Highbridge Street. You had no need to go in via the New Inn or Sun Street ... there was a cut-through. Sometimes in the summer, in the school holidays, we would walk to meet him, to have a picnic tea. From Waltham Road, opposite where the old Abbey church is, up on the hill, at Monkhams more or less, we would meet him up there with a picnic, and then he would go back to work. He would have half an hour or so, perhaps when we were haymaking. I wonder if they would do it today. I don't think so.

My father used to have his pleasures. He used to play quoits. He had his own two sets with different weights. They would throw them over a stick, and measure who was nearest. They played on grass at the King Harold's Head, against other public houses. The rings were quite thick and heavy, it depended on the weather which ones he took. They were all solid metal. We had the sets at home; I don't know where they went.

The 1911 census showed Henry Mead at home with Sarah Ann and their three youngest children, Annie Ada (Nance Colman, 1899-1982), Albert (1902-1972) and George (1903-1969).

The older children were all unmarried and away in service. William (1887-1964) was a footman at 3 Eaton Square, one of ten servants employed by Sir Walter Randolph Fitzroy Farquhar, a merchant banker. Harry (1889-1965) was a footman at 29 Portman Square London, one of ten servants employed by George Lawson-Johnston, the director of the Bovril Company and son of its founder. Arthur (1891-1976) was a gardener in the Leicestershire village of Kibworth Beauchamp, which featured in Michael Wood's *Story of England* television series. Between 1912 and the start of the war in 1914, Harry and Arthur Mead came back to Nazeing to work for F.W. Green at Collyers: Harry was a footman, later to become the butler, and Arthur was a gardener.

Harry and William Mead looking very smart, c1911

Alice (1893-1937) was a go-between maid ('tweeny') for Lady Georgiana Peel, at Westlea House in Wormley, Hertfordshire. Lady Georgiana was the daughter of Lord John Russell who was prime minister in the 1850s, widow of the nephew of Russell's predecessor, Sir Robert Peel, and aunt of the philosopher and activist Bertrand Russell. She wrote a book of recollections which was edited by her daughter.

The Mead Brothers in The Great War

Like his sisters, Ellen and Julia, Henry Mead had sons who fought in the Great War, but he was more fortunate in that all three returned home.

William was a footman at Holbrook Park, Horsham and joined the Royal Sussex Regiment in 1915. He then transferred to the Royal Flying Corps, where he was a driver and a mechanic, alongside his employer, Group Captain Alan John Lance Scott, CB MC AFC, who had originally been an officer in the Sussex Yeomanry before transferring to the Royal Flying Corps. After being wounded in action and receiving the Military Cross in 1917, Scott became the Commandant of the Central Flying School and acted as Winston Churchill's flying instructor.

At the outbreak of the war, Harry and Arthur volunteered for the 22nd Battalion of the London Regiment (The Queens), no doubt influenced by their employer, Green. They became batmen to his sons, who were already officers in that battalion. Neither Harry nor Arthur spent the full duration of the war at the front line. Having arrived in France in March 1915, Arthur sprained his ankle in May, probably in his first battle. He was sent back to a convalescent camp near Boulogne for three months and when he was given an 'unfit discharge' in August he was assigned work at the Base Depot in Boulogne. He then was shipped back to

England in 1917 to work in an Agricultural Company of the army. Harry was hospitalised several times during 1915 with kidney stones and influenza, and was transported back to England in December 1915, where he served for the remainder of the war in a 'Protection Company' guarding prisoners of war or strategic facilities. Both therefore got through the war and lived to tell the tale.

The Cook family

The Cook family moved around 1860 from Takeley in Essex to Broadley Common, where David Cook (1824-1899) was a shoemaker. In 1881 he was living in the cottage that became the Upper Town Post Office and by 1894 he was a sub-postmaster there. Rhoda Emily Cook (known as Emily) recalled her grandmother Sarah Cook née Bangs sitting at the window, 'her little face peering out'. Sarah had been a housekeeper at Nazeing Park and died in 1921, one day before her 100th birthday.

David Cook, shoemaker
and sub-postmaster

Sarah Cook c1910

In 1888 David's son Fred (1859-1930) married Mary Priscilla Pippard and they opened the Bumbles Green Post Office. The 1895 and 1899 Kelly's Directories show Fred Cook there, and his father at the sub-Post Office in Upper Town. In the 1911 census, Fred was listed as sub-postmaster and letter carrier with his wife and daughter, Emily, 'assisting'.

Marjorie Sykes remembered the shop:

> The stamps were in a wooden folder beside the small scales for the weighing of letters, and a pile of letters was lying there ready for the afternoon collection. Letters cost a penny for home mail, twopence-halfpenny for foreign. Postcards could be sent for a halfpenny. But the interest for us was on the right side of the counter where the large glass sweet jars displayed attractive wares...
> Some people said red-haired Em Cook read the postcards to keep herself informed on affairs of the village. I'm sure this was untrue, but of course all village people are interested in other people's affairs...

The Bumbles Green Post Office was also a telegraph office, a savings bank, and an annuity and insurance office. The first telephone exchange in Nazeing, run by the G.P.O., was a board hanging on Fred's living room wall. From 1899 to 1926 Kelly's Directories listed him as 'shoemaker and sub-postmaster'.

Chapter 16

The Hale Family

The 1911 census showed five Hale families living in Nazeing. All were descended from Isaac Hale of Much Hadham, who married Sarah Want, a Nazeing girl, at All Saints' Church in 1767. They were all involved with farming and/or the hay trade. Hay was a major crop because Nazeing is only a day's ride from London and it was needed to feed London's horses, which were still important in the capital's transport system. As early as 1841 there was a difference between Thomas (1811-1885), described as a farmer or hay dealer, and his brother Joseph (1819-1908), a farm labourer. That split between the two branches of the family could still be seen in 1911.

Thomas Hale (1811-1885) and His Descendants

In the mid-nineteenth century, Thomas built up his prosperous business as a self-employed hay dealer, living from about 1860 at Warleys where he also farmed twenty acres. He married Ann Dean whose family gave its name to Deans Brook in Middle Street. In 1861 three of their daughters were listed as working: Anna was a haymaker, Sarah a teacher and Elizabeth a servant.

In the 1870s and 1880s, their son **Joseph (1847-1935)** acquired two acres at the corner of Hoe Lane and Middle Street where he and his family built Hope Cottage where they were still living in 1911. He also owned a pair of cottages (now Nether Bowers) in Perry Hill Lane, which were occupied by two of his cousins. Joseph married Sarah Susannah Rodwell (1854-1933) in 1877 and they had seven children all born in Nazeing, but two died as babies.

In 1901 *William Thomas (1879-1958)*, was living with his uncle John at Low Hill Farm in Roydon, described as 'farmer's nephew'; ten years later his uncle had died and he had taken over the farm.

In 1901 *Joseph (1881-1914)* was living at home and working for his father, and in 1911 he was a shoemaker living in Tottenham. In 1904 he married Clara Elizabeth Freshwater in Edmonton district, where he died.

Annie (1884-1944) began working life as a domestic servant but by 1911 was a district nurse, living with her parents. She would have had a year's training in a hospital, six months in district nursing and three months in midwifery. In 1912 she married Alexander Vale Charge, a commercial clerk and widower who had moved to Nazeing two years earlier. Annie was listed on the 1911 census as a district nurse, but on their marriage certificate a year later no occupation is given. Alexander Charge had been born in Chelmsford in 1869, the son of a saddler. In 1891 he married Ada M Wheaton (1869-1907) and they had four children. In 1901 they were living in Willesden with two servants and he was described as a warehouseman upholsterer. On the 1911 census he is listed at Sunnyholme in Nazeing Road, where he was living with his children and a housekeeper. Soon afterwards, according to the *Lloyd George Survey*, he moved to occupy half of the White House in Hoe Lane, as the sub-tenant of John Argent Nicholls.

Frank (1886-1954) was also at home in 1901, but by 1911 he was a horse groom in Essendon in Hertfordshire where he met Gertrude Elizabeth Giddins. They married at St Marylebone in 1915, when he had made the career change from groom to chauffeur. They had sons Eric Frank and Alec Rodwell.

Bertie (1895-1951), later known as Bert, lived at Hope Cottage all his life and never married.

Descendants of Joseph Hale (1819-1908)

The other four Hale heads of household were the sons or grandsons of Thomas Hale's younger brother Joseph, the farm labourer, and all were born in Nazeing.

Hale family at their local with William Henry on the right

Isaac Hale (1848-1924) as a boy lived in Middle Street, possibly for a while at Shadwalkers, where he later farmed. In 1871 at All Saints' he married Elizabeth Cadmore, a 'semptress' from Ware. They moved to Nazeing Common but in 1886 went to Shadwalkers and stayed there. In 1911 Isaac listed his occupation as a farmer and an employer. The eleven-acre Shadwalkers was owned by Ralph Bury and the rent was £45 per year: 'A small freehold holding with timber built & tiled house. Three bedrooms in roof & five rooms on ground floor. The house is old but in fair condition and repair.'

The couple had six children, but only three were still alive in 1911 and all had left Nazeing. In 1902 Sarah Elizabeth married Frederick George King, brother of Langham King the North Street builder.

He was a terra-cotta fixer who had probably worked for Pulham's (see page 278) and he moved to a job in Croydon, where they had two children and remained for the rest of their lives. For a while William helped his father but by 1901 he had gone to work at the gunpowder factory. In 1898 Lizzie married William Reeves who in 1901 was running the White Hart pub at Witham.

Shadwalkers, where Isaac Hale farmed for most of his life

John Hale (1854-1941) was a farm labourer. In 1898 he married Margaret Parker in Walthamstow, where the 1891 census described her as 'Cook in charge, family away'. She was born at Hull in Yorkshire and they had no children. They were living in Perry Hill at a semidetached property, now Nether Bowers, with over an acre of land.

Joseph Hale (1852-1939?) was a farm labourer who in the 1890s took the family to Tottenham, where he worked as a council 'roadsman'.

His son Joseph junior (1883-1959) became a grocer's assistant. In 1903 in Tottenham, Joseph married Harriet Woodley, a neighbour of his Uncle John at Nether Bowers. Their four boys were Leslie,

Ronald, Laurie and Leonard. The two eldest were born at Haultwick in Hertfordshire and at Waltham Abbey, but by 1908 the family had come back to Nazeing and Joseph had returned to the family trade of hay binder. He was perhaps employed by his namesake, because they were known as Joseph Hale senior and junior, even though they were cousins rather than father and son. It was unusual for men who had left Nazeing to return permanently so perhaps he had been reluctant to move although the rest of the family apparently stayed in Tottenham.

In 1911 Joseph had moved next door to his Uncle John at Nether Bowers, described on the *Survey* as

> One of a pair of old brick built and slated copyhold cottages with good gardens. Damp and in much need of repair. Situate up Perry Hill Lane. This cottage has no frontage to the lane, only right of way over garden of house adjoining - but access could be from lane. 2 Bedrooms (one in roof) living room & kitchen. Lean-to horse shed.

Nether Bowers, clearly showing the division into two cottages

In 1881 *William Hale (1859-1945?)* was a lodger in the household of Joseph Brace at Broadley Common, and two years later he married Joseph's eldest daughter Caroline Charlotte (1863-1923).

In 1911 he was a hay labourer, as were his three eldest sons William Henry, John and Thomas. Also at home were five younger children including four-year-old Agnes, whose occupation was given as 'Baby'! Daughter Sarah was general servant to a publican at the White Swan in Hoddesdon and Alice was a housemaid at Mill Hill School, an independent day and boarding school which is still there.

William and Caroline Hale

William and his family were living at Riddens View, a semi-detached cottage with an acre of land next door to Salem. Four of William and Caroline Hale's sons went to war. William Henry had his finger shot off but John died of wounds in 1916. His great niece wrote a moving poem under the pen name Gertrude Schoen:

DEAR JOHN

Did you think John,

When your country called you to war

From your country cottage

Nestled in Nazeing's beautiful countryside

This would be the last time you would walk from your door

The last time you would see your Mother, Father

Your Brothers and Sisters

No, bravely believing, you would return

Once your task for your country was done

You John, amongst thousands of your comrades

So bravely fought for your country that you loved

Now your body lies in a war grave in France

Not for you the chance

To be a father, to see your family again

Instead a letter to your Mother from your Commanding Officer

'My dear Mrs. Hale, I am sorry to tell you

That your dear son John was killed in action

He was a brave soldier'.

Thank you John for what you gave for our freedom.

Chapter 17

Other Families

The Smiths of Cutlands, Marshgate and Netherkidders
John Smith (1842-1923) and his wife Rebecca Messenger both came from Buckinghamshire, where they married in 1864. They first lived in Nazeing before moving to Hoddesdon and Bayford between 1870 and 1877. By 1881 the family were back in Nazeing at the Lock House in Broxbourne Road and in 1891 they were living in North Street. John was a farm labourer and later a gardener, so he was quite bold when in 1895, in his fifties, he took on a substantial farm, Cutlands. The writing on his census form in 1911 suggests that he would not have found any paperwork easy.

In 1901, John's son Arthur Henry (b.1881) was living with his sister and brother-in-law in West Ham, working as a rubber moulder. His future wife Mabel Ann Berwick was living less than a mile away and they were married in 1904. Arthur became the farmer at Marshgate, which in 1910 he exchanged with his father at Cutlands. He was nicknamed 'Tractor' because he became a ploughing contractor. In 1913 Arthur and Walter Samuel of Pond House challenged the Trustees of the Common over their development of golf on the Common, claiming that '...we are being robbed of our very inheritance and many others besides'. It was a courageous action, for Smith's landlord was Ralph Bury and Samuel's was Ralph Palmer, both Trustees. Smith and Samuel were supported by the Commons and Footpaths Preservation Society and initially by Essex County Council, but Bury intervened and the council dropped the matter.

John Smith's son, John junior, married Jessie Ada Hills from Hertford in 1898 and in 1901 he was listed as a farmer-employer at Netherkidders in Laundry Lane. They had three boarders, all grooms born outside Essex. Jessie died in 1908 and two years later John married Ada Upson. In 1911 John described himself as a hay dealer and farmer, and had one live-in labourer.

During the Great War, John Smith junior twice had brushes with the law, once for driving with lights and once without. The first time, in October 1915, he was summoned for obstructing P.C. Reader in his duty under the Defence of the Realm Act. When Reader instructed him to put out the lights of his motor car, presumably because of the danger from bombing, Smith refused. The court found that it was a serious offence and fined him £5. Three months later he was summoned again, this time for driving his horse and cart without a light, presumably because of the danger to other road users. Smith said he had one light stolen and, because it was a foggy night, he found he could see better without. This time the Chairman found the excuse a good one, and the case was dismissed on payment of 2s costs.

The Bridgeman Family

Charles Bridgeman (c1802-1875) was born at Mildenhall in Suffolk. By 1836 he and his Nazeing-born wife Sophia were christening children at All Saints'. At first they lived at Broadley Common but by 1841 they were at Mulberries, where they remained. Charles was shown on censuses as a farmer and hay carter. After his death, Sophia was listed in Kelly's as the farmer but said on the 1881 census that she was 'retired from farming'.

Their son James (1838-1915) assisted Charles as a farm labourer and hay carter until 1865, when he moved across the road to Cutlands and married Mary Ann Pryor. In 1871 he was a hay carter and farmer occupying nine acres belonging to Henry Bury. By 1881 James was farming more land, some opposite Nazeingbury and on the marsh, and probably at Mulberries where his widowed mother lived until her death in 1888. He was listed in Kelly's as farming Cutlands from 1886 to 1908, so John Smith was probably his sub-tenant. He farmed Shottentons from 1890 and in 1911 he was living there and employing a horse keeper called Henry Bayford and his two eldest sons.

James' son Charles (1866-1952) married Ada Rose Potter in 1894 and they had twelve children, of whom eight were still living in 1911. By 1901 he was a hay dealer working on own account at Curringtons, where he remained until 1938. His evidence to Palmer v Guadagni gives an insight into his work. Three times a week he used his van to bring two hayricks from Harold's Park Farm as they stood. Altogether he bought thirty loads of hay and carted it to London at 50s per load. 'I would not have bought the hay if I could not have crossed the Common,' he stated. He was told that there was a right of way so 'if anyone stopped us we would knock them down'.

The Welch Family

The first reference to a Welch in Nazeing is in 1774, when Mrs Elizabeth Welch inherited White House Farm. In 1804, John Davies Welch (c1779-1832), possibly her son, married Mary Green (c1780-1861) and they had at least four children: John Davies II (1806-1866), William Burchill (c1810-1878), Esther (born Roydon c1811) and Louisa (born London 1819). There is no record that they were baptised, perhaps because the parents were nonconformists.

John Davies Welch I died in Nazeing in 1832, but by 1851 his widow Mary was head of a large household at 17 Annetts Crescent, Islington.

She and her unmarried daughter Esther were both described as annuitants and so were evidently fairly well off. Her son, John Davies Welch II, was a factor and warehouseman who later in 1851 married Charlotte Adams of Dunmow, where he died in 1866. In 1847 at St Mary Islington, Mary's daughter Louisa married Stanley Andrews, a commissioning agent. His father was described as a gentleman and hers as a minister, which may have been stretching a point in both cases. They had children Sarah Ann (1849-1911), Charles Townsend (1853-1880) and Louisa Elizabeth Charlotte (1834-1921).

William Burchill Welch married Hannah Pegrum (1815-1878) at Nazeing in 1835. They had three children: John Davies Welch III (1839-1923), Rachel (1844-1904) and Louisa (1848-1899). In the 1850s and 1860s William was living at Curtis Farm but by 1871 he had moved along Middle Street to Smalldrinks, where he was described as 'shoemaker and farmer of 10 acres'.

After his father's death, John Davies Welch III took over Smalldrinks. With him in 1881 were his sister Louisa and six-year-old niece Rachel Pasfield. In 1887 he married his cousin Louisa Elizabeth Charlotte Andrews, whom he had known since they lived in the household of their grandmother Mary Welch. For six years they had no children until, when he was fifty-four and she was thirty-seven, they had a daughter Mabel Andrews (1893-1948), to be followed by Andrew Davies (1894-1977) and Stanley John (1896-1957). He was still farming only ten acres in 1911 but for a while had additional income from a school run by his sister Louisa and from a Post Office, both housed at Smalldrinks.

During the Great War, Andrew served in the Royal Flying Corps and later used the knowledge gained there to establish Welch's Garage at Bumbles Green with Stan, whose son Michael was well-known in the village all his life.

Andrew Welch (back centre) in Royal Flying Corps Band

The Fairchild Family

In the late 1830s George Fairchild moved from Epping to Perry/White Cottage in Back Lane. He was initially an agricultural labourer but in the 1850s became a letter-carrier and grocer, and around 1860 he moved to a new cottage which is now Fairview. The land, on the corner of Betts Lane and Hoe Lane, was probably taken out of the 'waste' (see page 27) and donated by Sir Charles Wake to encourage Fairchild's trade, which was of general value to the village. In 1873 Fairchild owned the cottage, which was shown on the Ordnance Survey as 'Post Office' and perhaps also given to him by Wake. The census listed his wife Elizabeth as helping him, and after his death in 1878 she took over the grocery business.

Fairview was described on the *Survey* as

> Small detached freehold cottage with good garden, part of which is copyhold. Cottage is brick building, double span slated roof. Good condition generally. 4 bedrooms, 2 living rooms, kitchen & scullery. Wooden bays to ground floor front.

The bays could originally have been intended for use when it was a shop.

On the 1851 census George and Elizabeth's thirteen-year-old daughter Emma was listed as a scholar, and it seems likely that she showed such aptitude as a pupil-teacher that the Palmer family encouraged her to take up teaching as a profession. In 1861 she was a governess at a girls' school in Tonbridge and later in the 1860s she met a fellow-teacher called Sarah Ellen Mackarall. In 1871 they were teaching and sharing lodgings in Brighton, and in 1881 they were in Hackney. By 1891 they were at 9 Baalbec Road Highbury, where they lived for at least twenty years. Emma was initially head of the household but by 1911, as she became frailer, Sarah was head of the household and owner of Fairview. Sarah Mackarall died in the Tooting Bec Lunatic Asylum in 1919 and the cottage was sold for £240. Emma Fairchild died in 1922 aged eighty-four.

Emma's younger sister Jessie Maria was listed as a pupil-teacher on the 1871 census. In 1878 she married Harry Howard Raward, a solicitor's clerk from Brighton whom she possibly met while visiting Emma there. They had three children but he died in 1890 and she immediately became a teacher. On 7 August 1906, at the end of the school year, she married Richard William Little, a schoolmaster with the London County Council. Even though she was by then over fifty, she apparently had to give up teaching again, since no profession is given for her on the marriage certificate or on the 1911 census. Jessie died in 1935 and was buried with her first husband near her parents and sister Emma at All Saints'.

Part III

Nazeing Places

When, over a Bank Holiday weekend in April 1975, Mansion House Farm was demolished by its new owners, many in the village were shocked. It emerged that the house was not officially listed so no misdemeanour had been committed. The newly-formed Nazeing Conservation Society was concerned that other old houses might go the same way, and produced a preliminary report. Cecil Hewett, a senior officer in the Historic Buildings and Conservation Section of Essex County Council, visited the village to appraise local buildings for possible listing and was shown around by members of the society. Their enthusiasm persuaded him to bring forward the review of Nazeing's historic buildings before those of equally deserving Essex villages, so that forty-five buildings were listed in a schedule published in 1984.

In 1987 the Conservation Society published *Nazeing's Heritage Buildings*, which has become known as the Black Book. It covered not only the forty-five listed buildings but also all the properties (and buildings on the sites of properties) recorded in the Tithe Award of 1847. It was written by Adrian Gibson, an enthusiast for vernacular architecture who visited some of the properties to identify interesting features which were often unknown to their occupiers. In the preface, he wrote that 'Nazeing is a small area of Essex that has miraculously survived the expansion of London and is an example of rural life lasting right up to modern times'.

In this section we have built on the Conservation Society's work, using the Black Book, the *Lloyd George Survey* and other sources

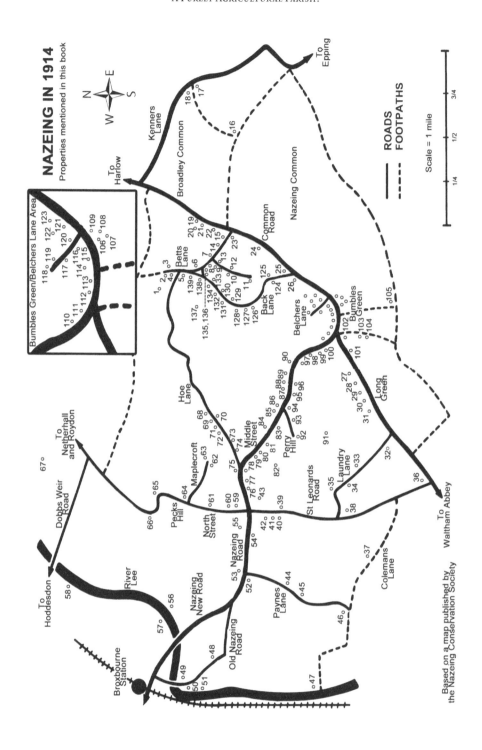

1 All Saints Church
2 Church Cottage
3 Old Vicarage and Glebe House
4 Fairview Cottage
5 Upper Town School
6 Mill House
7 Clematis, Heather and Vine Cottages
8 Longyard Cottage
9 Hubbards
10 Back Park
11 Nazing Park
12 Headmasters
13 Upper Town Post Office
14 1 and 2 Betts Lane
15 Golf House
16 Lodge Farm
17 Jacks Hatch
18 The Nook, Kenners Lane
19 Upper Gatehouse
20 Sun Cottage
21 Sun Inn
22 Collyers
23 Abbotts Cottage
24 Keepers Cottage
25 Kingswood Chase
26 Red House
27 Selways

28 Mamelons Farm
29 Wyndith/ Mamelons Cottages
30 St Lawrence Farm
31 Salem and Riddens View
32 Felstead/ Newmans
33 Netherkidders
34 Laun House/ Snows
35 Laundry Cottage
36 Coach and Horses Public House
37 Valley View/ Upper Langridge
38 St Leonards House and Farm
39 Mulberries
40 Cutlands
41 Shiree/ The Rookery
42 Pound House
43 The Ham
44 Paynes Farm
45 Langridge Cottages
46 Langridge Farm
47 Kings Weir Lock House
48 Keysers Farmhouse
49 The Crown Hotel/ Public House
50 179 Old Nazing Road/ Toll house

51 Broxbourne Boat House
52 Poona Lawn and Sunnyholme
53 Marshgate Farm
54 14 Elizabeth Close/ Rose Cottage
55 Nazingbury
56 Nazing Glassworks/ Goats
57 Carthagena Lock House
58 Dobbs Weir Lock House
59 36 North Street/ Whitehall Farm
60 42 North Street / Northcroft
61 60 North Street
62 Maplecroft Cottage
63 Maplecroft Farm
64 2 and 4 Pecks Hill / Curringtons
65 Shottentons
66 Meadgate Farm
67 Netherhall
68 Little End/ Camps Cottages
69 Camps
70 Greenleaves
71 The White House
72 Parkers Farm

73 Sunnyside
74 Hope Cottage and Barnfield
75 Wheelers
76 Crooked Billet Public House
77 Mayflower
78 Burnt Hall
79 Brook Cottage/ House
80 Mansion House
81 Shadwalkers
82 Old House, Old House Lane
83 Ninnings
84 Smalldrinks
85 Congregational Chapel
86 Trevone and Newlands
87 Darmers
88 The Poplars and The Cottage
89 Red Lion Inn
90 Curtis Farm
91 Porters,' Cemetery
92 Perry Hill Farm
93 Nether Bowers
94 Little Dormers
95 Feltre / Warleys

96 Rose Cottage, Middle Street
97 Convalescent Home
98 Goodalls
99 Walnut Tree Cottages/ Motts
100 Sturtsbury
101 Allmains South
102 Allmains
103 Callis
104 Beverley Cottage / Hawthorn Cottage
105 Harolds Park Farm
106 Old Post Office
107 Park View Cottage
108 Warwick House
109 Pindars Cottage
110 Bentons
111 Bumbles Green School
112 Welch Brothers Garage
113 Cranbourne Cottages/ Bumbles Green Post Office
114 Yew Tree Cottage
115 Havenslea/ Literary Institute
116 Common View/ Gardners Farm
117 Byners
118 Belchers Farm

119 Teys Farm
120 Belchers Lane Cottages
121 King Harolds Head Public House
122 Ivy Cottages
123 King Harold Cottage
124 Ravens
125 Nazing Park Cottage
126 Queens Cottage
127 Rose Cottage, Back Lane
128 Profits Hill Cottages
129 Little Profits
130 Park Cottage
131 Southside and Northside
132 Perry and White Cottages
133 Honeysuckle Cottage
134 Brewitts Farm
135 Pond House
136 Ricketts
137 Rookswood
138 White House Farm/ Homefield and Windrush Lodge
139 Church House Farm

to give brief descriptions of those houses for which we have contemporary photos, and a few others of particular interest. The Black Book is helpfully organised in a circular tour around the village, so we have used the same arrangement.

Chapter 18

Betts Lane and Nazeing Common

Church Cottage
Owned by the Churchwardens of Nazeing, this was also known as the Church Clerk's Cottage, and was occupied by the clerk rent-free. It was built in the mid-1700s, red brick and tiled. The *Survey* said: 'Walls bulged but have been tied in. 2 bedrooms, 2 living rooms, lean-to wash house. Good timber & tiled shed, stable & fodder store... Long garden.'

In 1911 the clerk of the ecclesiastical parish[23] was Arthur Reynolds, who had been a farm labourer. In 1902 he married Annie Mansfield and moved into the cottage, where he was clerk, verger and sexton. He was still living there in 1939 although he had had to give up his post and revert to being a farm labourer. His son Eric later became clerk to the secular parish.

The Vicarage
This fell down in 1442 but was rebuilt and later enlarged. The *Survey* described it as:

> An old brick, stucco & slate detached freehold house situate near Church. In really poor condition & repair. Orchard & paddock. 7 bedrooms, dressing room & bathroom. 3 rec. rooms (poor), kitchen & addition of scullery, dairy, pantry.

The house was not to be sublet without the Bishop's sanction. The outbuildings included stables, sheds and a coach house, and were

---

23 The secular parish had a different clerk.

in good condition. The vicar held eighteen acres near the church and vicarage and a further 2½ in the Meads. In 1956 the house was divided into two dwellings and sold off.

Mill House

In 1911 this was described as 'a very old freehold cottage (converted from a former mill granary). Brick built & slated. 4 rooms, shop & kitchen. Old timber & tiled stable & coach house. Lean-to cart shed. Pasture is good'.

The Nazeing windmill had been built in 1802 by William Palmer on his land at Betts Lane, for 'Grinding Grists for all the poor and other persons in the neighbourhood'. As the agricultural slump of the 1870s began to bite, the mill became uneconomic and fell into decay, apparently having entirely disappeared apart from the 'granary' by the time of the *Survey* thirty years later.

The miller had also run a shop which in 1885 was taken over by James Savage. He was originally a pig and poultry dealer but described himself in 1911 as a general dealer not working at home, so probably travelled around the area. His daughter Adelaide continued the shop until 1962, and also taught at the nearby church school.

Longyard Cottage

This timber-framed and plastered house was built in the 1500s and has an original brick chimney stack. In the mid-eighteenth century it was used as the village workhouse. It was bought by George Palmer MP in 1836 and remained in the family until the death of Archdale Palmer in 1950.

By 1871 it had been divided into two cottages, occupied by the Cordell and Mansfield families. In 1911 the occupants were widows Emma King Cordell and Sarah Mansfield, who were both pensioners of the Mercers' Company. It was described as 'a pair of very old timber & brick slated cottages', internally divided into two but with a single front entrance and common path. The two halves of the cottage had been reunited by 1955.

Upper Town Post Office and Park Farm

The oldest house in Nazeing, dating back to about 1475

It was described in 1911 as 'an old double-fronted gabled detached freehold weather-boarded and tiled house with four bedrooms, two living rooms, kitchen dairy & store room'. It was in fair condition, set in half an acre and surrounded by an old moat that gave it its former name of Moat Farm.

Until the 1870s it was the farmhouse for Park Farm but by 1881 Ralph Palmer had combined the management of Park Farm with that of Lodge Farm. The house was occupied by David Cook who in 1890 opened a Post Office and shop which remained in business until 1972. Its low rent of just £5 may have been a kind of subsidy from the Palmers for the social function of the Post Office.

Garden House (Headmaster's Cottage)

This was built in the mid-1600s and its original frame and red-brick chimney stack survive. In 1775 it was the first property bought by William Palmer after he moved to Nazeing. It remained in the family until the 1950s, when it was bought by Essex County Council to house the headmaster of the special needs school at Nazeing Park. On the *Lloyd George Survey* it was included with Nazeing Park and described as 'Good timber & tiled & plaster house with 4 rooms & lean-to wash house & coal places'.

For many years the cottage was occupied by the gardener for Nazeing Park, who from 1904 to 1927 was William George Payne. He came from Hampshire and in 1892 married Alice Jane Judd, a sister of Charles Judd the builder. Their son John William's interesting memoirs are among those that we have used in this book. In 1901 William George was a gardener working in Sutton, Surrey. The Judds and the Paynes were both Chapel families, so it may be that Charles alerted his brother-in-law to the job opportunity. John recalled that 'Father supplied from the large walled garden every kind of vegetable and fruit', while 'Mother made all sorts of jam... and bottled fruit for use out of season'.

Nazeing Park

In 1772 William Palmer moved into a farmhouse called Lucas Hill, and in 1794 had a classical style mansion built next door. The architect was James Lewis, whose best-known work is the Bethlehem Hospital for Lunatics (now the Imperial War Museum). Lucas Hill was demolished and some of the timbers re-used at Upper Town Post Office. The mansion was remodelled in the early 1800s and owned by the family until 1924 although George Palmer junior moved out in 1872 and they seldom lived there afterwards.

From 1872 to 1886 it was rented by Robert Henty, a retired brewer who was an uncle of George Alfred Henty, a war correspondent and prolific novelist best known for his adventure stories glorifying British imperialism. Then there were several short tenancies until 1904 when it was, as John Payne remembered, 'unoccupied and badly neglected'. His family lived in a suite of rooms there until the Garden House was ready, but in 1907 Walter Hargreaves became the tenant and the house's fortunes revived. The *Lloyd George Survey* described it as 'old but in excellent condition':

> Small freehold country mansion near Nazeing Common and standing back in its own park and approached by three entrances. The main entrance is by double iron gates from the Common. Brick built, stuccoed. Parapets to slated roof. Rather imposing entrance flanked with 5 Ionic pillars. 2nd floor – 10 bedrooms and

3 boxrooms. 1st floor – 10 bedrooms and 2 bathrooms. Ground floor – entrance hall with flag floor. Inner hall, light billiard room, library, large dining room...

John Payne, though, recalled 'a library of beautifully bound books that... were removed to the damp and unheated outhouses and eventually taken away by a dealer'.

Nazeing Park c1910

Nance Colman worked at Nazeing Park as a servant during the Great War and gave a vivid description of her life there:

When I left school at fourteen I went up to work at Collyers for Mrs Green with a friend of mine for a little while, to get me into doing housework. Then I went to work at Nazeing Park for Mr Hargreaves. I went as a school room maid, there were three daughters who had a governess. I looked after their bedrooms and so on. I wasn't their maid, the nanny did all that, looking after their dresses.

As the boys got home from school in the holidays, I used to have to work for them. I was taught how to do things properly. My own brothers were away at war. The family used to dress for the evening meal, and all that sort of thing. It was quite a big party when they were all home, all like one big family. There were about seven people working indoors, and six or seven in the garden. I remember seeing five of them hand weeding the path that runs to the gates onto the Common. We stayed at the Park all the time, we lived there.

We used to go to London every winter, when the fogs came because the trains used to get delayed. Mr Hargreaves had to go to work. So we all had to go to live in London. There used to be terrible fogs at that time. You could easily get lost in a fog. Sometimes we were in a hotel, with suites of rooms or we were in a rented house. We had a good life working in a place like that. It wasn't like *Upstairs Downstairs*, not a bit like that. It was strict in lots of ways, you had your set things to do, and you were expected to do it. It was all written out for you. You were shown the proper way to do it. You had to do it, or go back and do it again. It taught you to do things and be useful.

The kitchen people had to get up early before we did. I had to get up and call the nannies and the three young ladies. Then open up the fire and then get the fires going if it was winter. The nannies and young ladies used to breakfast together so I didn't have anything to do with them. They also all went to dinner together. I often laugh now when I hear when some of these people used to say 'Cor, I wouldn't go in service, I couldn't do that sort of thing'. But really, it's amazing, it's a good life, the lovely things that you see and enjoy. You enjoy them just as much as the people who are using them. Don't you think so?

In the summer the family would take a house along the sea front at Frinton. It is now Maplin Hotel. In the mornings before we started work we used to go for a dip, at about a quarter to seven. It was lovely, I always felt well there with all the seaweed. There were many different parties, including tennis parties, there were glasses, and violets in the finger bowls and the gardeners used to come in with flowers and do the tables. It was a good life, I thought we were well looked after.

We were allowed out once a week directly after lunch. We had to get back at seven o'clock as we all used to help wait on the people in the dining room. If you had anything special on you had to ask if you could stay out longer. As you got older and went up a peg or two you were allowed to stay out longer. Once a month you had a holiday, a whole day off.

Vine, Heather and Clematis Cottage

These cottages began life in 1796 as a poorhouse, built by William Palmer. After the new union workhouse was built at Epping, the poorhouse was advertised as containing 'eleven large rooms with two staircases which at a trifling expense may be turned into four good houses'. Estate agent hype is nothing new and William Palmer's son George, who bought it, in fact converted it into three dwellings.

In 1911 they were described as 'three old freehold brick & tile cottages. Each has a timber & tiled store shed & each contains 2 bedrooms & 2 living rooms. Very poor old property. Good garden.' They were occupied by James Sturnham, James Mansfield and Thomas Robert Pegrum and their families.

The Golf House

In the foreground is one of the gates to Nazeing Common, which were in use until the 1930s.

In 1911 the clubhouse was a 'substantially built one storied red brick & tiled building with glazed verandah along front'. It was in very good repair except the roof, and offered a large dining room, a smoking room, two dressing rooms and ladies' room.

The Nook, Kenners Lane

It was originally built in the late 1400s with timber-frame and weather-boarding. In 1822 George Palmer bought it with Lodge Farm, for which it was the gatehouse until 1883, when Ralph Palmer built the new track to Common Road. In 1911 it was described as 'small detached timber & thatched cottage. Very poor property. Large garden.' The tenant from 1896 until his death was Thomas Bysouth (1841-1925). He had been a farm labourer at Barkway in Hertfordshire before coming to be bailiff at Perry Hill, but after a few years he moved on to the Nook. In 1901 his daughter Emily was described as a dairy keeper working on own account at home, and is probably shown in the photo with her mother.

Later in 1901, Emily married James Warders, who in the 1880s ran the Lion and Lamb beerhouse, and then she went to help his widowed sister-in-law at the Red Lion. Emily died in 1906 but they may first have moved to Jacks Hatch, next door to the Nook, because James was living there as a widower in 1911.

Jack's Hatch

In 1922 the Faux brothers paid £350 for the property and opened the family garage business that is still there a century later, but the cottage burnt down in 1939.

The *Lloyd George Survey* describes it as:

> A very old timber built & thatched freehold cottage with buildings
> & land situate in the main road to Epping (which is about 2 miles
> distant). It contains 2 bedrooms, living room, kitchen scullery &
> dairy. There is a good timber & corrugated iron cow house for 6
> cows, also old timber & tiled rough shed & chaff shed. The land
> (all pasture) comprises 3 small hoppits with long frontage to main
> road, the total frontage of the property being over 1800 ft.

In 1911 it was owned by John Dear (1830-1911), a brewery manager
from Baldock in Hertfordshire who was apparently still working
at the age of eighty-one.

The tenant was James Warders, who described himself as 'Dealer
(Marine Store)', working on own account at home; he perhaps
serviced people using the River Lea, though he lived two miles away
from it. Soon afterwards the cottage was taken by Alfred George
Berg, a railway clerk who could have worked at Epping or another
station on the Great Eastern Railway. He was listed on Kelly's as a
private resident rather than in the commercial section, so evidently
he did not use the cottage for business purposes.

Upper Gatehouse

In 1901 this was a row of four cottages. Two of them housed the Lion and Lamb Inn, a small beerhouse which was closed in 1906 in exchange for the granting of a far more lucrative licence in the rapidly expanding suburbs of south-west Essex. In 1911 the premises were owned by McMullen & Co. who had converted them into a single cottage, which was 'brick built and slated, very old & in poor repair & condition'. It was occupied by William James Snell and his wife Julia née Mead, whose great-niece Nita Turner recalled 'This was a four-bedroom cottage on the edge of the Common ... The house had two kitchens, two staircases, and a cellar with a well in the centre that had a cover over it. I remember the slope that they would have rolled the barrels down from the road.'

In 1911 the rest of the terrace had become two 'very poor brick & slated cottages', each with two bedrooms and two living rooms. One was occupied by James and Hannah Osborn, both old age pensioners, and the other by widow Rebekah Atkinson. She had a lodger who was a builder's carpenter and a visitor who was a housemaid born in Sydney New South Wales, both aged twenty-one. The cottages are now Upper Gatehouse and Wyndicot.

In 1847 the property had been owned by Barnard Acres II and was described as seven cottages. They included a 'cottage formerly used as a butcher's shop, with an adjoining cottage, formerly part of Broadley Common'. The butcher in 1841 was Benjamin Harknett, after whom the area around the cottages was named Harknetts Gate. The cottages were at right-angles to the present terrace, parallel with Common Road. They were possibly there as late as 1891 but had certainly been demolished by 1911. In the 1970s Peter Lewis found their foundations after he purchased one of the terraced cottages.

Sun Cottage

There has been a dwelling on the site since the seventeenth century or earlier. By 1781 it was being used as an inn, but when in 1810 a new pub was built, the common right remained with the cottage. The *Lloyd George Survey* recorded: 'No direct frontage to road. Very old brick & tiled cottage. 2 bedrooms, living room. kitchen & scullery. Poor property. Small timber & tiled stables & loose box.'

In 1911 the cottage was occupied by Elizabeth, the second wife of James Samuels, a gardener who had lived there since 1851 and died in 1905, aged ninety-six. It was owned by Mrs Elizabeth Mills, whose late husband had bought it in 1899 for £469 from Christie's, the brewers who owned the Sun.

Collyers

Collyers with Harry Mead, butler to the Green family

Collyers was bought by William Palmer in 1813 and remained in the family until 1924, when Archdale Palmer sold it and the Golf House to F.W. Green for £5,000.

For most of the nineteenth century, it was occupied by farm labourers but around 1890 the Palmers improved it and either lived in it themselves or let it. Archdale was there until 1895, when it was let to Ranson Moore Cuthbert, a Russia merchant, and then to Archdale's sister Charlotte and her husband Herbert Wellesley until their tragic deaths in 1905. Archdale returned to the house until 1912, when he let it to Green. On the 1911 census, while Archdale was at his Kensington flat, Collyers was occupied by George Cordell, described as 'caretaker (domestic)' and later Palmer's chauffeur.

The *Lloyd George Survey* gives a detailed description:

> A small freehold country residence facing Nazeing Common. The owner has added a wing (brick built and tiled) to the other end of the old timber built and tiled house. The property is in an excellent condition. The house contains 7 bedrooms, 2 bathrooms, sitting hall and 3 reception rooms. Kitchen, scullery, larder, pantry and a long timber built corridor to the brick built and tiled lavatories.
>
> The extensive outbuildings are all good. A timber and corrugated iron coal house and lean-to lumber store. A good span roof coach house and harness rooms. A timber and tiled engine house provides electricity for lighting. A timber and corrugated iron garage. Timber and corrugated iron piggeries. A good span roof greenhouse (40ft x 15ft), fives court, tennis and pleasure lawns. Part of the grounds are tastefully and well laid out, enclosed by a 7ft wall. 80 young fruit trees and 1600 rose trees are growing in the garden.

Lodge Farm

The present Lodge Farm was built around 1715 with a timber frame and red brick. It still has the original frame with some original doors and ironmongery. Joseph Bird bought it in 1758 and in 1822 his family sold it to George Palmer senior for £4,680. It was the Palmers' largest property and they took a close interest in it, even though there was usually a bailiff in the farmhouse.

The land at Lodge Farm is very heavy
so it was always a dairy farm.

In 1847 it was described as 'in hand', meaning that George Palmer senior was managing it directly. The tenants of his son George junior were described as farmers, suggesting that he gave them a freer hand. Around 1850 Robert Hatton arrived from Leicestershire and then in 1858 George Derbidge became the only tenant to move to Lodge Farm from a farm within Nazeing, the much smaller Warleys. After Derbidge died in 1866, the tenants were all recruited from various places in Essex. John Clarke came from Clavering and, when he died in 1870, his widow Mary Ann succeeded him.

When Ralph Palmer took over the estate from his father, he adopted a more hands-on approach, employing a bailiff who would have had less autonomy than a farmer. Access to Lodge Farm had been from Jacks Hatch until 1883, when Palmer built a new road to Common Road. From 1874 to 1890, he listed himself in the commercial section of Kelly's as a farmer there, even though Henry Marking from Saffron Walden was described as 'farm bailiff to R.C. Palmer Esq.' On the 1891 census Henry lists his occupations as the unusual combination of 'farm bailiff & threshing machine proprietor'. From 1895 to 1905, the bailiff was Henry Unwin, who had been doing a similar job at Chrishall, Essex.

In 1905 Walter Brown, a farmer's son from Bobbingworth, married Annie Elizabeth Mugleston and came to Lodge Farm. He remained there until 1924, when the sale catalogue stated that he occupied the farmhouse only, and the owner worked the farm.

It was described in the *Lloyd George Survey* as:

> Freehold stock farm bordering on the Common and having a good frontage on the High Road. Land very heavy and wet - most of it poor. Good house - Brick & timber built & tiled with long lean-to addition at the end. 4 beds & box room. 2 rec rooms, large hall, kitchen, scullery & dairy. Timber and tiled coal and wood shed at rear. All in very good condition and repair.

The buildings were 'extensive and on the whole in very good condition'. They included: 'granary, tool shed, large workshop, wagon lodge, engine shed, a range of bullock and cattle sheds, cow house, piggeries and a range of buildings facing the house'. There was also a timber-framed and weather-boarded barn, built around 1700, that is now a Grade II listed building.

Abbotts Cottage

View from the Common with sheep grazing

This was originally built in 1542 as an open-sided grandstand for watching the hunt on the Common and was converted into a dwelling in the late 1500s, when the chimney stack was added. William Palmer bought it from Thomas Brewitt in the 1780s and it remained in his family until 1950. In 1911 it was 'a pair of similar freehold timber built cottages'. Each had '2 bedrooms (neither with fireplace), living room and wash house with lean-to timber and tiled shed at side'. They were 'old but in fair repair'.

They were occupied by widows Elizabeth Reynolds, a pensioner of the Mercers' Company, and Emma Cordell. They had lived there for at least twenty years, initially with their husbands, both farm labourers, and their families. Emma was the sister-in-law of Emma King Cordell who lived at Longyard Cottage, and mother of the George who became Archdale Palmer's chauffeur. She described herself as a poultry farmer working on own account and probably remained until her death in 1934, aged eighty. The Reynolds family lived there from the 1850s and the entrance to the Common from Betts Lane was sometimes called Reynolds Gate.

Kingswood Chase

This timber-framed and plastered building was erected in the late 1500s. In 1795 William Palmer bought it and the neighbouring Red House from the Banks family for £1,500. It was then described as Gores farmhouse but in the nineteenth century was occupied by Thomas King, a carpenter. A small plantation next to the house was known as King's Wood, and had possibly been planted by George Palmer senior with the intention that he and King should get some income from it. In 1947 the house was known as 'Kingsmead near Kings Wood', but by 1985 as Kingswood Chase.

In 1911 it was divided into two similar cottages described as 'old timber-built and tiled freehold cottage with good brick and tiled addition at rear. 2 bedrooms & 2 rooms on ground floor. Very good garden. Good condition.' The one where Thomas King had lived also had 'an old saw pit shed now used as wood & coal house'. The cottages were occupied by John Mansfield (1871-1956) and John Reynolds, who were both farm labourers. Reynolds was the son of John and Elizabeth of Abbotts Cottage, and he had lived at Kingswood Chase since his marriage in 1892 to Catherine Georgina Jenkinson. The 1911 census has a clue to family tragedy in that their younger son Arthur was described as 'feeble-minded from birth' while the name of the older, Alfred, has been crossed out and 'dead' written in although he probably died three years earlier.

Red House
This red brick house was built around 1770 and bought by William Palmer from George Adams in 1808 for £360. In the following year Palmer bought an adjoining piece of waste from Sir William Wake for £3 12s 6d. It was originally a pair of cottages, one of which was occupied by the Starling and Mansfield families from the 1840s until they bought the whole house in 1950 (see Chapter 14).

Red House

Chapter 19

Waltham Road, Laundry Lane and St Leonards Road

Mamelons Farm

This was also known as Malions, and the origin of the name is probably from John Maryon of Epping who held it in 1416. From 1824 or earlier it was owned by Elizabeth Palmer and then by Sir Roundell Palmer, later Lord Selborne. In 1886 the owner was George King, who in 1905 sold it and the next door cottages to Edward James Fowler for £1,400.

In 1847 the farmer at Mamelons was James Horne, whose daughter Frances married Matthew William Mumford, a plumber. After James's death in 1851, Matthew was listed as the farmer although Frances, as a farmer's daughter, is sure to have helped him. By 1881 they had moved to Stoke Newington, where Matthew reverted to his old trade of plumber, and Stracey Lake, said to be 'blind and without an occupation', moved into 'Millions' with his family. Stracey Lake was followed by farmer Susan Pegrum with her nephew A.J. Pegrum, and then by Fowler.

Marjorie Sykes visited her Pegrum relatives and recalled how the old farm house had been replaced:

> The old house was a brick built three-storey house that stood some distance from the road in a partly fenced, partly hedged enclosure to keep the farm animals out. The enclosure was surrounded by a wide ditch, a moat crossed by a fairly wide plank bridge that led through a wicket-gate to the front porch. In fact the layout

was very like that at Sturtsbury. In the outer frontage between the house and the road, animals were pastured. My father took a photograph of it during the nineties of the last century. In it you can see the cows and hens; and in the background, vast tall farm buildings, which were kept when the house was pulled down to be replaced by a more modern farm house by Mr Fowler, the new owner.

William Thornton's photo of Old Mamelons

The new building was described as:

> Small freehold pleasure farm, all grass in good heart. On the front meadow has been erected a new detached residence in excellent condition, a double-fronted, substantially built brick and tiled house with four bedrooms, bath room, two reception rooms with bays, kitchen, scullery and larder.

The farm buildings were built from timber with tiled roofs, and were all in very good repair and condition.

> **Pleasure Farms**
>
> A pleasure farm is one maintained for the enjoyment of the owner rather than to make a profit. In 1907 the journal of the Royal Agricultural Society explained their prevalence in the Home Counties: only half of occupiers of agricultural land described themselves as farmers, a proportion that decreased markedly for small farms of less than fifty acres and the nearer to London the farm was sited. The 22-acre Mamelons was thus typical.

St Lawrence and Warleys Farms

These were formerly two farms, acquired by James Bury in the early 1800s. Together they form a block of agricultural land, bounded by Long Green, Cemetery Lane, Perry Hill Lane and Middle Street. In 1911 the land was mostly pasture of a fair quality, but rather hilly with very heavy soil. The tenant of both farms was John Tayler, who was also farming Langridge. He, and before him his uncle, had probably managed the three farms for over thirty years. The owner, Charles James Bury, would have had to reorganise the management of his estate when the agricultural slump began to bite.

Warleys (now Feltre) on Middle Street was probably named after Thomas Warle, the occupant in 1475. In 1911 it was a very damp timber and plaster house with tiled roofs. There were five bedrooms, two living-rooms, kitchen and scullery. George Derbidge farmed thirty acres there in the 1840s and 1850s and was succeeded by Thomas Hale. After Hale's death in 1885, it was converted into two cottages occupied by labourers working on the farm. It had no farm buildings but next to the farmhouse was a pair of timber and tiled cottages under one roof, also tenanted by labourers.

The farm on Long Green had been called Lawrence's since the mid-sixteenth century and St Lawrence Farm since 1824, shortly after it was acquired by the Bury family. In 1851 John Haines was a farmer of 187 acres with seven labourers, so he must have been farming other land as well. He was succeeded by three men described as bailiffs but by 1891 the house was occupied by James Hutchings, a farm labourer. From 1904 the tenant was another farm labourer, Arthur Smith, whose grandson Robert died in the Great War.

In 1911 St Lawrence farmhouse was very old, damp and dilapidated. There were old farm buildings but also new, unfinished ones, showing that Ralph Bury was investing in the farm. These were a brick and slated five bay open bullock shed in one yard and a four bay stall in another, and a range of cow houses and a nag stable on the other side of the yard.

Newmans / Felstead

Newmans Farm was named from Walter le Neueman, the resident in 1275. From 1678 Thomas Chalkley and his son Thomas were owners and in 1824 it was still owned by their descendant Chalkley Gould. They were leading nonconformist ministers and one explanation for the name of Cemetery Lane was that on the field opposite the house they planned a nonconformist cemetery that never materialised. In 1847 it was owned by John Smith, the wealthy tenant of Harold's Park Farm and in 1872 by his son-in-law Henry Sworder. He or his daughter Katherine must have sold it to the Burys because Ralph Bury owned it in 1911.

The house was occupied from about 1840 to 1877 by a father and son, both called Alexander Felstead, who were farm labourers. After the Felsteads there were several tenants but the *Lloyd George Survey* called it 'Newmans known as Felstead' so evidently the new name was already in use, informally at least. From 1903 the house was occupied by James and Martha Hutchings, who had been at St Lawrence Farm. In 1911 he was seventy-three years old but still a farm labourer and apparently not drawing an old age pension.

The four-bedroomed, timber and tiled former farmhouse was very old and in a poor condition and repair. It contained two living rooms, a scullery and lean-to coal shed, with an old hip-roof timber and implement shed. The land was good pasture farmed by John Smith junior, no relation to the John Smith who owned it earlier. He also farmed Netherkidders and together they made a compact unit totalling sixty acres.

Netherkidders

The name Netherkidders was first recorded in the seventeenth century, when there was also a field called Upperkidders. They could be named from the Old Norse 'kida', a brother or friend. In 1911 it was owned by Ralph Bury and occupied by John Smith junior. It was described as a small freehold farm consisting of eight enclosures of pasture land, which were very heavy and wet. It required draining which would have much improved the grazing. The farmhouse was a four-bedroomed timber, plaster-and-tiled house containing two living rooms, wash house and scullery, in poor condition and repair. The farm buildings were for the most part very good and ample. They included a range of good brick and tiled buildings, one of them built in 1904 by Ralph Bury, as is seen from a plaque on the wall.

Snows (Laun House)

This had been named by the sixteenth century and was purchased by James Bury in 1798. It was occupied in 1911 by Miles Staveley Hopkinson, thirty-one-year-old stockbroker with his wife and daughter, whose age was given as 11¾ months precisely, and five servants. It was said to be 'partly old but in excellent condition'. Its description, 'a small freehold bungalow country residence', probably indicated that its ten rooms were spread out over a single floor although this may have been a joke at the expense of Ralph Bury, who complained about the 'bungalow craze' at Riverside.

Marjorie Sykes wrote: '[In 1928] an old farm called "Snows" was completely burnt out by fire and was the subject of much talk in the village. I was taken round to see the charred ruins, and felt a strong sense of something sinister as I looked [at] the pathetic remains of a family and home.' The Morrison and Hale families who lived there escaped and moved away.

St Leonards Farm

The *Lloyd George Survey* says that St Leonards Farm was owned and occupied by Ralph Bury and that it also included 'a homestead & 2 cottages', which it goes on to describe as a lodge and farmery[24].

In the late 1790s Ralph's great-grandfather James Bury (1766-1825) came to Leonards Green House and acquired Snows, Shadwalkers, Allmains, Lawrence, Warleys, Sturtsbury, Cutlands and Marshgate

---

24 'The buildings, yards, etc., belonging to a farm.' Oxford English Dictionary.

Farm, owning a total of 145 acres. By 1847 the family owned 337 acres in Nazeing, and also land just across the parish boundaries in Roydon and Waltham Abbey.

Censuses give an idea of how the Burys managed their estate. James's son James Frederick (1798-1860), who inherited St Leonards in 1825, was listed on the 1841 census as a farmer and in 1851 as a landed proprietor. The Tithe Award says that in 1847 the occupier was his brother William Shepherd Bury (1800-1852), a major in the East India Company's army. In 1861 the recently widowed Augusta Bury and her son Charles James were living at St Leonards House while William Lawrence, who had for many years been a baker and farmer in Roydon, was a farmer of 134 acres living at St Leonards Farm. In 1871 Charles James Bury was a magistrate and landowner and the farmer was his uncle Charles Bury (1806-1876), who lived at Snows. He was described as 'retired Bengal civilian farming 258 acres employing 11 men and 6 boys'. The 1881 and 1891 censuses list Charles James at St Leonards as a magistrate but nobody in the immediate area was described as a farmer, so he was probably managing the farm himself.

Certainly, after Charles James Bury's death in 1897, his son Ralph took an active role in running the estate. Although he was always listed in Kelly's as a private resident, he was shown on the *Lloyd George Survey* as the occupier as well as the owner of St Leonards and the adjacent fields, a total of 192 acres which included eight enclosures of good freehold pasture. Overall, Ralph Bury had twelve tenants working the 425 acres of land he owned, which were scattered around the village. The Survey described St Leonards House as:

> an old Freehold Country Residence with good grounds, orchards, gardens, park, farm house, buildings and agricultural land. House brick and timber built and plastered, with a slated roof. Fair condition structurally and in excellent repair.

The accommodation included: stone paved entrance hall, study (low pitch), good ante-room, morning room, small & large drawing room, large dining room, lamp room, store room, lobby, kitchen, scullery with flag floor, wine cellar, coal cellar and two larders; small servants hall, butler's pantry and back stairs leading to a room unused; 3 servants' bedrooms in the roof, 4 principal bedrooms and a bathroom, plus 4 other bedrooms.

'An old freehold country residence' : St Leonards House

The lodge was a 'substantially built brick and tiled new cottage with 2 sitting rooms, 2 bedrooms (partly in roof) and a back addition of a scullery', dated 1909 by a plaque on the front. Until at least 1939 it was occupied by Harry Treleaven, Bury's chauffeur.

The farmery was a 'large brick and slated double span roof house with brick and tiled addition at one end and brick and slated ditto at other end'. It contained 4 bedrooms, sitting room, kitchen, dairy, lumber room, large wash house and store at road end. It was formerly two cottages and was probably rebuilt on the instructions of Ralph Bury to house his farm bailiff, who from 1902 until the Great War was Peter Raithby.

There was also a very wide range of outbuildings including a brewhouse, a boot house and store, stables, granaries, horseboxes, cart sheds, bullock sheds and a wagon lodge. In the gardens were a walled kitchen garden, a double vinery, a garden frame and a brick and slated water tower.

Mulberries

In 1911 Mulberries was a 'small freehold poultry farm... substantially built brick & slated detached double-fronted brick house in good repair and condition'. It had four bedrooms, two reception rooms, kitchen and scullery. The few farm buildings were 'poor and much out of repair'. It was called Mulberries on the surveys of 1847 and 1911, but the 'Blue House' on Kelly's throughout the nineteenth century.

In 1901 James Henry Morrish paid £1,460 for Mulberries, perhaps so that he could supply stock directly to his butcher's shop at Turners Hill in Cheshunt. He died in 1906 and his widow Lucy returned to their native Somerset, but in 1911 she still owned Mulberries.

In 1907 the tenancy was taken over by William John Francis Overell, who was listed in 1911 as a farmer but also had a boarder called Walter Bott who was a 'poultry farmer working on own account'. In 1914 the new tenant was a milk dairyman, James Pigg, whose son David died during the Great War although the family remained at Mulberries until 1922.

Cutlands

This name is probably related to 'Scrutlands', held in the thirteenth century by the canons of Waltham Abbey. In the second half of the eighteenth century it was known as Wadeloves and owned by Robert Darley Wadelove, possibly the man of that name who was the Dean of Ripon. James Bury purchased it in 1819 and his tenant was John Backwith junior (1801-1864) a bricklayer, builder and farmer. James Bridgeman farmed Cutlands until at least 1908, but moved out of the farmhouse in the 1890s when first John Smith and then his son Arthur ('Tractor') Smith were the occupants.

The timber, plaster-and-tiled, three-bedroomed farm house built around 1600 still has its original red chimney stack. In 1911 it had a sitting room, living room, dairy and scullery, with a good range of farm buildings. The farm land was six acres of very good pasture close to the house, and Arthur Smith also farmed a further forty-one acres owned by Bury.

The Rookery (Shiree)

This was one of seven properties bought by William Palmer from Jacob Bosanquet in 1799 (see page 208). At that time it was a derelict cottage but by 1820 Palmer had replaced it with a block of four 'tenements', unlike anything else to be seen in Nazeing. Two faced on to St Leonards Road and two were at the rear. They were known as The Rookery and were in turn replaced in the 1950s, by Shiree.

The Rookery in 1915. Harry Hutchings is holding the horse with his wife Mabel seated near the wheel. Directly behind her is Ada, wife of Harry's brother Arthur, who may well be the man at the centre.

Pound House

It was described in 1911 as:

Substantially built brick & tile cottage freehold with good garden & small paddock – good repair and condition. 3 bedrooms, living room, sitting room, scullery & dairy. Detached brick built & tiled wash house. Good timber & tiled span roof in paddock.

It was acquired by John Smith of Harold's Park Farm in 1800 and inherited by his grand-daughter Julia, together with three detached fields, a total of thirty-one acres. She left the property to her son Henry Sworder who passed them on to his sister Katherine, just at the time the *Lloyd George Survey* was done - perhaps as her share of a substantial estate, or even as a tax dodge. She sold the cottage and fields in 1919 for £1,170. In 1911 the occupier for all of the property was listed as Nazeing-born George Pegrum who had farmed in Epping since 1880, although the house was sublet to George Mansfield (1830-1916). He and his wife Mary are probably the old couple in the photo.

The Ham

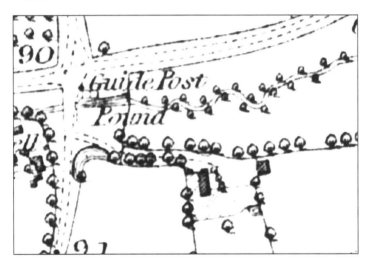

1873 Ordnance Survey map of The Ham and neighbourhood. The pound gave its name to Pound Close, and Ham farmhouse is the oblong building nearby.

Ham Farm was described in 1911 as 'two enclosures of freehold pasture with an old timber and thatched house in ruins'. The gates and hedges also were in a bad state of repair. Access to the land was over the green by the pound. It was bought by Randall Acres in 1787 and remained in the family until about 1911, when Ernest Acres had to mortgage it to Sworder & Longmore solicitors. It was therefore appropriate that the new housing estate built near the site was called Barnard Acres after several owners of that name.

It was occupied from 1832 until his death by William Watson (1786-1866), a labourer from Ugley in Essex who made good. He had since 1817 been the publican of the Crooked Billet and the adjacent orchard and meadow. He occupied Shadwalkers, farmed six acres of meadow at Porters in Cemetery Lane and twenty-two acres of meadow on Nazeing Mead, and was also listed as a corn and flour dealer. He was the grandfather of Emma Smith who married William Henry Mead and of Emma Selway and her brother William Lowe (see page 275). Watson was succeeded as tenant at the Ham by Thomas Argent and then by John Argent Nicholls. All lived elsewhere, so we do not know exactly when the house was abandoned.

Chapter 20

Paynes Lane, Old Nazeing Road and Nazeing Road

Paynes Farm

Paynes was described in 1911 as a 'compact good freehold stock farm'. The farm house was a large, old, timber-built and tiled house, much as it had been for three hundred years, part boarded and part plastered. Its three-span roof was in need of repair, otherwise it was in fair condition. There were seven rooms on the first floor and six on the ground floor, plus a conservatory.

The farm premises were 'on the whole a good sample for the area of the holding'. The land, totalling 104 acres, was in a very good state of cultivation. There was a right of way (now Paynes Lane) to Langridge Farm and cottages.

In 1781 Thomas Banks bought Paynes Farm and it remained in his family until 1878, when George Thomas Banks sold it to Richard

Bugg. When Richard retired, he recruited Thomas Chapman from Waltham Abbey, who stayed until 1910. Chapman was succeeded by Thomas Harker, a farmer from Swaledale, a rural area of Yorkshire in serious economic decline. In 1911 Harker's daughter Ruth was a dairymaid and three of his sons were working on the farm, with the two youngest boys still at school. Dairy farmer Thomas William Smith came from Stanstead Abbots in 1914 and was still farming there in 1939.

Langridge Farm

At 186 acres, Langridge was the third largest farm in Nazeing, and also extended into Waltham Abbey. It takes its name from the 'long ridge' that gives fine views as far as Hertfordshire to the west and over St Leonards Road to the east. The manor of Langridge dates back to the Middle Ages when it was a free tenement of Waltham Abbey.

Langridge farmhouse in 1940.
It had changed little since the nineteenth century.

The farmhouse was newly built in 1548 and part of it still survives, while the south side was added in the nineteenth century. In 1911 it was a 'roomy, brick built & tiled house containing six bedrooms, two living rooms, kitchen, scullery, dairy and beer cellar'. There was a brick and tiled detached brew house, used as a washing place and cooling room. A rectangular moat which surrounded the farm buildings was dry by 1961.

The farm was:

> A good freehold stock farm situate in an isolated position on the western boundary of the parish, close to the river and nearly one mile from the main road. Much of the land consists of marsh and three of the meadows are very hilly. The farm land is in fair state of cultivation. Hedges are well kept up. Buildings for the most part good, in fair repair and ample for the size of the holding. Cow house for 54 cows, piggeries, brick built granary and two sink grain pits outside, range of brick & slated buildings comprising coach house, stables, bullock shed, and horse boxes.

Included in the farm was a small plot of osier land in a loop of the old River Lea. Described as 'The Island', it had been owned by the War Office and its predecessors since 1824 or earlier. It was used to grow willow for basketry, perhaps to store or carry ordnance.

There were also three workers' cottages on the farm. The semi-detached Langridge Cottages were built in 1907 to house two cowmen and their families. Upper Langridge was a condemned cottage half a mile away from the main farmhouse up a steep hill, occupied in 1911 by the farm blacksmith, William Lowe

Langridge was owned in 1911 by Harold Smith (1848-1914), a retired varnish manufacturer from Coventry, and was probably bought as an investment by his father. It was inherited by his son Harold Nelson Smith (1880-1942), who in 1919 sold it to George Chapman for £5,000.

Langridge was farmed for nearly sixty years by three generations of the Tayler family. In 1862 James (1800-1881) came from Buckinghamshire where he had lived all his life, so it was a courageous move. He initially farmed 220 acres with six men and a boy, but when he died he was farming an extra twenty-two acres though employing only four men.

James's son John (1840-1927) assisted him at Langridge Farm and married Mary Belgrove, a Buckinghamshire farmer's daughter. By 1891 they had six children and were living in the house with a governess, two servants and a labourer. John was also farming ninety acres at St Lawrence and Warleys farms. He inherited his father's spirit of adventure and, in his late fifties, went to manage a model farm at Frogmore near St. Albans, which had been founded to explore innovative farming practices and animal husbandry techniques.

Langridge was taken over by John's nephew, also John (1863-1944). Although he had the middle name Carr, he did not always use it. In 1901 he was living at Langridge with his sister Louie and, in a separate household, the horse keeper Thomas Watts and his family, who had also come from Buckinghamshire. In 1911 John Carr Tayler was listed as the occupier of Langridge, St Lawrence and Warleys although by then he had moved to Ware Park Farm in Ware. He was farming predominantly pasture and very little arable. He left Nazeing when George Chapman bought Langridge and died in 1944, leaving £67,692.

Tatsford Farm

Tatsford was farmed in the eighteenth century with Paynes and in the nineteenth with Langridge, but by 1908 it was owned by Gerard Frogley, a dairy farmer at Spitalbrook in Broxbourne. The names Tatsford and Tatsfield seem then to have been interchangeable but after the Great War Tatsfield became the name of new cottages in St Leonards Road.

Tatsford was a freehold, detached, double-fronted, brick-and-slated house, formerly two cottages, in good condition and repair. It had four bedrooms, living room, kitchen and brick-and-slated washing room at the back. In 1911 it was occupied by Arthur George Josling, an 'authorised clerk' on the London Stock Exchange. Seven acres around the farmhouse included four taken from the Marsh under the Enclosure Award of 1861.

Also part of Tatsford were three fields totalling just over forty acres which were divided when Nazeing New Road was built in 1908. Initially Frogley asked Epping Rural District Council for a payment of £200 but the council refused. They argued that his property would be improved by the new road and he agreed to donate the land, which was indeed improved when in 1931 some of the fields became the site of the Herts & Essex Aerodrome.

Keysers Farm

Keysers farmhouse c1900

The farm was named from Robert Keyes who owned it in the sixteenth century, and the name Keysers evolved over the years. For much of the nineteenth century it was owned by Henry Cozens father and son of Broxbourne, landowners and farmers of over two hundred acres. The farmhouse was occupied by labourers, probably working for the Cozens.

In 1906 the farm was bought by Rachel Klenck, whose husband was an auctioneer and surveyor, with the intention of developing it for housing. After her death it passed to her daughter Florence Loughrey, who in 1907 moved with her surgeon husband to Charlton Mead in Hoddesdon, then a large house. Florence chose not to develop the land herself but to sell off individual plots although in 1910 over fifty remained unsold. In most cases people moved out from the London suburbs and built their own bungalows or had them built, often to a high standard.

The *Lloyd George Survey* gives no details about the farmhouse but the census says it had four rooms. In 1911 it was occupied by a City of London police pensioner who was one of the first people to retire to Nazeing. With him was his nephew, a house decorator who would have found plenty of work in the new bungalows being built.

Poona Lawn and Sunnyholme

Among the very few new houses built before 1914 in the older part of Nazeing were Poona Lawn and its neighbour, Sunnyholme. They were built in 1895 at a cost of £700 each. Poona Lawn was described on the *Lloyd George Survey* as a

> Substantially built brick & slated semi-detached freehold residence on main road about 1 mile from station. Good large garden nicely laid out. 2 attics, 4 bedrooms, 2 rec. rooms... Good condition & repair. Good brick & slated stable of 2 stalls with harness room & wood store with loft over. Fruit trees £20, timbered potting shed.

Sunnyholme was similar but without the attics.

In 1901 both were occupied by marine insurers working on own account, presumably colleagues who had been attracted to Nazeing even before the new road was opened. In 1907 one of the men, Henry Holford, was killed at Broxbourne level crossing while cycling home from the station. In 1911 they were occupied by clerks commuting to London.

Poona Lawn in the 1920s, showing the attics and stables

Rose Cottage (14 Elizabeth Close)

In 1911 this was described as 'A substantially built brick & tiled cottage (in fair condition & repair) with 3 bedrooms, sitting room & kitchen'. A frontage of 480 feet was 'divided by a running brook which greatly detracts from the value', and there was also 'settlement on east side of house', presumably caused by the brook.

The house had always been known simply as 'Near the Bury', but in 1911 on the census and the *Lloyd George Survey* it was called Rose Cottage. The name was possibly given by the tenant, David Wootton (1846-1923), a butcher who moved from Edmonton in 1905. Boarding with him was Vincent Moye, a nurseryman who was still living there in 1939.

The seven-acre plot had been in the family of Walter Pateshall Jones (1857-1920) since 1748. He was born at Roselands, a substantial eighteenth-century house at Turkey Street Enfield, which he sold in 1883 for £13,500 to the Bowles family of Myddelton House. Educated at Haileybury School and Trinity College Cambridge, he lived entirely off a private income. After his death, the cottage was sold for £800, possibly to Wootton. In 1976 it was demolished to make way for Elizabeth Close.

Nazeingbury

The Wake family, as lords of the manor, had owned Nazeingbury since the late seventeenth century. In 1822 William Collins became the farmer and a co-founder of the Chapel. When he died in 1838, Edward Collins took over and was still there forty years later. By 1881 the farmer was Joe Pegrum, who at the age of twenty-five was employing eight men and two boys.

In 1911 Nazeingbury was, at almost 340 acres, by far the largest farm in Nazeing. The *Lloyd George Survey* described it as:

A good freehold farm part arable & part pasture with a large old farm house situated close to the cross roads ... very old, brick built and tiled and in fair repair and condition ... The land is very well farmed and is in the most part in good heart. Part of the land is marsh land and about eight acres have been excavated for gravel.

The farm house was of timber frame construction, much of it built before 1550 with rebuilding during the 1700s.

The Bungalow (Goats)

This was built, owned and occupied by Herbert Edward Hughes who was born in 1870 in Hackney, where his father was a toy merchant. Herbert was a clerk in 1891 and a 'toy agent' in 1901, but by 1911 he had taken over the firm and was giving his occupation as 'toy merchant and manufacturer'. In 1896 he married Rose Perkins in Hackney and they had five children. In 1901 he and his family had just moved into 'The Bungalow' with his wife's sister.

The site was on Nazeing Mead with frontage to the towpath and Occupation Road at the side, adjacent to Nazeing Wharf. Hughes was also listed as owner-occupier of three nearby enclosures totalling eleven acres.

The impressive property was described in 1911 as

In good repair & condition, timber & tiled bungalow with substantially built brick & tiled two storied addition at side giving altogether the following accommodation: 3 bedrooms & bathroom, hall, billiard room & 3 other rooms on ground floor, verandah & balcony on two sides of new addition, double span large conservatory, well laid out garden.

The buildings consisted of:

> old span roof double greenhouse, brick & tiled engine house (with
> 3 HP oil engine & dynamo for making electric light) & workshop,
> greenhouse adjoining, rough timber & corrugated iron pony stable
> & chaise house, well-built span roof (with lantern light), brick &
> corrugated iron goat house for 48 goats with stalls and feeding
> gangway, lean-to roof timber & corrugated iron fowl house, brick
> built & tiled goat house with loft over, lean-to large goat [sic],
> corrugated iron shelter for billy goats.

The house was sometimes known as Goats, because Herbert kept
goats in the sheds there and was a prize-winning breeder. In the
Royal Association of British Dairy Farmers Handbook of 1915, he
won first prize in Class 26 for his goat 'Broxbourne March Maiden'
for Anglos Swiss She-Goats as well as first prize for Class 28 She
Goats of any other variety with 'Broxbourne Fairy Queen'. He was
breeding his goats not only for their pedigree, but also their milk
production.

Chapter 21

North Street and Hoe Lane

Maplecroft Farm and Cottage

Maplecroft Farm was not quite the place of gothic
horror this atmospheric photo might suggest.

In 1781 John Banks died and left Maplecroft Farm to his great
niece Sarah Banks of Paynes Farm, who married Joshua Crow
(c1770-1850), a farmer from Roydon. By 1795 Joshua was listed
as owner/occupier of Maplecroft and later as joint owner of many
properties in the village, presumably from his wife's inheritance.
With him in 1841 was his son George (1813-1890), who became
a farm servant at Paynes Farm. In 1851 George married Hannah
Dellar and moved back to Maplecroft, where in 1861 they were
living with their three children and her widowed mother, a nurse.

In 1881 at Christ Church Highbury their son George (1855-1943)
married Jane Galloway, a baker's daughter. He described himself as

a carman and this may well be how he met her. Initially they lived in Bethnal Green but later George returned to Nazeing as a farm labourer and his two brothers-in-law joined him. The Galloways were a Hoxton family and their arrival in Nazeing may be typical of how some people came to the village.

The neighbouring two-bedroomed timber dwelling, Maplecroft Cottage, was bought by William Palmer in 1801 and owned by the family until 1950. In the nineteenth century it had a rapid turnover of occupants but by 1901 it had been taken over by the growing Crow family. Living there were George's brother-in-law William Galloway and three of his sons, as well as a lodger. In the main house were George and Jane with their five youngest children.

In 1911 the extended Crow family was still filling the two properties. The eldest son William, who worked at Pulham's terra cotta works, and his young wife Jessie had the four-room cottage to themselves, whilst George, Jane, her brother and five children squeezed into the five-room house. All of the men worked on the land except Ernest Edward, a house painter who was probably employed by his neighbour, Langham King.

George Crow was listed in Kelly's as a farmer at Maplecroft from 1899 until 1937. The family continued to live in both dwellings although George did not take the opportunity to buy the cottage in 1924, when Archdale Palmer sold off much of his estate. His daughter Ethel married a private in the 8th Essex Regiment and the name of their son, Jack Verdun Pearce, reflected one of the darkest periods of the Great War.

The *Lloyd George Survey* says that Maplecroft Farm was less than four acres. The two-bedroomed detached brick house, with tiled roof, was old but in fair repair. It contained two living rooms and a lean-to timber-and-tiled wash house and larder-cum-dairy. The farm buildings were old and in poor condition. In the early 1960s the house was replaced by a new building, now 38 Maplecroft Lane.

The neighbouring cottage was described as 'A detached timber built & tiled freehold cottage – 2 bedrooms, 2 living rooms – brick & timber & tiled. Wash house at rear. Good garden'.

Maplecroft Cottage in 1961, taken by George Holeyman shortly before it was demolished to make way for new houses in Maplecroft Lane.

Shottentons

In 1911 'Shottingtons' was described as a small mixed freehold farm, just under fifty acres which included twenty acres on Nazeing Mead, with access to the towpath by Carthagena Lock. It had been owned by the Acres family since 1791 and the tenant was James Bridgeman.

The timber and thatched two-bedroomed cottage had two living rooms and a wash house but was described as dilapidated. The farm buildings were sufficient for the size of the farm with some in good condition, others very poor. James Bridgeman also occupied fields north of Shottentons at Stoneshot and Northfields, which brought his total acreage to eighty-five acres. The agricultural land was described as fair, with one arable and two pasture enclosures. In 1912 Sworder & Longmore on behalf of Ernest Acres sold Shottentons, Stoneshot and Northfields to Essex County Council for £2,000. The council may have intended to use the land for housing but, if so, nothing came of it.

'Very old span timber and thatch cattle barn' at Shottentons.
The photo was probably taken in the 1920s or later, because the dilapidated thatched cottage described on the Survey has been replaced by a more modern building.

Netherhall

Netherhall is now entirely in Roydon, but part of it was in Nazeing until 1946. In 1500 there were two adjacent but separate houses there, one moated and brick-built, the other smaller and timber-framed. They were built by Thomas Colt, whose eldest daughter, Jane, married Sir Thomas More. By the eighteenth century the owners lived elsewhere and the brick house was falling into ruins, leaving only a three-storeyed gatehouse. Netherhall became a farm whose tenant lived in the timber-framed house.

Ruined gatehouse at Netherhall

In 1911, Netherhall was owned by George Archer-Houblon, who described himself as a 'Colonel Militia retired'. The Houblon family migrated from Flanders to England during the reign of Elizabeth I, and rose in the commercial life of London. In 1694 Sir John Houblon was appointed the first governor of the Bank of England. The family lands were greatly increased through the marriage in 1770 of Jacob Houblon and Susannah Archer, sole heiress of the Archer family of Coopersale, whose ancestor John Archer had bought Netherhall in 1680.

In 1905 the Colonel recruited George White Barrett to farm Netherhall. The second son of a Wiltshire farmer, he moved with his family from Donhead St Mary in the Blackmore Vale, famed for its dairy farming. Family legend has it that he brought his cows on the train and walked them from Broxbourne station to the farm, probably along the towpath. The *Lloyd George Survey* records him as farming sixty-five acres.

Netherhall farmhouse c1900

The Colonel died in 1913, leaving £57,904. The main part of Netherhall was sold in 1920 for £11,000, with two small later transactions totalling £165.

Camps

Camps was built originally in the 1500s with a number of alterations over the years. The house and the three-bay barn of timber-frame construction built in the 1700s are both Grade 2 listed buildings. In 1911 it was described as 'A small farm, all grass. Old brick and tiled house with four bedrooms, two sitting rooms, kitchen, dairy and coal cellar. In fair repair and condition.'

The Camps were a leading Nazeing family until the 1780s, and the house name dates back to 1673 or earlier. Abraham Nicholls bought it in 1803 and it remained in the family until the death of Sarah Nicholls in 1917, when it was sold for £1,100.

Camps. The women may be Sarah Nicholls
(in porch) and one of her daughters.

Little End (Camps Cottages)

This pair of cottages was built for the labourers working at Camps
Farm and was originally called 'Camps Cottages'. It was bought by
Abraham Nicholls in 1803 and in 1873 was owned by his grand-
daughter, Charlotte Nicholls (1810-1875?), who in 1871 gave
her occupation as 'House property'. She bequeathed it to her half-
brother George (1832-1901) who owned and farmed at Camps.
In his will he left instructions that it should be sold for the benefit
of his widow, Sarah, and it was snapped up by John Banks. It was
occupied in 1911 by Herbert Mansfield, a horse keeper, and Ted
Coleman the builder.

No details of Camps Cottages are recorded on the *Lloyd George Survey* but the photo shows that it was weather-boarded and brick.

Greenleaves

Greenleaves was originally built in the 1400s and altered in the 1500s with the insertion of the first floor and by raising the roof. The house was described in 1911 as being 'in fair condition considering its age', with five bedrooms, two living rooms, kitchen, dairy and scullery.

The farm buildings at Greenleaves were described as very old and in poor condition, and included:

> Timber and thatched bullock shed, four bay open bullock shed, stables with four stalls and loose boxes, cow shed with lean to fowl house at side, open three division shed and barn with piggeries at end, timber and tiled calf pens, wood store, small granary and three bay wagon lodge.

The barn, built in the 1400s, and outbuildings, with timbers from the 1200s, nevertheless survived and are Grade 2 listed.

Greenleaves was described in 1911 as a freehold mixed farm in a good state of cultivation, with heavy land and good pasture. It had been farmed with Darmers since 1874, a total of sixty-nine acres. It was tenanted by the Pegrums since 1770 and bought by Edward Williams in about 1840. In 1911 it was officially occupied by Joe Pegrum although his sisters Mary and Martha lived in the house. By 1916 his son David managed the farm and lived in the house.

David Pegrum and his wife Dorothy at Greenleaves

The White House

The farm was owned and occupied by the Nicholls family from 1793 until the 1840s, when it was bought by William Robert Smiley. He was the manager of A.B. Savory & Sons, a leading firm of goldsmiths and clockmakers who were eventually taken over by Mappin & Webb. He was succeeded as manager by his son Samuel (1825-1882), who was a gold-and-silversmith of some distinction.

Samuel and his family were born in the Clerkenwell area of London and none of them were ever listed on the census in Nazeing, yet they owned property in the village and probably lived in it between censuses or used it as some kind of country retreat. Samuel was elected a Trustee of Nazeing Wood or Park in 1878 but four years later was buried at All Saints' where his headstone quotes a rather gloomy verse from Psalm 107: 'They fell down and there was none to help', hinting that he came to a sad end.

His son Samuel junior (1860-1930) was apprenticed to his father as a goldsmith but decided to become a cycle-maker and agent and for many years had a shop in Wood Green High Road. He was never listed on Nazeing electoral registers but evidently still felt an affinity with the village because he was buried alongside his parents and brother at All Saints'.

The farmhouse was built in about 1580 with a heavy oak frame. On the April 1911 census it was divided into two parts, occupied respectively by Susan Pegrum and Ted Coleman, but a few months later the *Lloyd George Survey* recorded the house and outbuildings as being in the single occupation of Alexander Vale Charge. He was the sub-tenant of John Argent Nicholls, who lived next door at Parkers and farmed twenty-two acres of pasture attached to the White House.

The Survey described it as a

> Small copyhold farm with house (formerly 2 cottages) & 5 enclosures of good pasture land ... The detached house is timber built & plastered, tiled roof – in good condition. 4 bedrooms & boxroom, 2 rec. rooms, kitchen, scullery.

The outbuildings were 'in very poor condition generally'.

Hoe Lane c1900, with the White House on the right and entrance to Greenleaves on the left. A century later, the nature of the traffic is rather different.

Parkers

The name Parkers dates back to 1582 or earlier. The present house was probably built in the 1700s, with some framing dating from the 1500s. In 1911 the farm was described as:

Small freehold holding consisting of - Old timber built & tiled house. 4 bedrooms, 2 sitting rooms, scullery & dairy. Very old but in fair repair and condition. Buildings very poor. Timber & tiled coal & wood shed, small timber and thatched barn used as stables, timber & thatched double hen house.

The farm also had six enclosures of good pasture totalling fifteen acres.

Parkers was bought in the 1780s by Randall Acres and remained in the family until about 1911. Thomas Nicholls became the tenant of Parkers in 1780 and members of his family farmed there for the next 150 years. They did not always live in the house, but John Argent Nicholls moved in after his marriage in 1890 and stayed there until 1930.

Barnfield

In 1873, as a result of George Palmer junior's financial problems, a triangle of land bounded by Hoe Lane, Middle Street and Nazeing Brook was put up for auction. Known as Barnfield, it was bought by Alexander McKenzie, a well-known Hoddesdon auctioneer, who immediately divided the land into twenty plots and put them up for sale. He sold Lot 15 to Joseph Hale who built Hope Cottage at the back of the long, narrow plot, which fronted on to Middle Street.

The *Lloyd George Survey* shows that by 1909 the land bought by McKenzie in 1873 had been divided into several hereditaments. Joseph Hale owned Hope Cottage and all of the land to the west of it. The description was 'Good brick & slated detached cottage, double-fronted. 3 bedrooms, 2 living rooms, lean-to scullery, lean-to timber & tiled store shed. 8 fruit trees. Number of old dilapidated buildings of no real value.'

Sunnyside was owned and occupied by George Lipson. It was about five years old in 1900 when he bought it for £650 and on his death in 1920 it was sold for £750. It was described as 'a freehold detached brick built and slated double fronted house in good condition and repair, with 4 bedrooms, box room, 2 sitting rooms, kitchen and wash house'. The house was demolished and replaced by the present houses in 1970, and no known picture survives.

Lipson was also the tenant of two small adjacent fields. They, along with 1½ acres of freehold pasture land owned by Christie & Co, the Hoddesdon brewers, were described as Barnfield allotments.

Hope Cottage seen from Brook House in 1926, with recently-built Barnfield on the left. Halesmere was built at the front of the plot in the 1930s.

Chapter 22

Middle Street

Mayflower

Mayflower was described in 1911 as:

> Old freehold double-fronted detached brick-built and slated house.
> 4 rooms on first floor. 2 living rooms. Shop with bay. Old but in
> fair condition. Buildings in bad repair – timber & tiled fowl house
> & coal shed, ditto store shed & wood shed. Rent [£15] fair.

The house was a shop by 1839 when Thomas Argent (c1795-1881)
was listed as 'shopkeeper & dealer in sundries', which he remained
until his death. In his time it was owned successively by Robert
King, George Banks, George Thomas Banks and the Reverend
John Price Alcock Fletcher of Broxbourne, who in 1893 sold it
to Miss Martha Pegrum for £400. After Thomas Argent died, his
daughter Mary Ann ran it until her own death in 1892, describing
herself on the census as 'keeper of village provision shop'.

Mayflower with 'Shop Gran'

In 1879 John Herbert Ashby (1843-1923) married Eliza Annie Lewis (1858-1940), known as Annie or 'Shop Gran'. He was born in Islington and she in Netteswell near Harlow but they had moved to Nazeing by 1881 when Alice was born, the eldest of four children. John Ashby then moved from Laundry Lane to Mayflower and was listed on directories as a 'shopkeeper', but on censuses as a 'bricklayer'. His brother William was a carpenter who lived with them and is said to have built the staircase at Mayflower. John's wife Annie certainly ran the shop after his death, and probably whilst he was still alive.

Wheelers

Wheelers with the extensive outbuildings that were later
demolished and replaced by Wheelers Green

Wheelers was named from a Robert Wheler [sic] who lived there in 1475. By 1780 it had a blacksmith's shop and the *Lloyd George Survey* mentions a workshop although nobody described as a blacksmith had lived at Wheelers for many years. John Banks bought it from his cousin George Thomas Banks in 1877 and lived there until 1886 when he let it to James Judd, a haybinder who, with his family, remained until 1904.

In 1895 Joe Pegrum bought Wheelers for £800 and also paid £126 for its enfranchisement. He apparently decided more money was to be made from letting this pleasant house to middle-class outsiders, rather than to a local farm worker. From 1911 to 1914 the tenant was George Felix Dudbridge Green, a blouse and robe manufacturer who briefly changed the four-hundred-year-old name to Elm Cottage. During the war it was let to Mrs Laura Johnson, whose son Alan was killed in action.

In 1911 the farm was only five acres which were next to Nazeingbury, so Joe Pegrum probably managed it himself. It was described as:

> A freehold detached brick & slated house in good & substantial repair. 5 bedrooms, bathroom, 3 rec rooms, kitchen, scullery & larder. Lean-to timber & tiled workshop at end. Small lean-to glasshouse, brick and slated coal shed & potting shed. 50 fruit trees. Buildings: span roof timber & tiled open cart shed. Range of old timber & tiled stables with hen house at end. Good orchard. Enclosure of good pasture land.

Burnt Hall

Burnt Hall was built and named in the late 1600s, and rebuilt in 1799. It is timber-framed and weather-boarded, described in 1911 as: 'Timber and tiled freehold detached cottage. 4 bedrooms & box room, 2 sitting rooms, kitchen & scullery.'

In 1827 George Palmer senior paid John Banks £1,405 for Burnt Hall and some land in the Meads. It was then a separate farm of about eighty acres occupied by the Dean family, who gave their name to the section of Nazeing Brook that ran in front of the farm. After his wife's death in 1874, Charles Dean went to live with his nephew at Stratford St Mary in Suffolk, and was apparently still a working farmer at the age of 82. Ralph Palmer took the opportunity to combine the farming of Burnt Hall with Mansion House Farm.

From 1894 the tenant was William Alfred Pulham, a terra cotta finisher working for the family firm in Hoddesdon. In 1911 his wife Caroline and son Herbert were both described as 'worker at home' although for Herbert the enumerator has added 'farmer & cowkeeper [working] on own account'. William's daughter Beatrice was a much-loved teacher at the Council School for many years.

Mansion House Farm

William Sinclair at Mansion House Farm

In 1799 William Palmer paid Jacob Bosanquet, lord of the manor of Broxbourne, £5,302 for Mansion House Farm, Whitehall Farm and five cottages – probably Brook Cottage, 42 and 60 North Street, Maplecroft Cottage and the Rookery.

Mansion House Farm was known as Haywards or Hawards until at least 1820 but had been renamed by 1847. The *Lloyd George Survey* valued it with Whitehall Farm in North Street and both were being farmed by George Sinclair. Mansion House was described as 'a small freehold farm, all under grass'. The pasture was good and the hedges well kept up. A small orchard contained eighteen trees.

The four-bedroomed house was brick, timber and tiled, with two living rooms, scullery and dairy, old but in very fair repair. The farm buildings were all in fair repair and included a small barn which was built in the early 1700s with Baltic pine frame and weatherboarding. It was listed as an historic building in 1984 and later sympathetically converted into a dwelling.

Across Middle Street, owned and occupied by Joe Pegrum of Nazeingbury, were two enclosures that had been part of Mansion House Farm in 1847 and were again later included in it. Two enclosures, Grass Garlands and Ploughed Garlands, adjacent to St Leonards Road, were also part of the farm.

Brook House (Brook Cottage)
This timber-framed and plaster hall house was built in the late 1600s and has an original red brick chimney stack. The *Lloyd George Survey* described it in 1911 as:

> A good freehold timber & tiled detached cottage with nice garden
> let by the owner with Mansion House Farm but sublet by the

tenant of the farm as a weekend residence. In excellent condition. 3 bedrooms, 2 living rooms & lean-to scullery.

The occupier of the 'weekend residence' was William Innocent, who was not there on census night but appeared on electoral registers in 1910-11. He was probably one of two cabinet makers, father and son, who lived in South Tottenham.

Smalldrinks

Smalldrinks was built in 1580 and first so named in 1733. It was a T-shaped plan hall house with a timber frame. In 1911 it was described as:

> Copyhold small holding including 3 enclosures totalling 10 acres. Old timber & tiled house in rather bad repair. 3 bedrooms, 2 living rooms, kitchen, dairy, brick & timber built wash house with tiled roof. Buildings: old timber & slated open cart shed, barn with cow house & stable, lean-to fowl house & old timber & thatched shed. 9 elm trees and one oak tree value £30.

In 1847 it was owned by Thomas Collin of Netteswell, who also owned Netherkidders. The tenant was Charles Dean junior, a haycutter who occupied four enclosures around his home and three elsewhere, mostly meadow. The house was bought by Joseph Pegrum senior in 1870 and bequeathed to his daughter Mary, who owned it in 1911. By 1871 the tenant was William Welch, a shoemaker and farmer working on own account, who did not take on Charles Dean's other enclosures. William died in 1878 and his son John Davies Welch lived and farmed at Smalldrinks until after the Great War.

Ninnings

Ninnings was of timber-frame and weather-boarded construction, built originally in the late 1400s. In 1911 it was described as

> A small freehold farm. All pasture in very good heart. Very old large farmhouse, timber built and tiled. Poor condition. 7 rooms on first floor, 4 unusable. Shearing rooms. [Ground floor] Kitchen, pantry and dairy. Buildings very old...

There was exceptional continuity in the ownership and occupation of Ninnings, or 'Ninnetts' as it was sometimes known earlier. It was owned by the Camp family from before 1558 to 1776, the Acres family until 1831 and the Williams family until 1918. From 1841 until his death in 1891 the tenant was Samuel Pegrum, and then until 1920 his widowed daughter Ann Head. In 1881 Samuel was farming seventy-five acres but by 1911 Ann had only the twenty acres around the farm.

From the Pegrum family album.
They lived and farmed at Ninnings for at least eighty years.

Trevone and Newlands

In 1911 the cottage on the site of Newlands was described as

> A very old timber built & slated freehold cottage containing 2 bedrooms, living room, scullery & wash house. Small shop attached to house. Old timber & tiled shed near house. Other buildings are claimed by the tenant. An enclosure of freehold meadow land is rented with house. 24 elms value £60.

Its neighbour was similar but with no buildings or land.

The sweet and general shop was started in 1901 by Charles Judd (1837-1911), who lived in Middle Street all his life. Shortly before his death it was taken on by his daughter Jane, who continued it after her marriage to Alfred Ford in 1912 and until the cottage was demolished.

In the 1850s the cottages were purchased by John Draper, a wholesale stationer who was born in Harlow and moved to Wormley via Lambeth. In 1911 they were owned by John's daughter Charlotte Emily Draper and grand-daughter Gertrude Gilbertson. In 1919 they sold them for £290 to Joe Pegrum, who demolished and replaced the cottages, moving into Newlands.

Cottage on the site of present-day Trevone
or Newlands, seen from Clappers Weir

Porters/Cemetery Cottage

When Barnard Acres II bought this property in 1814, it was described as a

> very valuable and desirable estate pleasantly situated on an eminence in the respectable village of Nazing, commanding extensive and uninterrupted views over the counties of Essex and Hertford, and the house might, at a very small expense, be converted into a sporting box.

The agent was suggesting that the cottage would make a suitable headquarters for the activities of the local hunt, but that did not happen and it remained a dwelling, probably occupied by farm labourers. One of them in the 1820s was called Porter, a name which seems to have surfaced almost a century later when given to the cottage on the *Lloyd George Survey*. On the 1891 census it was described as 'Near Perry Hill (The Cemetary)' [sic] and in 1901 as 'Cemetery Lane' - the first known references to a cemetery in the area, which are still unexplained.

The Survey describes: 'Small old brick built cottage, condemned (formerly let @ 1/6 per week). Materials worth £30.' This suggests that it was about to be demolished but it survived until 1937, described on electoral registers as 'The Cemetery Cottage, Middle Street'.

Perry Hill Farm

The name Perry came from John atte Pyrie in the 1300s, meaning a pear tree on the hill. The small freehold farm was owned by the Jones/Williams family from 1737 until 1918. From 1841 or earlier until 1883, when he retired, the tenant was James ('Peg-leg') Pegrum, who employed two men and a boy for the fifty-five-acre farm. The land was very heavy and wet but the pasture was fairly good. Included with the farm was about fourteen acres of 'rather rough' marsh land which was situated nearly two miles away on Meadgate Lane.

The L-shaped timber-built and tiled four-bedroom farmhouse was built in the 1500s and in 1911 was in fair condition with three living rooms, kitchen, scullery, dairy and lean-to conservatory.

The outbuildings were 'Quite ample for the size of the farm and in good condition.' They comprised:

a two bay wagon lodge; a range of timber and slated buildings included a harness room, four stall stable and a lean-to fowl house; an old timber and slated granary and a lean-to barrow shed; two brick and slated bullock boxes; lean-to timber and corrugated iron bullock shed; timber and tiled piggeries adjoining a timber and corrugated iron barn with an adjoining cow house; another lean-to timber and tiled enclosed shed.

The greenhouses, motor garage and other sheds not mentioned belonged to the tenant.

Perry Hill Farm with outbuildings

When James Pegrum retired, the Cattermole brothers, who owned Thomas Pegrum's shop at Nazeing Gate and the neighbouring Park View Cottage, became the tenants of Perry Hill Farm. After the death of Edward Henry in 1896, Walter was there until 1918. He always described himself on the census as a contractor and was never listed at Perry Hill. He and his brother put up several sheds of their own in addition to the farm buildings and probably used them as cheap storage for their removals business. Walter evidently had some involvement with the farming, because in 1917 he was among the buyers at Messrs Chalk's annual sheep sale at Cambridge Cattle Market.

The Cattermoles also sublet the farming to a series of bailiffs who lived at the farm. Thomas Bysouth, a farm labourer from Barkway in Herts, came in 1889 and in 1896 moved to Kenners Lane, where he reverted to being a farm labourer. In 1900 Charles Woodley, who was a bailiff from Ashdon in Essex, came but stayed only a year or two. For the next few years no tenants were listed on electoral registers, which may mean that they did not bother to register or that Walter Cattermole sometimes lived in the farmhouse himself. By 1911 James Trussell had moved in with his wife, three children and widowed mother. The son of a farm bailiff from Great Parndon, in 1901 he had been living in Islington and working as a railway shunter, but evidently preferred country life.

Little Dormers

Sometime between 1824 and 1847 Barnard Acres II acquired two adjoining cottages, where Little Dormers now is. They stood on land taken from the waste, and Acres may have built them himself. In 1911 the old timber and slated cottages, similar in construction, were in fair repair and condition. Both had wash houses and extra-large gardens, but one had two bedrooms and living rooms and the other only one of each.

The tenant of the smaller cottage was Stephen Beadle, a farm labourer who in 1878 moved with his family to Nazeing from Little Munden near Ware. Though aged only sixty in 1911, he was rather sadly described as 'retired, afflicted and bedridden'. His wife, daughter and mother-in-law were also living there, so it must have been quite cramped. Next door Thomas Burton, his two sons and a boarder were all farm labourers.

Darmers

Darmers is an open hall timber-framed house built in the 1400s, with the roof raised and a floor inserted in the 1500s. It was called

Daman's Farm in 1730 and Darmers by 1852. On the *Lloyd George Survey* it was described as 'an old roomy cottage timber built and tiled containing 4 bedrooms, 2 living rooms, cellar, coal place, dairy and wash house. Poor property.' The occupants were the Pegrum family from 1789 until 1874 and then Alfred Coleman until shortly before his death in 1923. It was owned by the Williams family from about 1840 until David Pegrum bought it in 1918.

Darmers showing Alfred and Sarah Coleman
and their daughter Sarah

The Poplars and the Cottage

The Poplars (closest to camera) and the Cottage, with the sign
for the Red Lion on the right and Curtis Farm in the distance

The Poplars is described on the *Lloyd George Survey* as 'A substantially built double fronted freehold house. 4 bedrooms 2 living rooms with kitchen, scullery.' It was built about 1902, replacing an earlier cottage. It also had an 'Old timber & tiled workshop' used by the tenant, Alfred Pegrum the carpenter. Next door was 'Small freehold semi-detached brick & slated old cottage in poor condition, 2 bedrooms, 1 living room, pantry, lean-to wash house', occupied by the Drane family. In 1911 they were owned by Joe Pegrum.

Curtis Farm

Curtis Farm was so named by the 1620s when it was purchased by the Beaumont Charity, which still owned it three centuries later. The charity was founded by King James I 'to bind apprentice poor children in the Parish of Cheshunt, for the benefit of the decrepit, aged and impotent poor of the said parish'.

The tenant from 1905 until the 1930s was Jim Pegrum (1873-1946). His son Bernard recalled:

> Move to Curtis Farm – there came a day when we left Queens Cottage and went to live at Curtis Farm. I remember absolutely

nothing of the morning, only that my father carried me from Queens Cottage to Curtis Farm, across the fields, snuggled in his coat and I slept, only waking when we arrived at the back door of our new home.

Curtis Farm was described in 1911 as a small freehold pleasure farm whose land, about 16½ acres, was in good heart and condition. The four-bedroomed double-fronted farmhouse was brick built with tiled roof. It included two sitting rooms, kitchen and wash house, all in excellent condition.

Goodalls

The people are probably members of the Webb family,
which farmed at Goodalls for over fifty years

Goodalls was first named in the late 1500s. A new house was built around 1715 and extensively rebuilt in the 1920s. From about 1850 until 1924 it was also called Brick House. It was owned and sometimes occupied by the King family from 1825 to the 1870s but at some point was acquired by John Banks in one of his sharp business deals with his King cousins. After his death in 1909, it was owned in trust for his great-nephew, Lewis Claude King.

The farmer from 1871 to 1900 was Thomas Webb, whose family had lived in Nazeing since 1400 or earlier. The tenancy was taken over by his son Oscar James (1871-1948), who had been born in the house. He was one of the most versatile farmers. As well as eleven acres at Goodalls, he farmed sixteen acres of Belchers Farm, across the road from Goodalls, sixteen acres of meadowland and four acres in Nazeing Mead for Banks's nephew Lewis King, and eight acres of pasture in the Mead for the Clarnico confectionery company.

Oscar's first wife, Annie Jane née Hollow, died in 1906 and two years later he married Ada, the widow of Arthur Carr, who worked at the Gunpowder Factory and lived at Claverhambury. In 1911 Oscar lived at Goodalls with his three children and his wife's four. Three employees lived on the premises, two of them sleeping in the barn.

Walnut Tree Cottages (Motts)

Originally known as Motts, this block of four cottages was built in 1790. Upstairs was lath and plaster with a tiled roof, and on the ground floor two were brick-built and two weather-boarded. They were in fair repair but rather damp. They had long front gardens with smaller gardens at the side and rear. Lewis King inherited them from his uncle John Banks and in 1917 sold them for £120, possibly to Edward Fowler who owned them in 1941. They are now an attractive pair of cottages displaying many original features.

In 1911 they were occupied by three families. The Turners and Thurlows had been there for over twenty years, and the Fields for ten. Arthur Turner was a blacksmith while Charles Field and George Thurlow were farm labourers. In 1901 between them they had eighteen children at home – and a boarder! By 1911 the three families had had twenty-seven children and, in a time when infant mortality was high, they may have considered themselves fortunate to have lost only two. But the Great War was to bring to the little cottages tragedy greater than anywhere else in Nazeing, when no fewer than five of the boys died: Charles Arthur Turner, George Turner, Sidney Turner, Frederick Thurlow and James Edward Field.

The *Lloyd George Survey* states that the two weatherboarded cottages were occupied by George Thurlow, so the photo probably shows him with his wife Emily and daughters Alice, Winifred and Ada.

Sturtsbury

Sturtsbury was described in 1911 as

> Old detached timber & tiled small freehold cottage. 3 bedrooms, 2 living rooms & wash house. Rent full. Fair repair and condition. Timber & tiled cowshed for 6 cows – fair. Timber £20. Good pasture.

In 1782 the Young family sold the farm to Hester Darley who married Christopher Sturtsbury or Tutsbury, and the property passed to him when she died. In 1809 he sold it to James Bury but it kept his name, even though he and his wife had owned it for less than thirty years.

In 1904 A.J. Pegrum (the Midnight Milkman) became the tenant and remained there until his death in 1939. The house was inconvenient in many ways but his niece, Marjorie Sykes, loved the old place: 'Dear Sturtsbury, centre of love and good fellowship, the love of people and animals, and the good life. The door ever open, the old black kettle on the boil, the beds made and a sincere welcome to all friends.'

'Dear Sturtsbury' and A.J. Pegrum

Chapter 23

Bumbles Green

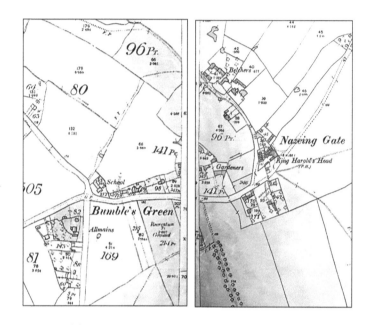

The Bumbles Green area as shown on the *Lloyd George Survey*

Harold's Park Farm[25]

The farm is named from King Harold, who owned land in Waltham
Abbey before the Norman Conquest. It has a superb high location
with views over Hertfordshire, Essex, London and Kent. Though
always a single farm, its 512 acres were spread across three parishes

---

25 This section is based on: *Abstract of the title of Mr J. Mackie to Harold's
    Park Farm Nazeing* (1966, kindly lent by John Carr), a copy of which
    is in the Nazeing History Workshop archive; the excellent website of
    Alice Barrigan at http://northyorkshirehistory.blogspot.co.uk/2012/12/
    chapter-10-1831-mr-barlows-first-year.html; the Guadagni family history
    website at http://www.guadagnifamily.com/archives/images/

- 311 acres in Waltham Abbey, 180 acres in Nazeing and twenty-one acres in Epping Upland. The timber-framed farmhouse has eleventh-century foundations but was mostly built in the 1700s and extensively altered over the years. It was situated just in Waltham Abbey although access has been from Bumbles Green for at least two hundred years.

Harold's Park farmhouse

The owners
The estate was bought in or before 1780 by Joseph Bird (1715-1793) and in 1825 passed to his great-granddaughter Marian D'Oyley Bird (1814-1885).

Her first husband was James Barlow Hoy, MP for Southampton (c1794-1843). They often went abroad for her health and in 1843 they visited the Pyrenees. While crossing a ravine with a shooting party, James slipped and his gun went off, shattering his arm. His companion Captain Richard Meredith, who had been a witness at the wedding in 1831, rapidly applied a tourniquet but within a day James had died of tetanus. Marian stayed with James until she had to have the body buried at Toulouse. Soon after her return to England, Marian married Richard Meredith and James' brother Robert claimed that they had conspired to murder James with that intention, but the care both gave him after the accident seems to contradict that accusation.

Richard died in 1850 and within a few months Marian was married again, to John Richard Digby Beste (1806-1885). He was a devout Catholic and she converted to Catholicism. In 1860 her only child, Louisa Barlow Hoy (1838-1900), married Guadagno Guadagni, a nobleman from one of the oldest and wealthiest families in Florence. His mother was English and the Guadagni website claims:

> It seems that Louisa Barlow Hoy was very beautiful and charming. The famous well known 'Guadagni Charm' might also come from her. And then, Guadagno himself was half English because of his mother Luisa Lee. So, all our Guadagni grandfathers and their siblings were 25% Italian and 75% English.

Guadagno Guadagni (1833 -1905) in his uniform as an officer of the Garibaldi Army, which helped free the Kingdom of Naples and unite Italy as one country

Marian D'Oyley Bird aged seven

The Beste family moved to Olmo in Tuscany where Marian established a charity school for poor children in the Villa and built a chapel. Under her will she provided for the school and chapel to be continued and, if they ceased to exist, the money was to be spent on the Roman Catholic Church nearest to her 'paternal estate in Essex, called Harold's Park'. When Louisa died, her eldest son Guitto inherited Harold's Park and, as a party in the case of Palmer v Guadagni, became one of the more unlikely figures in Nazeing history.

Selective Bird / Hoy / Guadagni family tree

Guitto Guadagni married Dorothy Schlesinger, who was born in Newcastle-upon-Tyne into a family of shipowners. In 1920 he and his mother-in-law, Gertrude Harriette Schlesinger, put Harold's Park Farm up for auction and it passed out of the family after 140 years. Guitto and Dorothy Guadagni spent most of their time in Florence where they both died during the Second World War, in which their native countries were on opposite sides.

The Tenants

From 1792 the farmer was John Smith, who died in 1820 and was followed by his son, also John (1784-1864). Both were men of substance who were elected Trustees of Nazeing Wood or Park, owning Pound House and other property in Nazeing.

In the 1850s there were three tenants who were not farmers and did not always live at Harold's Park. Augustus Balls (1820-1853) married Emma Matilda Kempfer and lived in Hampstead. He was an upholsterer by trade and a famous bird fancier, who won a first prize at the Great Yarmouth and Eastern Counties Show but died the next day, ten days before his 33rd birthday. His widow Emma was the tenant until 1857 when she married Jules Joseph Duplessis, a wealthy French landowner, and he took over. In 1859 they moved away to a large estate at Lymington, with easy access to France.

The next tenant was Thomas Luke Rippin from Stretton in Rutland, where his father farmed 280 acres. He was the resident farmer, employing twelve men and three boys. He was probably affected by the agricultural depression in the 1870s, and he gave up the farm in 1875. In 1881 he was a humble cowkeeper in Nazeing, but by 1891 he had returned to his native Rutland as a farmer and grazier.

Rippin was succeeded by Thomas Garratt, who farmed and continued to live at Hunsdon in Hertfordshire, where he was tenant of 1,185 acres. Garratt apparently tried to manage Harold's Park from there with the assistance of a bailiff, but he was a cantankerous individual much given to writing to newspapers. Eventually he went too far and attacked his landlord, Charles Phelps of Briggins Park Hunsdon, who evicted him for non-payment of rent and he was declared bankrupt.

In an 1885 *Spectator* article, William Westall described Harold's Park as untenanted because it had been 'brought into such a condition by neglect and bad management that nobody would buy the hay, which is the only thing it produces'. Louisa Guadagni inherited the farm in that year, and she followed the practice of other Essex landlords by recruiting a Scottish farmer, William Graham from Ayrshire. Ayrshire cows were highly regarded in Essex and Graham would have brought his with him on the train. The presence of an experienced and capable young man on the farm meant that its fortunes immediately began to improve, helped by his carrying on 'an extensive milk trade for miles round'. He remained until the farm was sold in 1920.

The change from arable to pasture

In 1847 Harold's Park was a mixed farm with over 40% arable. This probably did not change in the quarter-century of high farming when arable farming reached its peak although, by the time William Graham arrived in 1886, a further thirty-five acres had converted from arable to grass. Graham was primarily a dairy farmer and in 1914 only fifty-four acres of arable remained. Then, as part of the government's war-time drive for increased food production, a different thirty-one acres of pasture in Waltham Abbey were ploughed on the instructions of the Essex War Agricultural Committee under the Defence of the Realm Act.

	arable	pasture	increase	% arable
1847	178	261		40.5
1886	143	296	35	32.5
1914	54	385	89	12.3
1920	85	354	-31	19.3

Table showing changes in acreage between arable and pasture on Harold's Park Farm in all three parishes

Callis Cottage

In 1911 Callis was described as

Old copyhold timber & tiled cottage containing 2 bedrooms, 2 living rooms and lean-to wash house. Timber & tiled detached span roof living room. Small timber & corrugated iron stable with lean-to fowl house. Very poor property situate up an old green lane. Good garden & small paddock.

George Holden bought it in 1808 and bequeathed it to his daughter Sarah, who married William Rodwell. In 1854 their daughter Sarah married James George Barnes from Islington and they had a son, also James George (1855-1937). Rodwell became the landlord of the Red Lion, where in 1861 young James was listed with his mother and grandparents. Callis was inherited first by Sarah Barnes, then by her son James who lived in north-east London but may have felt a connection with Nazeing through early memories of his grandparents.

From 1860 the tenant was Thomas George Hampton (1831-1909), a hay carter, but Callis was best known for his daughter Emily and her enormous pet pig Totty (see *Five Miles from Everywhere*, pp176-178). George built the detached living room for Totty but, after her death, the main cottage became so dilapidated that Emily moved into the room. She claimed that the pig was killed by the cruelty of the local authority in refusing her permission to keep it in the house, but the usually kindly Marjorie Sykes was unsympathetic:

> It was apparently not cruel to overfeed and exhibit this pampered creature for money... Another animal of Em's, less pampered, was a diminutive and long suffering donkey. We often saw Em, a great mountain of a woman, squeezed into the small space of a little, back-sloping governess cart, which the poor donkey had to pull. Her companion, the shrimp-sized Bill Dellar, walked beside her like an attendant in a royal procession. I remember thinking that it would be better for the donkey if she had walked and let Bill ride. All of which made me ask; who was she to complain of cruelty to animals?

On the 1911 census, Emily was described as 'feeble-minded' and Bill as her boarder.

Emily Hampton and Totty

Callis Cottage in the 1920s with Florence and Lily Hampton.
Florence's husband William was Emily's cousin.

Beverley and Hawthorn Cottages

Unusually, these were always treated as a pair, even though they
were detached. In 1814 William Palmer bought them from John
Banks for £410. Hawthorn Cottage was described as 'Old freehold
timber & tiled cottage with good garden. 2 rooms in roof. 2 rooms
on ground floor ...Old but in fair condition.' No description was
given for Beverley Cottage but it was probably similar.

From 1886 the tenant of Beverley Cottage was Thomas George Hampton's nephew William, who remained there until his death in 1931. Charles and Mary Perry moved into Hawthorn Cottage in the 1860s and Mary was listed as the tenant on the *Lloyd George Survey* although she may have died or moved away.

Cranbourne Cottages (**Bumbles Green Post Office**)
The *Lloyd George Survey* described it as

> Freehold brick built semi-detached cottage with lean-to brick & slated erection used as Post Office & workshop. Good repair & condition. 2 bedrooms, 2 living rooms & lean-to wash house. Very good garden.

It was one of a pair, the other being similar but with no Post Office or workshop. The tenants were the Cook and Mead families (Chapter 15). Next door to it was a 'Freehold corner site with timber & tiled builder's workshop & stores [with] open timber & corrugated iron ladder store'. It had been Dellar's wheelwright's shop for many years, but from 1907 was rented by Charles Judd the builder and later became Welch's Garage.

In 1911 the three properties were owned by Jules Gaston Duplessis (1859-1956). He was the son of Jules Joseph Duplessis and both men were listed on censuses as being of private means. The properties were bought by Duplessis senior or his wife Emma or her first husband, Augustus Balls. The strange thing is that the Duplessis family owned and kept them for over sixty years, even though the father only rented Harold's Park and soon left it.

The Post Office is on the right and the builder's workshop is in the centre of the photo

Common View and Havenslea
(Formerly Gardners and the Institute)

A Mr Carter at Gardners Farm, c1900

In the nineteenth century these neighbouring properties were owned by the King family who ran the King Harold's Head. By 1911 the owner was John Bambridge (1844-1926), a boot manufacturer and later a publican, who was then the landlord of the Five Bells at

East Finchley. He married Clara Barling London (1846-1914) at Shoreditch in 1866 and both described themselves as of independent means. She died in Epping district, but otherwise they had no known connection with Nazeing. A report in the *Times* for 13 March 1914 says that 'Gardeners Farm' was sold at auction for £615. It is now a pair of houses called Common View.

Gardners had been given that name by 1685. The *Lloyd George Survey* described it as:

> Small freehold holding. Two old timber & tiled cottages formerly a farmhouse. Mansfield's cottage contains 2 bedrooms & 2 living rooms. Perry's, 2 bedrooms, 2 living rooms & wash house. Two enclosures of good pasture. 6 small elms worth £10... 2 large ponds. Property very old.

William Thomas Perry was the son of Edward of Allmains. He was an upholsterer when in 1899 he married Ada Beatrice Boyes in Shoreditch so may have worked there for a few years. By 1901 he was a labourer in the building trade living at Felstead, and he moved to Gardners in 1905. William and Ada had a son who, like him, was deaf and four daughters. John Mansfield was a horsekeeper on a farm and married Catherine Thomas Hollow.

There had been a cottage on the site of the Institute for many years, but it was built new and given that name in 1854. The *Lloyd George Survey* called it the 'Literary Institute' but extensive research has failed to reveal any explanation for the name. The Survey described it as

> A small old one storied freehold cottage brick built & slated. Very old & in need of repair. 4 rooms & lean-to wash house. No frontage to road. Access by right of way over front meadow of Gardners.

It was demolished and a replacement house now has its own frontage to the road.

It was occupied in 1911 by Edmund Brace, a carter on a farm. He married Mary Ann Stalley in 1892 and they had eleven children of whom seven were then living. Before they were married, Mary Ann and her neighbour Catherine Thomas Hollow both had sons who were shown on the census under their birth surnames, but both boys were living in the households and described as 'son', so evidently their stepfathers accepted them.

Old Post Office and Park View Cottage

Park View Cottage (back right), the Old Post Office (formerly Pegrum's shop, front right). This image and the next two are aerial photos taken in the 1960s.

The cottage and what became a shop were built by John Backwith in 1818 on land taken from the waste. In 1847 his son sold them to Mrs Elizabeth Kain, who was possibly the wife of a Bethnal Green plumber. In 1882 Edward Henry Cattermole bought them from her for £100 and paid the cost of enfranchisement, £54 7s 8d. Two years later he purchased the adjacent four-acre field on the corner of Bumbles Green Lane for £250 and also started to rent Perry Hill Farm.

In 1911 the cottages and field were owned by his widow, Amelia. Park View Cottage was occupied by John Daniel (Jack) Coleman and described as 'an old brick built & slated cottage, 2 bedrooms, 2 living rooms, wash house and coal house. Damp and much out of repair. Stands back from road & approached by a long cart path. Good garden & orchard.'

In 1911 the shop was described as

> Freehold house, shop and premises brick-built and slated containing 4 bedrooms, 2 living rooms (one with bay), shop. Buildings: 4-bay open lean-to brick & timber & tiled cart shed, brick-built & tiled 2 storied shed. Good stable range with loft & stores. Well built & in fair repair.

It was the first at Bumbles Green, opened by Thomas Pegrum III around 1860. After his death in 1895 the 'corn & coal & general shop' was run by his son Alf and Alf's wife Sarah.

Warwick House

This was built in 1824 and owned by John Banks from 1896 until his death in 1909. It was then purchased by William Henry Cross, a butcher who had retired from a prosperous business in Tottenham High Road. Warwick House was formerly called Coburg House and the obvious explanation is that the name was altered during the Great War because it sounded German. In fact Cross had already made the change in 1911, perhaps because he was born in Warwickshire, at Nuneaton.

The *Lloyd George* description reads more like an estate agent's advert:

> This property consists of a white brick-built & slated residence detached standing well back from the road with a large garden. The house which is very pleasantly situated near the common contains <u>four bedrooms</u> [their underlining], 2 good sitting rooms, kitchen, scullery, detached brick & tiled wash house. At rear of house is a range of timber built & tiled span roof buildings (40ft x 12ft) consisting of hay & straw store, chaff room, pony stable & coach house. Attached to these buildings is a lean-to timber built & tiled open cart shed & coal store. In the rear is a lean-to roof timber built cow house with piggery. There is a large pond in garden (now being filled in). 25 fruit trees worth £6. The frontage to Middle Street [sic] is 117ft with an average depth of 248ft.

When Cross died in 1915, Martha Pegrum bought Warwick House for £325 and then sold it to Frederick William Lawrence for £450 in 1920.

Pindar's Cottage

Pindar's Cottage (left) and Warwick House

This cottage was built by the Trustees of Nazeing Wood or Park in 1784, soon after the reorganisation of the trust by William Palmer. It was a home for the 'pindar', the shepherd who managed Nazeing Common, and it was given a common right even though it was not one of the original houses that were entitled to common rights.

In 1911 it was

> a substantially built red brick & slated detached cottage near Nazeing Gate. Good condition. 2 bedrooms, 2 living rooms, detached brick & slated wash house & coal store. Timber & tiled stable with lean-to shed at end.

From 1909 to 1919 the pindar was Henry Gentry, who had previously been a farm carter at Cranham, Romford. Marjorie Sykes recalled:

> Though little, I generally managed to pull the heavy lever and open the great gate to the Common; this involved climbing on the bottom bar and a swinging ride out and back. If the Gentry boys... were not about (and they generally were) I occasionally got a penny from a passing driver for holding the gate open and shutting it again. The Gentry family considered this tribute to be theirs by right.

Belchers Farm

Belchers belonged to the Knight and Lucas families from 1666 until 1830, when it was inherited by Laura Lucas. She married Charles Deacon but died shortly afterwards and he – lacking her attachment to the property – sold it to George Palmer for £1,995. It remained in the Palmer family until 1924, when Archdale Palmer sold it and neighbouring Teys to Walter Hargreaves for £3,700.

Teys Farm (front right), Belchers Farm (next to it), Byners (opposite Teys). Most of the land behind is now part of Nazeing Golf Course.

The Palmers' tenants were the Nicholls family until the death of William Nicholls in 1887. After a succession of brief tenancies, William Lawrence came from Great Parndon in 1905 and remained until his death in 1924, when his widow Clara took over until she retired in the mid-1930s.

The farmhouse was built in the early 1500s with a jettied and gabled first floor on brackets, and original red brick chimney and staircase tower. It was described in 1911 as 'Timber built & tiled, old but in fair condition and repair. 4 bedrooms, 3 living rooms, kitchen, scullery, dairy & cellar.' The buildings, which were ample for the size of the farm and in fair condition, were described in exceptional detail.

In 1847 Belchers comprised only forty-three acres but by 1911 had grown to 110 acres, taking in land previously associated with Queens, Bentons and a house behind Darmers, which is no longer there. The land formed a good mixed farm with about forty-five acres arable, the rest being pasture. Although the land was of a very heavy nature, it was in a good state of cultivation.

Teys Farm

In 1811 William Palmer bought Teys and King Harold Cottage from Susannah Abell for £1,800 and the family owned it until 1924. George Judd was the tenant from 1903 until his death in 1939.

Teys was described in 1911 as 'a small compact grass farm of 25 acres, a valuable small holding for which there is a good demand in the neighbourhood'. The land was all under grass and in a good state of cultivation, and there were twenty elm trees valued at £60.

The timber and tiled house was very old but in fair repair. It contained three bedrooms, three living rooms, wash house and scullery with a lean-to timber and tiled office. The buildings were ample for the size of the holding, old but in fair repair.

Chapter 24

Back Lane

Ravens

Ravens is a timber-framed three-storied house with weatherboarding, built of reclaimed beams around 1740. In 1911 it had '2 attics, 3 bedrooms, 2 reception rooms with lean-to kitchen & scullery and large garden'.

George Palmer bought it in 1835 from the Hunt family for £398 10s. It is named from John Raven, a tailor who lived there in the mid-1800s. After the church school reopened in 1891, Ralph Palmer made the house available to the head teacher, sometimes a master with his wife as assistant.

Nazeing Park Cottage

This open hall house with cross wings was built before 1500 and altered in the early 1600s, when a floor and a red-brick chimney shaft were installed. William Palmer bought it from William Pegrum in 1809 for £400. The section of Back Lane from Kingswood Chase to Nazeing Park Cottage was then called Deighton Hill after a man who had lived in both houses.

In 1911 the cottage was recorded as 'Chauffeur's cottage. Old timber & tiled detached cottage in fair condition. Porch, 3 bedrooms, 2 living rooms & timber & tiled lean-to coal & wood shed.' The chauffeur was James Sadler whose employer was Walter Hargreaves. In 1901 he was a traveller working for Christie's brewery and staying in Hoddesdon High Street with Richard Surridge and his daughter Edith, whom he married in 1905.

Queens Cottage and Rose Cottage

In 1614 Queens Cottage was known as Quernes after the owner, but the name became corrupted in the eighteenth century. Rose Cottage was called Colliers Croft in the seventeenth century and later Lakes, after the family from whom William Palmer bought both properties for £345 in 1813. Both were demolished by Ralph Palmer c1880 and replaced by the present red-brick buildings (see illustrations on page 34).

Queens in 1911 was a pair of cottages, each having three bedrooms and two living rooms. The tenant of one was Henry James Starling, the carpenter on the Palmer estate who with his wife Mary Elizabeth and daughter Adelaide later took over the Upper Town Post Office. The other was occupied by horse keeper George William Wallis and his wife Minnie Eliza, who had four sons and a daughter. Her brother Joseph Samuel Wright, a farm labourer lodging with them, was killed in the Great War.

Rose Cottage also had three bedrooms and two living rooms. It was occupied by Fred Myson and his son Alfred, who were both assistant gardeners. A hidden gate in Back Lane enabled estate workers like Henry Starling and Fred Myson to slip into Nazeing Park via the back door. Fred's son Ernest had moved to Haslemere in Surrey but was killed in the Great War and is among those listed on Nazeing memorials.

Pond House

This small timber-framed, plastered and weather-boarded hall house was built in the 1400s. In 1820 William Palmer bought it and another property from Randall Flowers for a total of £700.

Unusually, the *Survey* description began with the field rather than the house:

Small irregular shaped freehold pasture field facing Upper Recreation Ground. Small timber & thatched cottage. Old but in good condition containing 2 bedrooms, 2 living rooms, wash house & dairy. Good timber & corrugated iron cow shed. Timber & tiled fowl house. Other rough buildings belong to the tenant.

The tenant was Walter Samuel (1861-1956), a wheelwright and cow keeper who had lived there since 1895. In 1945 his brother-in-law George Whitbread bought Pond House from Archdale Palmer, who made the proviso that Samuel was to be allowed to stay there.

Pond House, Nazeing

In 1911 Pond House was one of five thatched cottages in Nazeing but the only one described as in good condition.

Ricketts

Ricketts Hill is the local name for the short stretch of road between Betts Lane and Back Lane. It takes its name from Ricketts, the cottage that can just be seen on the extreme left of the photo. It was probably built around 1744 by Thomas Ricketts and used as a workhouse until 1796, when William Palmer bought it and built a new poorhouse nearby.

Although Pond House is at its centre, this photo is entitled
Ricketts Hill

From 1861 another Ricketts family, possibly descendants of Thomas, lived there. Charles Ricketts was then listed as a farm labourer with his young wife Ann, and fifty years later they were still there, both as old-age pensioners. Their son William James was with them, but his wife Minnie Louisa and son William George were in the Epping Union workhouse.

Honeysuckle Cottage, White and Perry Cottages,
Brewitts Farm, painted from behind Hubbards

Honeysuckle Cottage

This can just be seen through the trees near the site of the current house, which was built in the 1960s. William Palmer bought it in 1806 from Smith Hollingsworth for £172 9s. It was described in 1911 as 'A very old freehold detached cottage timber built & tiled. 2 bedrooms, living room, store room. Timber & tiled wash house. Fair condition ... Orchard & garden.' It had been occupied by George Mansfield for at least forty years.

Kate Henty, 1837-1925

The water colours in this book were painted by Catherine Eliza (Kate) Henty, the eldest of the eight daughters of Robert Henty, who occupied Nazeing Park from 1872 to 1886. Kate attended the Brighton and Sussex School of Practical Art where she was awarded a Second Grade prize in 1860. She never married and lived off a private income.

Nazeing Park Cottage. The woman in the doorway is Sarah Cook. When Kate Henty left Nazeing, she gave her paintings to Sarah and they have passed down through her family.

Chapter 25

Pubs and Churches

Probably the feature of Nazeing that has changed least over the last hundred years is the pubs. They were all owned by independent local breweries – the King Harold's Head by Chaplin's of Harlow and the others by Christie & Co. of Hoddesdon.

The Hoddesdon Brewery was started in 1700 by William Plower and taken over in 1781 by William Whittingstall, who was responsible for developing the Sun, the Crooked Billet and the Coach and Horses as pubs. After his death in 1803, his sons sold them to William Christie and George Cathrow. The firm was known as Christie & Co. from 1860 until 1903, when it became a limited company. A note on the *Lloyd George Survey* entry for the Coach and Horses states that it and other properties were sold for £565,435 10s 6d. In 1928 the company was bought by the Cannon Brewery of Clerkenwell and brewing ceased at the Hoddesdon site, which is commemorated in the name of Brewery Road.

The 1911 census described landlords either as publicans or as licensed victuallers. None of them or their wives were natives of Nazeing so evidently the owners recruited them from outside, but most described themselves as 'employers' so they presumably had a considerable degree of autonomy. The census recorded them and their live-in staff although other people working on a casual basis might have come in. The *Survey* gave more detail about pubs than about private properties, with a full list of facilities and simple sketch-maps.

In addition to the standard features of pubs that have changed little, they all had variously named separate rooms that were perhaps designed to cater for teetotallers and families – an assembly room at the Coach and Horses, club rooms at the Red Lion and the Crooked Billet, and tea rooms at the Sun and the King Harold's Head. Although owned by different companies, the tearooms were both 'matchlined' – *lined with matchboard,* a type of wooden board that became a cheap and popular building option around 1900. In the summer they attracted passing trade with day trippers from London and its emerging suburbs.

Red Lion, Middle Street

The Red Lion was the only one of Christie's four Nazeing pubs that was not opened by William Whittingstall. In 1810 George Holden bought a pair of cottages in Middle Street and later bequeathed them to his daughter Sarah, who married William Rodwell in 1816. By 1841 they were running the New Inn in Roydon, and in 1848 Sarah was also listed as having a beerhouse in Middle Street. In the 1850s it was occupied and run by Joshua Paul, who had been a carpenter in Bishop's Stortford, but in 1861 William and Sarah moved into the beerhouse which was by then called the Red Lion. In 1868 their widowed daughter-in-law Ellen married John Warders and he became the licensed victualler. Ellen Warders in turn died and in 1877 John married Mary Turner. One of the witnesses at the wedding was her niece Ellen Redington, who in 1881 was a barmaid at the pub. John died in 1888 and Mary probably sold the pub to Christie's, although she continued to run it until the late 1890s when Ellen Redington took over, assisted by John Warders' brother James. Ellen moved away shortly afterwards, ending ninety years occupation by one extended family.

The publican in 1911 was William Jocelyn, a police pensioner assisted by his wife and a general servant.

The *Lloyd George Survey* described it as

> Substantially built brick & slated house in fairly good repair and
> in good structural condition. Contains 4 bedrooms, bar, tap room,
> bottle & jug department, kitchen & private parlour. Cellar in
> basement. At side & communicating with house is a one-storied
> double span roof, brick built & slated club room – good.

There was also a coach house, fowl house, workshop, fifty fruit
trees, cesspool drainage and 'water from well'.

Next door was a 'small timber weather-board & tiled cottage
adjoining stables' in fair repair and condition. There were two
bedrooms (one over part of the stables), living room, shed and
wash house. It was occupied in 1911 and probably all of the time
by the publican.

The Red Lion closed in 1967 and is now a private dwelling, the
White House.

Christie & Co. probably bought and refurbished the
Red Lion in 1888, the date displayed over the door.

Coach and Horses, St Leonards Road

Originally a private house, the Coach and Horses had been named by 1792. In 1849 Peter Christie and Robert Hunt were presented to the manorial court for enclosing waste beside it and it may have been around this time that a new building was erected. It was enough of a landmark that on the 1891 census St Leonards Road was called Coach and Horses Road.

The *Lloyd George Survey* described it as

> Brick timber & slated house in fair condition & repair containing – 5 bedrooms, bar tap room, small parlour, kitchen & pantry, timber £10, fruit trees £5, good garden & orchard. The outbuildings: stable cart shed, cold store, store, WCs, granary, fowl house [all] timber & slated…Good brick-built & slated Assembly Room with communication from house.

The publican for over thirty years was William Bailey then from 1910 it was John Caryl, a widower who had previously been a farrier in Camberwell. With him was his son Walter, a gold-block bookbinder, daughter-in law Julia Alice and daughter Maude, a schoolgirl. The family may have helped out in the pub, but the only person listed as doing so was fifty-year-old Mary Ann Burton, the widowed sister of Thomas Robert Pegrum.

Crooked Billet

The name Crooked Billet derives from the ancient custom of hanging a green branch outside premises where wine and beer were for sale. When all the leaves and smaller branches had fallen off, the billet was what remained. The Nazeing pub had been named by 1803.

In 1911 it was described as

> An old brick & timber built house (tiled roof) with new extension in front & brick & slated extension to private parlour. Poor condition – good decorative repair. Contains – 4 rooms 1st floor. 4-ale bar, private bar, club room. private parlour, addition of kitchen on ground floor, cellar in basement. Water from well, cesspool drainage... 'coal place'... stable ... and open cart lodge.

The pub also owned Charpickles, an adjacent field either side of the brook as far as St Leonards Road, and land across Middle Street at Barnfield.

The recently-arrived licensed victualler, Henry Weare, was born at Goodrich in Hereford but had worked for many years as a coachman for wealthy families in the West End. He was probably assisted by his Scottish-born wife Catherine and certainly by Laura Hooper, a seventeen-year-old domestic servant born in Hackney.

The Sun

In 1810 Christie & Cathrow erected a new building which, considerably altered, is the present pub. The old house next door became Sun Cottage and retained its common right. A hundred years later the *Lloyd George Survey* regarded the new pub as 'old but in fair condition':

> Brick built below, timber & plaster above with slated roofs. Brick & slated addition of scullery at rear. Licensed rooms, tap room, bar & parlour. Span roof corrugated iron detached match-lined tearoom on south side. 4 bedrooms, kitchen, scullery & beer cellar.

The outbuildings constituted a cart shed, fowl house and stable for four horses, with small paddock at rear and meadow adjoining Collyers.

It was managed by Charles Horne, who had previously been a farm bailiff at Aimes Green in Waltham Abbey. He was assisted by his wife, son and grand-daughter. A hundred years earlier the landlord had been the wonderfully named Titmouse or Titmus Horn but this seems to be a coincidence, for Charles Horne was born at Copford near Colchester and had no known connection with Nazeing.

King Harold's Head

The King Harold's Head replaced a pub called Harts which was converted into present-day Ivy Cottages. It was built new in 1797 by Robert King and had its own brewery, which for a while gave its name to the adjacent road, now called Belchers Lane. In 1852 Robert King's son, William King, sold it to Thomas Chaplin, who had recently established a brewery in Harlow. The firm later became Chaplin & Co., and closed around 1927.

The *Lloyd George Survey* recorded:

> Situate just inside Lower Gate to Nazeing Common. Very old property – condition generally fair. House brick built & slated (part stuccoed). 4 bedrooms, small bar, bar parlour, passage and tap room with flag floors, kitchen. Timber-built match-lined tea room with timber & corrugated iron addition at side. Coach house stable, 2 WCs & coal cellar.

There was also a wood house, coal shed, cart shed and fowl house, and two enclosures of pasture in Galley Hill Lane.

The licensed victualler from 1875 to 1903 was James Bainbridge Riley. In 1875 he married Maria Benton, who was related to the King family that had owned the pub. In 1861 they were in service together in Westminster, where in 1871 she was a cook. In 1907 he gave evidence to the Palmer v Guadagni court case, recalling that, to prevent carting across the Common, James

Pegrum had dug a ditch so that men had to carry hay across the fields on their heads.

From 1908 to 1913 the tenant was Arthur Cutler, who probably had the help of his wife Elizabeth and certainly of George Lester, a 'Hostler Domestic'. The information he gave on the census about his birth and marriage does not tie up with other sources, so we know nothing more about him.

This postcard seems designed to advertise the
Nazeing countryside as well as the pub

The Crown Hotel
The Crown was built in the late eighteenth century, when the land was taken out of Keysers Farm. Until the 1930s, when it was demolished and replaced by the present pub, it was a substantial hotel. It catered for people on short breaks from London and had a frontage of about 520 feet for fishing on the Lea.

The owner in 1911 was Horace Harry Broughton, who had bought it in 1897 for the substantial sum of £11,500, which included a premium for the goodwill and the right to collect tolls for the bridge across the Lea. He was a licensed victualler whose family had been in the trade in south London for many years. On the 1901 census he was listed at the Crown, but later he returned to Southwark. Broughton owned the toll house opposite, where the toll-keeper was allowed to live rent-free in exchange for his services although it had a bad roof and was 'generally out of repair'. Broughton also owned the adjacent Keelings Field, an enclosure of very good pasture with a long frontage to the towpath.

The Crown from across the River Lea

In 1911 the hotel was managed by James Henry Macaire, who had been a licensed victualler in his native West Ham. Several of the staff were living on the premises, including Macaire's step-son, who was head barman, a German waiter and a general labourer. There were also two domestic gardeners, George Parker living in the hotel and David Shepherd in the toll house. They would have maintained the 'extensive ornamental flower gardens [which were] laid out with exquisite taste and effective, and kept up at considerable expense'.

In 1911 the Crown was 'Very old rambling low pitched contains 1 attic, 9 bedrooms and boxroom'. (See plan and

incredibly detailed description on page 10). There was also a
remarkable variety of outbuildings including three tea-rooms,
two conservatories and stabling for some twenty horses. It was
'At one time a very noted House, much patronised by anglers
and others, but since the new road from Broxbourne to Nazeing
has been opened, the house is very little used'. The tolls were
'now of practically no value', presumably because casual trade
no longer passed the door.

The Crown billiard room and ornamental gardens

Bridge and toll house

The Broxbourne Boat House

The Crown also owned a rough field with a footbridge which, for an annual rent of 30s, provided the only land route to the boat house of the Broxbourne Rowing Club. Otherwise access was by ferry from the towpath. The timber boat house had a tea and club room and dressing rooms above, with an adjoining boat house, bathing shelter and paint shop. The Island on which it was built was owned by George Smith-Bosanquet of Broxbournebury, and one of the three occupiers listed on the *Lloyd George Survey* was Frederick William Green, then of Cheshunt and later of Collyers. They paid £8 rent and the property was valued at £200. The Club, which had been founded in 1847, had 450 feet of frontage to the river.

Churches

Church graveyards are sometimes called 'God's Acre' so it was appropriate that All Saints' parish church and its burial ground occupied just over an acre. It was 'situate in Upper Town in a rather isolated position' and commanded 'extensive views of surrounding country' but was 'very old and not in good repair'. The square tower was built from brick and the walls from brick and rubble. The old porch was timber-built and the roof was tiled. The total valuation was £2,780, with the stained glass windows valued at £130 and the peal of five bells at £150.

All Saints' Church c.1918

Near to the Church was a corrugated iron, match-lined 18ft x 55ft school room with a urinal and two earth closets. Valued at £160, it was owned by the Lord of the Manor and occupied by the Reverend Thomas Goddard, who paid a peppercorn rent.

The Congregational Church in Middle Street was described on the *Survey* as a substantially built, brick and slated building, with stone dressings and stepped buttresses to the front and sides, valued at £890. It was owned by Cheshunt College and occupied by the Trustees of the church, Thomas Nicholls of Parvills, Joe Pegrum of Nazeingbury and William Lawrence of Belchers Farm. Next to it was a substantially built school room 30ft x 65ft, brick with a slated roof, valued at £877 10s. At the rear of the building were two brick and slated WCs, which were valued at £10.

The Chapel hall, built in 1908

The present Chapel before the building of the hall

Chapter 26

Summary of the Lloyd George Survey for Nazeing[26]

Compared with other places, Nazeing is very fortunate in the quantity of information available from the *Survey*.[27] Over 60% of entries gave full details about the condition and structure of the dwellings, 20% gave some information and for only 16% was there little or nothing.

Of the dwellings that were described in the field books, 105 were cottages, fifty-seven were houses and ten, mostly at Riverside, were bungalows. A house was defined as 'a structure serving as a dwelling for one or more persons, especially for a family' and a cottage as 'a small simple house, especially in a rural area'.[28] In Nazeing, farmers had lived in houses and labourers in cottages, a distinction made by William Palmer in lists of common right holders compiled more than a century earlier.

The properties with the highest valuations were Nazeing Park at £5,865 and Collyers at £2,550. At the other end of the scale, the ruined Ham Farm House had no value and Porters, the condemned cottage in Cemetery Lane, was valued at just £30.

In 1911 it was still normal to rent rather than buy dwellings. Rent in Nazeing ranged from £807.50 for Nazeing Park to just £2 for

---

26 This section is based on a very thorough statistical study by Jacky Cooper.
27 Short, p 212.
28 http://www.thefreedictionary.com

a timber-built bungalow near Carthagena Lock, which may well have been a country retreat and the first of the plotlander dwellings that developed between the wars.

The average annual rent for houses was £68 12s but for cottages was only £10 14s. Six tied cottages were listed as rent-free because they went with their tenants' jobs and there were probably others that were not recorded.

About 60% of returns included information about the length of tenancies. They varied between weekly and multiples of seven years, with the majority yearly or quarterly. The traditional day for contracts to begin was the Michaelmas Quarter Day, 29 September when harvest was over, and 72% of Nazeing contracts started then. George Mansfield and Charles Ricketts in Upper Town had been tenants of their homes since 1874, just before Ralph Palmer began running the family estate; this suggests that he was content to leave old open-ended contracts in place, but negotiated new ones as they came up.

Fabric, Condition and Size of Buildings
Three-quarters of buildings were described in some detail. Each owner entered their own description of their property, so for walls there were various combinations of brick, timber, weatherboard and plaster. Almost half of the dwellings were built from brick and more than a third from timber. Other properties were combinations of two or more fabrics and eight were weather-boarded with either timber, plaster or both. The Vicarage and Nazeing Park were built from brick and stucco, a decorative weatherproof covering which showed off their status in the community.

From about 1875 many old cottages were rebuilt in red brick, by Ralph Palmer and others. There was no major brick works within

Nazeing but bricks would have been produced at Claypits Weir (now Clappers Weir, near the Scout Hut) and two fields called Brick Field. Bricks could also have come from local firms in Roydon, Epping and Waltham Abbey, or from further afield on the train.

Two-thirds of roofs were tiled, and slate was common. Five dwellings were thatched, of which just Pond House in Upper Town was described as in good condition, while the others were dilapidated. There were thatched outbuildings on fourteen properties, mostly farms or smallholdings.

Gardens were an important resource, providing vegetables and fruit. Many properties stated 'good garden', and orchards and fruit trees were also mentioned. A cottage on a plot of just under half an acre was described as having a small garden, giving an idea of the average size. Eleven had a pasture or paddock. Others make no mention of the garden but list a potting shed or fruit store. There were allotments in Broadley Common, Bumbles Green and Hoe Lane.

Astonishing detail about outbuildings was provided for seventy-three properties, giving an idea of what ordinary householders got up to on their own plots, besides growing their own fruit and vegetables. Thirty-six dwellings had one or more sheds on their plot, and twenty-nine had a separate building to store wood or coal, the main source of heat. Thirteen had hen houses or fowl houses, which provided eggs for the householders and their neighbours. Five had one or more glass houses, four a cattle shed, three a dairy, two a piggery and one a granary.

The number of rooms in the 170 dwellings where figures are provided gives a clear indication as to the size of the property. They varied from forty-two at Nazeing Park to just two in four dwellings. The average was six, of which there were twenty-two.

Over half of the fifty-seven houses had seven or eight rooms and 78 of the 101 cottages four or five. Four of the eleven bungalows had four bedrooms, while five had fewer and two had more.

The number of bedrooms tells a similar story, but the most striking figure is that sixty cottages (two-thirds) had only two bedrooms. Many of them were occupied by farm labourers with large families and sometimes also lodgers, so the overcrowding must have been considerable. More than half of the fifty-seven houses had four bedrooms, most of them farmhouses rather than new build.

Chapter 27

A Walk Through Nazeing's Countryside in 1914

In 1914 the prolific travel writer Benjamin Prescott Row published *Wayfarings Round London: Field-path and Woodland Rambles in the Home Counties with Directions and Maps*. It was the sixth in his series of Homeland pocket books, in which he gave directions for walks starting at one railway station and finishing at another. His Ramble no.6 was entitled *Some Cowslip Uplands in Essex*. He started at Cheshunt and finished at Broxbourne, going via Waltham Abbey, Galleyhill Wood and Nazeing. He visited on an April Bank Holiday so he probably came at Easter 1914. His vivid description of the Nazeing section shows just how much the village has changed in the last hundred years.

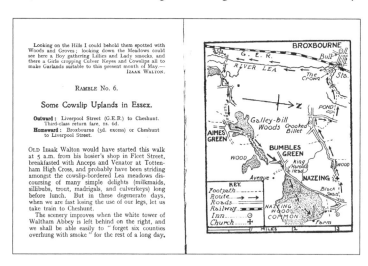

Row crossed the Common on 'a faint green track' towards Lodge Farm and then went straight ahead on a path that emerges at Kenners Lane. He turned left past what is now Weatherwhites and along Common

Road as far as the Black Swan, where there was a footpath that 'leads across some cowslip-broidered fields to the church'. Marjorie Sykes recalled that 'in the fields we could pick paigles, which in other places they call cowslips, and use for making wine'[29]. You can still walk this route but it is no longer the pleasant experience that Row enjoyed. Traffic on the roads has multiplied and the path alongside the Black Swan is sometimes impassable with rubbish and vegetation. After that the fields are walkable but the once prolific cowslips are just a bedraggled remnant.

As Row set off from the King Harold's Head, he would have passed the Common pound (left) and Nazeing Gate.

Then into the churchyard, where one thing has not changed: the 'wonderful westward view across the Lea valley: one that will well repay those in search of the picturesque'. Row continued down a 'beautiful winding remote' lane, a description which does not entirely apply to Hoe Lane today, and then up another 'lane', North Street. It is noticeable throughout the walk that, even when he had the alternative of a footpath across the fields, Row did not often take it, because what we know as busy roads were quiet country lanes.

---

29 'Paigle' is a word used mostly in Eastern England, and is the only example we have found of a dialect word in use in Nazeing before the Great War.

The section from 'the top of the rise' at Pecks Hill to the river has changed out of all recognition. On the right, Row saw a house called Curringtons, replaced by modern houses in the 1950s. Opposite was a gate and stile, from which a faint path dropped downhill past a fairly large pond to another stile. He then crossed a ploughed field to a footbridge over a stream, and followed wheel marks in the next field to the towpath. Nowadays, the extraction of vast amounts of gravel for post-war reconstruction has left three large lakes which feature a variety of birdlife, so this is one place where changes to the Nazeing landscape have undoubtedly enhanced the walker's experience.

Finally Row turned left 'down this extremely pretty stretch of the river to the Crown Inn, where you may enjoy yourself in the delightful gardens – famous for a hundred years or so – of that noted house'. Row continued to the Bull at Broxbourne, before returning to the station. The third-class return fare from Liverpool Street to Cheshunt was 1s 6d. The rambler could either pay a 3d excess at Broxbourne, or walk a further three miles along the towpath back to Cheshunt.

The River Lea at Broxbourne, with the toll-house (right) and part of the Crown Hotel

Part IV

A Changing Village

Chapter 28

Farms and Farming

In 1900 and again in 1912 the parish council declared that Nazeing was 'purely an agricultural parish'. The building of Nazeing New Road and the development of the Keysers Estate made commuting to London much easier, both for local people finding new job opportunities there and, even more significant, for Londoners moving out to Nazeing. But although things were changing, even in 1912 the parish council's claim would still largely have been true.

Nazeing is a parish of just under 4,000 acres bounded on the west by the river Lea and on the east by the steep slopes of Nazeingwood Common and Epping Long Green, with gently undulating hills between. In earlier epochs, extreme changes in temperature and also land movement deposited London Clay on the north and east side and gravel on the west, where the River Lea was much wider than it is now. When the river narrowed, it left fertile silt deposits that became the Meads, which were parcelled out in strips for grazing. South of these were the Marshes, bogs which were gradually drained and cleared of reeds and rushes but were of no use until centuries later. The brook, which divides Nazeing roughly in half, flows westwards into the Lea.

Common Land
Nazeing was always rich in pasture. The villagers enjoyed rights of common not only on Nazeingwood Common but also in Stoneshot Common, the Mead, the Marsh, and in open arable fields after harvest. The right to pasture in the Mead and the Marsh was restricted to the owners of certain dwellings, and in 1861 there were 666 of these 'cowleazes'.

The 1847 Tithe award map shows that the 186 acres of the Mead were divided into 141 separate strips, an average of 1.3 acres with the smallest 0.25 acres and the largest 7.4 acres. This was similar to the medieval open-field system where each tenant of the manor cultivated several strips of land scattered around the open, unfenced field. There were twenty owners and twenty-three occupiers. The Palmers owned 65 acres with eight tenants, and Sir Charles Wake 50 acres with four tenants.

Rider Haggard

Sir Henry Rider Haggard was an author best known for colourful adventure stories such as *King Solomon's Mines* but he also wrote about agricultural and social reform. At the turn of the century he toured the country and in 1906 published two volumes called *Rural England*. He spoke to leading landowners and farmers in Nazeing, noting that only about a third of the land had a local owner. The first interviewee was:

> Mr Palmer, a gentleman renowned for his great skill as a judge of Hereford and other cattle at the larger agricultural shows. He had some beautiful Herefords, young things of thirteen months that weighed half a ton and a bullock of two and a half years preparing for the Christmas shows which was a positive monster. His farming was excellent, and of barley especially he grew very heavy crops per acre. It was not his custom to use artificial manure, as he preferred to rely upon large dressings of farmyard muck. Of labour, he had sufficient, but said that the men must be gently handled. Mr Palmer also believed that hay which was cut directly the grasses flower, that is, earlier than usual, has much superior feeding properties to any other. But of course the crops secured in such circumstances must be lighter.

Rider Haggard next spoke to Ralph Bury who, by contrast with the traditionalist Palmer, was experimenting with artificial manures on his pastures. He showed Haggard a field that had received four dressings in as many years of basic slag, valued as fertilizer in gardens and farms. It was the best piece of grass on the farm, and 'looked as though it would cut 1½ ton per acre'.

Joe Pegrum told Haggard that:

> the district was badly off for cottages, so that the elderly men had to live in what there was and take in the bachelors to board, not always a satisfactory arrangement. Mr Pegrum had kept cows for a good many years and at the same time been engaged in building up young pastures. Two thirds of his 600 acres was under grass. He reported that in 1900 potatoes were very good, but it was a difficult crop to market through the London salesmen. Hay on the contrary was easily marketed, but he made complaints of the salesmen's fees at Whitechapel market, as had many other local farmers. Milk was sold at ten pence a gallon in winter and seven pence halfpenny a gallon in summer, but out of this amount farmers were obliged to pay carriage. Mr Pegrum estimated the drop in rentals of grass lands in his neighbourhood at about 30 percent. There was difficulty in finding skilled labour or finding labourers who would learn ploughing (to walk the clods) or milk the cows. To earn a living a farmer had to work like a labourer so that few of his sons would be willing to continue in the business[30].

Pegrum had no cottages for his labourers and showed Haggard where they lived

> ... a brick shed, measuring twelve or fourteen feet square, which might have served as a wagon house and was, I think I am right in saying, windowless. In this place, upon sacks that lay around the

---

30 This comment was prescient. After the Great War, Joe's son David gave up farming and went into property development.

wall, slept the twenty men upon the floor. No washing apparatus was visible and no fireplace.

Haggard described the problem of labour shortages as 'universal', but if these conditions were typical it was scarcely surprising.

Haggard was unimpressed by the state of Nazeing Common.

> It was covered with tens of thousands of ant-heaps that greatly damage, if they do not ruin, the pastures, while the surrounding land is practically free of these pests… [It was] an instance of the evil of unenclosed land over which a number of persons have certain more or less limited rights. What is everybody's business is nobody's business, therefore the emmet-heaps remained unlevelled. The individual owner of a piece of property, knowing that he is working for his own benefit only, takes a different view of the matter, and is rid of them.

Drainage

The higher ground away from the river was often described in the *Lloyd George Survey* in 1910 as very heavy and wet, being mostly London clay. This was despite improvements in drainage that were a major development in agriculture in the mid-nineteenth century. The manufacture of cheap machine-made pipes in the 1840s and the availability of £2,000,000 in loans under the Public Draining Acts of 1846 and 1850 resulted in a total of some four to five million acres being tackled between 1846 and 1876. This included land owned by George Palmer senior, who applied for loans totalling £2,000, and Mrs Marion Meredith [later Beste], owner of Harold's Park Farm (£1,000).[31] The cost of drainage was only £4 to £5 per acre but returns were low and loans had to be repaid, which may have contributed to the financial problems of George Palmer junior.

---

31 *London Gazette*, 30 August 1850. Issue 21131, page: 2351.

The heavy clay was traditionally described as 'three horse land'[32] and required lots of feeding, for which there was plenty of suitable manure to be brought from London, just a day's carting away.

Newspaper advert for a sale at Harold's Park Farm in 1859.
The 'clod-crusher' and eight cart horses would have
been very appropriate for heavy Nazeing clay.

The lowland marsh and mead adjacent to the River Lea (almost 10% of Nazeing's total acreage) was prone to flooding. In 1892 an

---

32 Hunter, p22.

Act of Parliament created a Commission for the Improvement of the old River Lea and its tributaries, and the drainage of the lands in the river valley[33]. Nazeing would have benefited from this but farming in the village was never far from crisis.

Agricultural Boom and Bust

The years between 1850 and 1875 were a golden age of 'high farming', which has been defined as 'good quality farming achieved by using the most efficient methods, the best rotations, the best seeds, the best fertilisers, and by the way in which the land was organised'.[34] The introduction of machinery and steam engines enabled more land to be brought into cultivation and produced greater yields, although the percentage of workers employed full-time in the countryside fell by 30%, and women and children found less casual work at harvest-time.[35]

But then from about 1875 a combination of some exceptionally wet summers and a drastic fall in wheat prices due to cheap imports from the USA brought the good times to an end. In twenty years over five million acres of farmland fell out of arable cultivation: 'Essex was described as "the heartland of the depression" and it was the heavy clay that suffered the most.'[36]

This led to many farmers going bankrupt – seven hundred in 1881 alone, when the first Nazeing casualty was Thomas Garratt of Harold's Park. There were several outbreaks of foot and mouth disease in 1883 and 1884 near the River Lea, including the Mead and Marsh where many farmers grazed their stock; although none

---

33 London Gazette: 24, November 1891 Issue: 26226 Page: 6381
34 https://www.victoriacountyhistory.ac.uk/explore/themes/agriculture/high-farming. Sourced 11 July 2017.
35 Wormell, p135, 146.
36 Wormell, p177.

of them formally went bankrupt, they would certainly have been affected. In 1888 the *London Gazette* reported an outbreak of highly contagious pleuro-pneumonia, also known as lung plaque. The infected cattle of Augustus Champness, farmer at Brewitts, were slaughtered and the movement of his neighbours' cattle was restricted, so he was made bankrupt and left Nazeing. Ernest Henry Webb, hay and straw merchant of Goodalls, was declared bankrupt in 1902, as was ploughing contractor Arthur 'Tractor' Smith of Cutlands in 1923.

In 1907 the National Farmers Union reported that the depression had hit landowners more than farmers or labourers. Land had become difficult to sell and its value had decreased.[37] Even though rents were lower, struggling farmers often could not pay them, but landlords would rather have a tenant maintaining the property than have an empty farm going to rack and ruin.

Ralph Palmer reduced the acreage of arable fields and sometimes removed hedges to make larger fields. He combined Shepherds Farm with Brewitts and Queens Farm with Belchers, and replaced the farmhouses with new dwellings for farm labourers. He invested in other housing stock, rebuilding many of the cottages. Ralph Bury also built several new houses. Housing for farm workers was nevertheless a problem and censuses show that many lodged with families.

The number of working horses probably reached its peak around 1902 and the need for hay in towns began to fall as motor transport increased. Much of Nazeing's agricultural production was for hay transported to London, so Nazeing farmers needed to adapt or go under. Some were unable or unwilling to change

---

37   Searle, p 179

their ways and invest in dairy farming so newcomers came to the area, encouraged by the low rents and with the confidence and experience needed.

In 1916 a nationwide agricultural census was carried out, as part of the government's drive to maximise wartime food production. It recorded that in Nazeing 2,737 acres (85%) were laid to grass, and 411 (13%) were arable. There were 295 cows, 604 cattle, 212 horses (including 31 ploughing teams), 1,381 sheep and 93 pigs.

Farm Work

Of exactly four hundred Nazeing people listed on the 1911 census as working, no fewer than 179, or almost 45%, were employed in farming and related trades.

	Males	Females	Total
Farmer employers	15	1	16
Farmers own account (self-employed)	13	4	17
Farm managers	5		5
Family working for farmers	12	6	18
Nursery workers	7		7
Gardeners	16		16
Farm workers – specific jobs	46		46
Farm labourers - general	48		48
Farm-related crafts	5	1	6
	167	12	179

Most of the farmers did not own their farms but were tenants working for the leading Nazeing families – five for the Palmers, three for the Burys and two for the Wakes. Three were the tenants of absentee landowners, two were working for themselves and one was retired. The seventeen farmers 'working on own account' (self-employed) were tenants of the Palmers and Burys, and of various small absentee landlords. The main difference between them and the farmer-employers was that they had few if any employees of their own although some of them employed family members: wives helped with the paperwork, while sons were probably farm workers in all but name and two daughters were dairymaids.

Leading local farmers at a court leet, a manorial court for the punishment of minor offences. By the time of this photo in 1890 it had become largely ceremonial. Harry Bugg (seated) with his banking experience was an obvious choice as scribe.

Most farmers were born in Nazeing or nearby and the exceptions were all dairy farmers, reflecting the inability of some Nazeing farmers to switch from arable to dairy after the agricultural slump of the 1870s. Two recruits from Cornwall were Thomas Hollow of Brewitts Farm and Richard Power of Church Farm, both in Upper Town. Thomas Harker came from Yorkshire to Paynes Farm and George Hewitt from Norfolk farmed nearby Tatsfords for the Frogley family. Will Graham came from Scotland to Harold's Park and George Barrett from Wiltshire to Netherhall, both large farms of which less than half was in Nazeing.

Dairy short-horn cows at Harold's Park Farm. c1900

Five farm managers worked directly for the Palmers and Burys, although they seem to have experienced a greater turnover than the farmers. Of those listed in the *Lloyd George Survey* in 1909, only Walter Brown, working at Lodge Farm for Ralph Palmer, was shown on the census two years later. But Peter Raithby, originally a Lincolnshire farm labourer, had recently arrived at St Leonards via North Weald and was to stay in Nazeing for many years.

Still, in 1911, ninety-four Nazeing men were farm labourers – almost a quarter of the workforce. Of these, fifty-five were born in Nazeing and, of them, forty-six were employed on specific tasks. As more skilled men, they were paid a little more than the standard twelve shillings a week. They included twelve cowmen, ten hay-binders, eight horse-keepers, three stockmen, two shepherds, a gamekeeper, and ten men described variously as carmen, carters and waggoners. There were also seventeen gardeners, mostly said to be domestic and probably working at the large houses – Nazeing Park and St Leonards.

Six people were working in farming-related trades: a harness-maker, two wheelwrights and three blacksmiths. The harness-maker was Sydney Ernest Bassett, who was born and brought up in Hampstead, where in 1901 he was already working at his trade. There in 1902 he married a parlour maid called Marian Curtis, who was born in Waltham Abbey. It would be intriguing to know whether this connection is why he moved out to Nazeing, and who was his employer in what was already becoming a fairly specialist occupation. John Dellar and his son Arthur were self-employed wheelwrights working at home at Bentons in Middle Street. From 1841 or earlier until 1907 the family had a wheelwright's shop round the corner in Bumbles Green which became Welch's Garage.

Two of the blacksmiths were brother and sister. The Lowe family had for over a century been blacksmiths and farriers at Selways, in Long Green. In 1911 the recently widowed Emma Selway née Lowe described herself as self-employed. Although the business had nominally been in her husband's name, he was a carpenter and Emma may have been the actual blacksmith, learning the trade from her father. Selways was still described as a blacksmith's shop in 1947.

William Lowe, Emma Selway's brother, was a tenant of Harold Smith at Langridge Farm. Marjorie Sykes wrote: 'In Coleman's Lane... the village hermit of our day, Billy Lowe, lived in a little shack much overgrown with creepers and brambles.' The *Lloyd George Survey* said that it was a 'very poor cottage in out of way position', and had been condemned. It was demolished soon afterwards and by 1925 Valley View had been built on the site. Perhaps it was because of Billy's eccentric nature that Emma returned from Cheshunt to take on the business when their father died in 1891. This may be when the family bought the premises from Henry Sworder, which they certainly did between 1873 and 1910.

The other blacksmith, Arthur Turner of Walnut Tree Cottages, was possibly employed by the Palmers or the Burys, whose estates could still have provided plenty of work.

In 1911 the nursery trade, which was to become so big in Nazeing, was in its infancy, near the river at Rushymead. Five nursery workers lived in various parts of the village and others could have come from across the river in Hertfordshire. The first of many Scandinavian nurserymen was Olof Hansen from Denmark, who was working on his own account at Keysers Lane. He was growing tomatoes and cucumbers in eight glasshouses (five 27ft x 200ft, three 15ft x 225ft.) He was living in a timber built bungalow situated beneath a water tower and there was also a workshop and engine shed. Nearby, Sydney Rich owned his own business. He erected eight glasshouses, each 200ft x 30ft, a packing shed, stables and engine shed with oil engine.

Chapter 29

Other Work

Local Businesses

Probably the largest employer in the area was the Royal Gunpowder Factory at Waltham Abbey. In 1911 nine Nazeing men worked there, probably walking a mile or two to the factory. Another seven, born in Nazeing, had moved to live in Waltham Abbey. Their job titles give an idea of the variety of jobs on offer, some of them rather hazardous: two dangerhouse men, two manufacturers of gun cotton, a nitroglycerine maker, a gunpowder weigher and an explosive cordite labourer, as well as five general labourers and five other men. All of them were born in or near Nazeing, so none had come any great distance to work there.

Henry Mead (centre) with the predominantly female workforce in Press House no.2 at the Royal Gunpowder Factory during the Great War. He spent over thirty years working as a labourer, mechanic and foreman. [38]

---

38   With thanks to the Royal Powdermills, where a large version of the photo is on display.

Only one Nazeing-born man worked at the Royal Small Arms Factory in Enfield although another had moved to the Royal Ordnance Depot at Weedon in Northamptonshire. Three Nazeing women were married to men who worked at the RSAF, including a gun mechanic and a sword setter.

A leading local firm was James Pulham & Son, whose terra cotta works at Broxbourne was founded in 1845 to take advantage of the brick clay on the valley floor of the Lea and of the newly-opened Eastern Counties Railway. Working on rock gardens, churches and cremation urns, they built up a fine reputation and obtained a Royal Warrant. The firm was continued by James's son and grandson but closed in the late 1930s. Living at Burnt Hall in Middle Street, William Alfred Pulham, a grandson of the firm's founder, was a terra cotta finisher and his son Walter was a gardener, perhaps also for the family firm. Three other Nazeing men also worked for Pulham's: William Whitton, who lived nearer the firm at Keysers, was also a terra cotta finisher, George Francis of Middle Street was a plasterer, and William George Crow of Maplecroft was a labourer.

In 1911 Nazeing Common Golf Course gave employment to five Nazeing men. The professional was James Savage of the Mill House in Betts Lane, who had risen from being an attendant in 1901. William Snell was a steward, while George William King and George William Mansfield were labourers, all living within a few minutes' walk of the course. Percy Mussell was a domestic gardener by trade but lived at 1 Betts Lane which was said on the *Survey* to be occupied by the Golf Club, and he evidently had some duties there.

Builders
With Nazeing beginning to develop, there was scope for builders to provide new housing, and most of them were local.

Langham King (1867-1954) was living in an old common-right cottage at 60 North Street. His cousin Marjorie Sykes remembered 'a lovely garden full of the scents and colours of an old English garden, complete with beehives and butterflies'. But there were also signs of things to come in a large builder's yard where Langham ran a business with his brother Thomas and brother-in-law William Thomas Perry, both working for him as labourers. He described himself on his letter-head as 'Builder, Plumber, Painter, Glazier, Paper-Hanger, House Decorator etc', adding 'Special attention given to well-boring'. With Langham was his nine-year-old son Leonard Francis (1901-1975), who later developed the engineering side of the firm as L.F. King & Son.

Chapel members Charles Judd and Ted Coleman both listed themselves on the census as employer-builders. Judd had since 1907 been renting the former wheelwright's shop near his home that later became Welch's Garage. It was described on the *Survey* as 'Freehold corner site with timber & tiled builder's workshop & stores, open timber & corrugated iron ladder store'. Around that time the two men got together and formed the firm of Judd & Coleman, which built many houses in Nazeing and in villages further afield.

The development of Keysers gave new opportunities for builders. Arthur Joseph Button was a self-employed carpenter living at Keysers in a six-roomed house, Sunnymede. He also owned Model Villas, which were two semi-detached houses. One of them was unoccupied on the Survey and may at some point have functioned as a show house. At that time his wife was listed as renting out a pair of houses: Marion Villa to William Whitton of the terra cotta works; and a house, shop and garden, which later became the Post Office, to T Gray[39]. The Buttons then owned

---

39 Kelly's 1912 directory shows Mrs Sarah Gray as the shopkeeper, so probably the legal agreement was made with her husband but she ran the shop.

only one other building plot, but they later acquired more and built Buttondene Crescent. Langham King had already built and rented out one house, and he also owned two adjacent plots that were as yet undeveloped. Builder Alfred Steed and his decorator brother William rented out Lea Bank to their father Thomas although all three were listed on the census in Highgate; the brothers also had a then undeveloped plot.

Eleven other Nazeing men worked in trades related to the building industry, possibly employed on some of the new dwellings at Keysers. There were five carpenters, three bricklayers, two house decorators and a builder's carman. In addition, bricklayer Benjamin William Starling and carpenter Henry James Starling did maintenance work for the Palmers, who were their landlords.

As well as men working in specific trades, there were just nine general labourers. Four were sons of Arthur Turner the blacksmith, three of whom were to die in the Great War.

Servants

After labourers, the next largest category of worker comprised the sixty-seven people in various forms of service. A tax on male servants remained in place almost until the Second World War so only wealthier people were able to employ them and there were just fourteen in Nazeing. Ten worked with horses as grooms and coachmen but it was a sign of the times that Ralph Bury, though himself a keen motorist, employed a coachman-chauffeur, Harry Treleaven. Harry's father was a horse-trainer on Dartmoor and Harry's career progression from horses to cars was a common one at the time. Walter Hargreaves, Frederick Green, Ralph Palmer and Archdale Palmer also had chauffeurs.

Apart from a 'house boy domestic' who was apparently a non-resident visiting his grandfather, there was only one other male servant listed in Nazeing. He was twenty-five-year-old James Biles, the butler of Anna Loftus Bury and her son Ralph at St Leonards. Biles was later killed in the Great War.

The fifty-three female domestic servants comprised eighteen general domestic servants, twelve housemaids (including two kitchen-maids and two parlour-maids), seven housekeepers, five cooks, five domestic nurses, three charwomen, one governess, one companion and one laundress. No fewer than thirteen of them were born in Hertfordshire, which may suggest that already the River Lea was not the barrier it had been before the opening of Nazeing New Road. Nine were born in Nazeing, seven elsewhere in Essex and nine in London and Middlesex. One came from Australia and the rest from various parts of England. In addition, three women described themselves as 'mother's help' and another five said they worked on domestic duties at home.

Alice Mead in servant's uniform (see page 128)

Only four households had more than two servants. The highest number was eight, at the largest house, Nazeing Park, which had twenty-eight rooms: a governess and two domestic nurses were presumably employed to help bring up the five Hargreaves children, while the job titles of a domestic cook, a maid, a housemaid, a kitchen-maid and a parlour-maid reflect a clear division of responsibilities. Nance Colman described herself as a 'school room maid', which may be yet another gradation. The Bury household at St Leonards was surprisingly small, with only the butler, a cook and two maids to service the twenty-room house although others from cottages on the estate would have worked for the family. One of them was undoubtedly Eliza Starling, a laundress at the cottage which gave its name to Laundry Lane. Snows had only ten rooms but Miles Hopkinson, a stockbroker, also employed four servants – a nurse for his daughter, a cook, a parlour-maid and a housemaid. At the vicarage, Thomas Goddard had three domestic servants.

There were six live-in housekeepers, all single and all employed by single or widowed men. Ralph Palmer at Hubbards had an aunt and niece from Warwickshire, Edith and Alice Bomford, as housekeeper and housemaid.

Fifteen females lived in as domestic general servants, only four of them aged over thirty. Five of them worked for farmers and seven for middle-class newcomers to Nazeing. Three worked in pubs, two of them widows in their fifties and presumably well able to look after themselves if necessary.

The youngest, twelve-year-old Florence May Patrick, worked for widowed farmer, Ann Head, at Ninnings. Florence had been listed on the Nazeing 1901 census as a 'nurse-child' living with the Ellis family at Brook Cottage in Middle Street, one of three foster children who probably came from London. In 1916 she married William

Hampton, who later became the pindar on Nazeing Common, and they had ten children. Their grand-daughter, Josie Watson, assumes that Florence was fostered out because her mother was unmarried, and was sent out to work - when legally she should still have been at school - because she had no real family to care for her.

A further five female servants were listed on the census living with their families, and probably worked for some of the leading figures in Nazeing. In Back Lane, housekeeper Martha Webb and nursemaid Dorothy Flack could well have been employed by Walter Hargreaves. Alice Burton, who was a cook, and Margaret Sturnham, a housemaid, both lived in Betts Lane with their respective parents and probably worked for Ralph Palmer; Hubbards is a relatively small house and he would doubtless have been happy for them to come in to do their work.

Three older women were charwomen; two were widows and one supported an infirm husband. Like cleaning ladies today, they probably worked a few hours a week for several employers.

Public Services

Few professionals were living in Nazeing and serving its people. The Reverend Thomas Goddard was with his wife, grand-daughter and three servants in the twelve-room vicarage, one of the largest houses in the village. In addition to his work at the Chapel, George Lipson was clerk to the civil parish and Overseer to the Poor although on the census he gave his occupation as solicitor's law clerk. When he died in 1920 aged only 58, the tribute on his gravestone – 'Life's Work Well Done' – was richly deserved.

There was no resident doctor in the village but there was a district nurse, who would probably have served Nazeing and perhaps the surrounding area. This was Annie Hale, who lived with her parents at Hope Cottage in Middle Street. Fanny Hewitt was described as a 'trainer nurse' but gave no place of work such as a hospital, so she too may have worked locally. Nazeing was covered from Hoddesdon by Dr John Wells, and by Dr William Love who occupied Back Park, near Nazeing Park. The obvious conclusion is that the cottage was his surgery and dispensary while practising in Upper Town, several miles from Hoddesdon, but the *Lloyd George Survey* says, curiously, that he used it as a 'summer tea room'. The two-roomed timber and tile cottage was described as in good condition but perhaps, as living standards improved, it was considered too small or remote because soon afterwards it was pulled down[40].

Back Park

This was a time when the numbers of white-collar civil servants and local government officers were increasing considerably but, surprisingly, none of them were in Nazeing in 1911. The only local government employee was William Mansfield, a road labourer with Epping Rural District Council.

---

40 It was probably vacated in 1893 when the widowed Martha Whay married her neighbour Thomas Robert Pegrum and moved in with him at Vine Cottage.

Shops

Nazeingbury Parade was not built until the 1950s, and earlier in the century shops and other commercial enterprises were scattered throughout the village. The fortunes of the village shops, and of the post offices with which they were sometimes combined, ran in broad parallel with the overall development of Nazeing. For many years each of the scattered hamlets had two or three shops which usually carried a huge variety of stock. Some of the shops and their owners were long-established village institutions and are described in Parts II and III, while others were transitory and made little impression.

There were several other small shopkeepers and traders. George James Banks of North Street and his son George William were both fish hawkers, and would have served a wider area. Henry Robertson of Wyndith in Long Green moved from Scotland in the 1890s. He was a milk carrier and probably had a milk round; on the 1901 census he had been listed as 'milker on farm' so was perhaps working for his landlord, Richard Bugg of Paynes Farm. Some shopkeepers from elsewhere increased their trade by taking their goods to Nazeing customers by horse and cart. Bernard Pegrum recalled that before the Great War Horace Pemble visited Queens Cottage weekly, delivering one order and taking the next. Pemble, who had a shop at Waltham Abbey in Sun Street, had one of the longer occupational entries on the census, describing himself as 'Grocer Draper Wine Spirit Beer Merchant, Clothier, Insurance Agent, Fire Life Etc'. In his memoirs John William Payne of Upper Town remembered groceries being delivered by Archer and Turner from Hoddesdon, as did Jacky Cooper fifty years later.

Pensioners

The *Lloyd George Survey* was partly designed to fund Lloyd George's newly-introduced pension scheme for people aged seventy and over, and there were twelve old age pensioners in Nazeing. Four men had formerly been farm workers and there were seven women for whom no occupation was given. One of them was Sarah Pegrum, whose husband Alfred was apparently drawing his pension while still working as a self-employed carpenter. As a married couple they would have received 7s 6d a week (single people were paid 5s). In addition, James Sturnham and James Westley, in their early sixties, were police pensioners.

Three widows had pensions from the Mercers' Company and had lived with their families for at least forty years in houses owned by the Palmers. This was no coincidence because the Palmer family had been leading figures in the Mercers' for well over a century. The late husbands of all three women had worked locally as farm labourers rather than directly for the Mercers', so there is no obvious reason why they should have had pensions when other women did not; perhaps it was a combination of long-term loyalty and individual circumstances. Emma King Cordell and Sarah Mansfield lived in separate households at Longyard Cottage.

Elizabeth Reynolds lived nearby at Abbotts Cottage for most of her married life, but with an interesting break: in April 1901 she was working as a servant at a convalescent home in Hove with her daughter Emily and Emma King Cordell's daughter Jane, who had both been there for at least ten years. Elizabeth returned to Nazeing later in the year. On the original census entry, 'visitor' has been crossed out as Elizabeth Reynolds's relationship and replaced by 'servant', suggesting that she was not just visiting but working. Similar arrangements may have been commonplace but are now lost to us because they did not coincide with censuses.

At the other end of the social scale, several people lived off private means, including Mrs Anna Loftus Bury of St Leonards. Ralph Charlton Palmer, still the largest landowner in Nazeing, had retired from his civil servant post as a Visitor in Lunacy. The sisters Martha and Mary Pegrum lived at Greenleaves, which they rented from the Williams family, although they in turn rented out Poona Lawn and Sunnyholme in Nazeing Road, and several properties in Middle Street. John Arthur Rufus of Old House was a retired master printer from Walthamstow. William Henry Cross was a retired butcher from Tottenham.

Women

Women may have helped out on a casual basis at peak times such as harvest but not been in regular work, and some people still felt that it was not entirely respectable for them to work at all, so female employment was not always reported on censuses. From women who were listed, though, we can get an idea of the kinds of work that they did.

Widows sometimes took over farms from their husbands. Mary Ann Clarke took on Lodge Farm when her husband died in 1870. She stated on the 1871 census that she farmed 162 acres and that she had three women labourers as well as three men and a boy. Increased mechanisation meant that overall fewer women were employed on farms, but it would be fascinating to know whether it was the employment of women that was unusual, or the recording of it on the census. At Camps Farm in 1911, eighty-one-year-old Sarah Nicholls had been widowed ten years earlier but was apparently still running the farm. Both women were the daughters of farmers and would have understood the land.

Several women had their own small enterprises, working at home. Sophie Pegrum and Harriet Elizabeth Dellar were both unmarried daughters in Middle Street working as dressmakers. At Newlands in Middle Street, Jane Judd had a 'sweet and general shop'. Along the road at Mayflower, there had been a shop since about 1840 and from 1898 directories listed it as John Ashby's although on the census he was described as a bricklayer and his brother William as a carpenter. His wife Annie certainly ran it after his death, and had perhaps done so while he was still alive. Matilda Starling and Emma Selway officially took over Post Office and blacksmith's businesses when they were widowed and may in practice have run them even when their husbands were alive.

Eleanor Hodges was a self-employed poultry keeper at her home, Rose Cottage, in Middle Street which, unusually, she owned. Her mother, Charlotte née Standingford, had farmed at Teys Farm since the death of her husband in 1870. Eleanor built the cottage for herself in the 1890s and on the 1901 census was recorded as living there 'on own means'. Three other women were also poultry farmers, including Emily Hampton who a few years earlier had her moment of fame as the owner of Totty the Nazeing pig.

Chapter 30

Migration

In 1911, no fewer than 359 (43%) of the 818 Nazeing residents were born in Nazeing, most of them farm workers and their families. But even in an isolated place like Nazeing, there was always movement in and out of the parish, usually for work or marriage. Though not perfect, a good way of getting an idea about migration is to look at birthplaces as seen on censuses. Remarkably, the 466 Nazeing natives who moved away were almost exactly balanced by the 459 outsiders who moved in. We have divided migrants in both directions into five groups: Essex, Hertfordshire, London and Middlesex, elsewhere in England, others.

People Moving Out of Nazeing

Nazeing natives living elsewhere on 1911 census

Place of Residence	Total	Head	Wife	Children born 1895 and later	Others	Children as % of total
Essex	105	27	20	22	36	21%
Herts	145	34	32	23	56	16%
London/ Middlesex	163	60	36	10	57	6%
England (rest of)	68	14	19	10	25	15%
Others	3	0	1	1	1	
Total	484	135	108	66	175	14%

In the above analysis, if no occupation was given in the census for a Nazeing native, then the occupation of a spouse or head of household was used. The numbers of children suggest where families were more likely to go.

Only a fifth of natives of Nazeing who moved away went to live close to where their spouses were born. Of those that did, almost twice as many Nazeing women were to be found near their husband's birth place than vice versa, which is a normal pattern. Just ten couples where both were born in Nazeing were to be found elsewhere, three south of the Thames, one in North London, the rest less than five miles from their birthplace.

Not surprisingly, the most popular destination for Nazeing migrants was London and Middlesex, but more unexpected is the finding that Hertfordshire was close behind. Four out of five migrants were within five miles of Nazeing, very quickly taking advantage of the opportunities presented by the new road and bridge across the railway.

One fifth of migrants were in domestic service, with four times more women than men. The women were mostly single with an average age of twenty-eight, whilst the men were older and much more likely to be married. More than a third of them were working within five miles of Nazeing, with the proportion of men growing higher the further away the move. There were also twenty-one gardeners, mostly domestic. Thus a quarter of those who left Nazeing were involved with maintaining the homes and gardens of others.

Agriculture and horticulture employed sixty-two people. Of the forty-four working in agriculture, thirteen were living in neighbouring Waltham Abbey, Roydon and Parndon and another eleven were within five miles of Nazeing. Only three had moved more than fifty miles: Thomas Henry Rippin was a farmer in his father's native Rutland, while James Mansfield had gone to Yorkshire and Arthur Mead to Leicestershire, both as gardeners. Sixteen men and two female 'nursery hands' were in the glasshouse industry in Wormley, Cheshunt and Waltham Cross.

There were some sixty-eight professional people including solicitors, architects and school teachers, as well as shop keepers, publicans, policemen, postmen and other service providers. Thomas Tyrwhitt, who was born while his father was vicar of Nazeing, became an architect, but Nazeing natives also were beginning to benefit from education. William John Boreham, who was from a family of farm labourers, became the superintendent of a life assurance company. Albert Edward Perry, son of Edward of Allmains, was an assistant manager to an engineering company. William Frogley was a theological student.

Over thirty were skilled craftsmen. Twenty were carpenters, builders and in allied trades. Twelve worked on the railways and three on the electric tramways in London. A.J. Pegrum's brother Joseph became a motor engineer and Alfred Coleman's nephew David a wood bender at a wheel and pulley factory in Hoddesdon. More unusual trades included an ivory turner at a piano works in Enfield and a cue tipper in Willesden, who presumably put tips on snooker cues, so Nazeing exiles were doing their bit for the leisure industry. 17% of men were general and other labourers.

Four boys were living in institutions. Nineteen-year-old Arthur Wilson was an inmate of the Stanley Home at Stonebridge Park in Willesden, a probation home run by the Church Army. About twenty boys were set to various trades but his job of industrial chemist suggests that he may have had a bright future despite the misdemeanour. James Stokes was born in 1900, the son of John Thomas Stokes, a farm bailiff for Ralph Bury; John apparently died in Surrey in 1906 and by 1911 James was in the Reedham Orphanage, Purley. Horace Stebbing was born in Woodford in 1899 but by 1901 had been boarded out with an elderly farmer and his wife in Waltham Road, next door to the Stokes family. In 1911 Horace was a boarder at Ongar Grammar School, stating mistakenly that he was born in Nazeing. Ongar Grammar School was a private school with 164 pupils and how his education was financed is a mystery. No such mystery attaches to Norman Knight, who was a boarder at St Winifred's, a minor public school at Kenley in Surrey; Norman's father was a Lloyd's underwriter and insurance broker who lived with his family at Sunnyholme in Nazeing Road for about ten years but then moved to Banstead in the Surrey stockbroker belt.

Only two people are known to have been living abroad. Ellen Mary Graham née Gladden married Thomas Benjamin Graham, a serving soldier who was posted to Egypt where their son Leslie was born in 1910. Thomas Ford was a petty officer in the Royal Navy, serving on board *H.M.S. Irresistible* since 1901.

Though the world of work still belonged largely to men, women were beginning to make an impression. Three women and one man were schoolteachers. Four women were office workers and three were shop assistants. Two were dressmakers and one a milliner's apprentice.

Two Nazeing women were trading in Epping High Street. Harriett Foster née Cordell ran her own confectionery shop, assisted by her daughter Alice. Bertha Nicholls was the manageress of a dairy owned by her brother-in-law, George Pegrum of Shaftesbury Farm, also in Epping. Bertha must have learnt the trade from her family at Camps Farm, though she was never listed on Nazeing censuses as working.

Nine men were described as pensioners and/or retired from their jobs. They were: a Prudential Assurance agent, a water warder, a distillery engineer, a detective inspector, three farm labourers, and two just described as old age pensioners. William and Sarah Boreham were living in Lambeth with their son, the life assurance superintendent. Seven people were 'living on own means' and, at the other end of the scale, three were in the Epping Union workhouse and one on parish relief in Hoddesdon.

People Moving into Nazeing

Nazeing residents on 1911 census - birthplaces

Birthplace	Total	Head	Wife	Children	Others
Nazeing	359	77	22	240	20
Essex	152	51	45	41	15
Herts	90	15	24	30	21
London/ Middlesex	97	26	23	24	24
England (elsewhere)	99	25	32	15	27
Others	21	5	8	3	5
Totals	**818**	**199**	**154**	**353**	**112**

The largest group of incomers was the 152 coming from other parts of Essex. Almost half were born in the neighbouring parishes of Roydon, Parndon and Waltham Abbey. This suggests the existence of a 'country' – something larger than a parish but smaller than a county, not a formal administrative unit but a rather nebulous area where people had things in common. Roydon and Parndon were rural villages similar to Nazeing so labourers and their families would probably have moved between them with little difficulty, particularly as some Nazeing landholders also owned land in the wider area. Waltham Abbey was a draw in several ways: the authorities there had long held Nazeing, it housed the gunpowder factory and it was a market town. Surprisingly, very few came from the other nearby market towns of Epping and Harlow, suggesting that Waltham Abbey was of greater significance in Nazeing. Most of those from other parts of Essex lived in rural villages similar to Nazeing. The Smith, Flack and Wallis families came from the neighbouring north Essex villages of Chrishall and Elmdon to Back Lane and may well have known one another. But in most cases there is no obvious explanation for their moves, except perhaps that Nazeing was closer to London and conditions were rather better.

Most of the heads of household who moved to Nazeing from Hertfordshire did fairly specialised jobs and none was a farm labourer. Frederick Willmott and David Shepherd were gardeners at the Crown Hotel and William Lambert was a lock-keeper, all living and working next to the Lea. James Savage was a shopkeeper, James Sadler a chauffeur, and James Pulham was working for his family's terra cotta works, along with William Whitton. Several of them had small children, suggesting that younger families were already beginning to take advantage of the new road.

James and Edith Sadler of Nazeing Park Cottage were among those who brought their young families to Nazeing

Unsurprisingly, ten heads of household who were born in London and Middlesex were commuters taking advantage of the recent improvements in Nazeing. Five were in farming and related trades, two worked for the Lee Conservancy Board, two were publicans and George Francis came to work for Pulham's. Of the others born in London and Middlesex, ten were living with their families, including James Greatbatch who was 'feeble-minded' and 'being maintained by relatives'. Six were the children of men from Nazeing, Roydon or Parndon who had lived for a few years in London and its suburbs, and then returned to the country. Six were servants and six were boarders or visitors.

The Wives of Nazeing
In 1911, of the seventy-seven male heads of household born in Nazeing, only twenty-two married Nazeing women.

Even after the Second World War, it was normal for couples to marry in the bride's parish and settle in the groom's. For example, Anna Loftus Tottenham was born in Ireland into a family that was among the largest landowners there but when, in 1869, she married Charles James Bury, she moved into the relative modesty of St Leonards House.

Some Nazeing men met their future wives in London and its suburbs. In 1901 Mabel Berwick was living in West Ham with her parents and seven siblings, a mile away from Arthur 'Tractor' Smith of Cutlands who was staying with his sister and brother-in-law while working as a rubber moulder. Arthur and Mabel were married in late 1904.

It is perhaps surprising how far women travelled to take up positions as servants. Some were recruited from other parts of the country through personal contacts and then married Nazeing men. From 1859 to 1874 the farmer at Harold's Park was Thomas Rippin, who was born and lived at Stretton in Rutland, England's smallest county. He certainly brought one and probably two female servants from his native county. Mary Munton, who in 1871 was working for him at Harold's Park, came from Empingham, which is four miles from Stretton. In the following year in Nazeing she married Ben Starling of the Red House. Martha Ball from Edith Weston, also in Rutland, married James Whay in Nazeing in 1866 and lived with him and their children in Betts Lane. Though in 1861 she was still at home with her parents in Edith Weston, it seems likely that she too worked for Rippin, and when she married James may even have been replaced by Mary.

Often girls moved to Nazeing with their families as children and married local boys when they grew up. Three daughters of Thomas and Agnes Hollow were born in Sennen, Cornwall, where they lived until 1890 when Thomas became tenant of Brewitts Farm, one of the first Cornish farmers to take on an Essex farm. By 1911 Catherine was married to John Mansfield, Eva to Ernest Webb and Mary to George Standingford. On the night of the 1911 census one of Mary Standingford's daughters was staying with her aunt Eva Webb.

Harriet Woodley came to Nazeing in 1900 when her parents Charles and Eliza moved to Perry Hill Farm, where Charles was the farm foreman. She met and married Joseph Hale junior, presumably because Joseph's uncles Isaac and John were immediate neighbours. In 1881 Charles Woodley was living in Ashdon, Essex, with his parents and seven siblings, one of whom was Selina. For a while she was a domestic servant in London but she married Alfred 'Sammy' Coleman, whom she probably met whilst visiting Charles in Nazeing.

Herbert Mansfield married Rebecca Ann Saville in 1896. There is no sign of Rebecca on the 1891 census but her father David and sister Maria were in Ware workhouse while her mother Mary Saville was living with her brother Charles Field and his family in Back Lane. Herbert was with his parents and siblings further along Back Lane, and that is presumably how he and Rebecca met. In 1901 Herbert and Rebecca were living at Camps Cottages with their children, the widowed Mary Saville and Rebecca's brother William.

In some cases women may have known the area already. Ada Potter was born and brought up in west London, but in 1881 was a domestic servant staying with William and Mary Ann Nicholls née Bridgeman at Belchers Farm. Later Ada was a servant living nearby in Broxbourne High Road and in 1894 she married Mary Ann's nephew Charles Bridgeman, so evidently kept in touch with the family.

Commuters

It was the development of Riverside and the building of Nazeing New Road in 1908 that made commuting to London much easier and led to the opening up of Nazeing for outsiders but, even before that, working away from Nazeing and the local area was not unknown. Archdale Palmer was the managing director of the Slazenger Sports Company and, on censuses, was always to be found at his flat in Kensington. Ralph Palmer and Ralph Bury were both barristers by profession, and John Banks was a barrister's clerk, all working in London.

Professional people, clerks and tradesmen were beginning to move into Nazeing. Walter Hargreaves of Nazeing Park was an insurance broker. George Felix Dudbridge Green was a blouse and robe manufacturer living at Wheelers. Miles Hopkinson at Snows and Arthur George Josling at Tatsford Lodge were stockbrokers. Edgar Sykes was an electrical engineer staying with Susan Pegrum in Hoe Lane. At Sunnyholme in Nazeing Road, Alexander Charge and his son Herbert were both commercial clerks, Alexander in an upholstery warehouse and Herbert in a mantle warehouse. A commercial clerk for a household furnisher, Walter Middleton, would have had a fair trek to the station from his home at Fairview in Upper Town, and later moved to North Street. David Wootton of Rose Cottage in Nazeing Road was a butcher but is not listed in trade directories for Nazeing, so was probably continuing the business he had in 1901 when living in Edmonton; he also had a visitor who was an engine driver. Walter Caryl was a bookbinder who moved to the Coach and Horses when his father took on the pub. James Kimpton was an iron foundry employer who moved from Stepney to the Rookery in St Leonards Road, although he did have Nazeing connections: his father, Peter, was baptised at All Saints' and his grandfather, John Jennings, lived at 42 North Street for at least thirty years. Few if any houses were built in the older parts of Nazeing in the decade before the Great War, but the new development at Riverside was a major change that will be described at greater length in our next book.

Conversely, Nazeing people were beginning to take job opportunities outside the village. Seventeen-year-old Mabel Welch was a student of shorthand and her father, perhaps rather proudly, noted that she was working in London. Arthur Coleman was an agent for the Wesleyan and General Assurance Company. Both of them came from old farming families that continued to be influential in the village.

According to the 1911 census, there were 127 farmers and farm labourers in Nazeing; seventy-six were born in the village, but a mere four in London and its suburbs. By contrast, only fourteen of the seventy-nine people in broadly professional and commercial jobs were born in Nazeing, but twenty-five in London and suburbs. This suggests that Nazeing was still a deeply conservative society, but its transformation by outside influences had begun. Without this influx, emigration would have exceeded immigration and population would have declined.

Chapter 31

Transport

Horses and Bicycles

Before the Great War, horses were the main means of transport for most of the villagers although bicycles were becoming more popular. The *Survey* gives information about outbuildings and shows that, excluding farms and smallholdings, almost one in three dwellings had a stable for horses. Seven had a coach house and seven a cart shed. The owners of three properties in Riverside Avenue specified that they had a cycle shed, possibly to house their transport to the nearby station. Bicycles were probably kept in the sheds listed for some of the properties.

Emily Cook (left) and Nellie Starling were obviously proud of their new bicycles. They were good friends who were later buried next to one another in All Saints' churchyard.

Peter Brent recalled that one of the ways of getting out of the village was the horse and trap. Villagers often shovelled up the manure from horses to use on their gardens, where they grew their own vegetables and fruit. 'A few people had a bicycle but you were always getting punctures as the roads were made up with gravel. In the summer months they were very dusty and during the winter they were very muddy and had potholes six inches deep.'

Nance Colman recalled:

> The trains ran very regularly, we walked home from Broxbourne station, or you could go by horse and cart, or have a fly (single horse light covered vehicle) from the station. I remember we went to a wedding once by fly, and when we got back to Broxbourne the old man was drunk. He said he couldn't get us back home. My mother said 'we paid you when we went, to make sure that you would come for us'. The horse knew his own way along the road. Animals do get used to routines, as we do, and parts of the road. My husband's father used to be a hay binder. He used to go up to Ponders End with the load of hay with the horses. The horses used to go along the tram lines and directly they hear the tram bell go, they would turn off the rails.

But times were changing and horses were requisitioned for the war effort.

Roads

Before the Great War, the Nazeing road network had changed little for centuries. Even a hundred years later, Nazeing New Road remains the only major addition. Nazeing roads in 1911 were still gravel. Other than the amount of traffic, little would have changed from fifty years earlier, when maintenance was undertaken by the parish. According to their Highway Account

Book 1862-5, John Mead was employed on a regular basis over the winter months and paid 1s 10d per day. Charles Judd received 2s 4d a day and his assistant Jacob Patmore 1s 6d a day. Bricks and pipes were obtained from Charles Foster at Epping Plain. Gravel was carted by Nazeing farmers from Broxbourne, Ware and Parndon.

At the front of the book are remarks and suggestions for repairing old roads, including how to use 'The Rake':

> If any ruts appear, this tool must be used to keep a regular even surface, but caution must be observed in its application. The labourer, if left to himself, when a rut shows itself, will gather all the loose stones he can find and draw them into the rut, with the view of levelling it; but this does mischief, and it should not be allowed, because by doing so he causes the road to be harder in those places than the rest of the road. In the summer it will present an uneven surface, showing longitudinal ridges where the ruts were, and be the means of forming a barrier to the escape of water. In using the rake, then, let it be worked backwards and forwards on each side of the rut, and across it.

Early in the new century, cars began to make an appearance in the village. At Epping Rural District Council in 1903 there was a motion to restrict speeds to twenty miles per hour. Ralph Bury, who was one of the first people in Nazeing to own a car and who listed one of his recreations in *Who's Who* as motoring, said: 'I think cars might go at any speed on a straight wide road with no one about'. 'Ah, but what if there *is* someone about?' commented the chairman, and the motion was carried 9-4.

Before the war, Bury, Ralph Palmer, Archdale Palmer, F.W. Green and Walter Hargreaves all had chauffeurs.

Frederick Mason Green with Alfred Eldred, the family chauffeur

The River Lea[41]

The river was still an important means of transporting goods to and from Nazeing. The parish had wharves at what is now Nazeing Glass, and at Occupation Lane, off Green Lane. From 1868 to 1948 the River Lea in Nazeing was managed by the Lee Conservancy Board, which provided tied cottages for its lock-keepers at Carthagena and Dobbs Weir, and a weir-keeper at King's Weir.

King's Weir marks the junction of the old river course and the channel of the Lee Navigation, cut through in 1767. The present weir house was built in 1886 but sadly the keeper, Harry Norton, was not able to enjoy it for long, because in 1891 he drowned in

---

41 This section summarises the relevant parts of Richard Thomas's splendid website at http://www.leeandstort.co.uk/, and adds some new material.

the treacherous waters there. His widow and five children had just one month to leave the house although she was given £5 funeral expenses and a pension of 7s a week. William Turner then gave thirteen years' reliable though uneventful service, but his successor's short period of office was decidedly the opposite. The engineer, Charles Tween, reported to the Board:

> This path was very seriously damaged by flood water being allowed to rise considerably above its proper level on the 17th December 1906, a length of about 30ft of the path being washed into the adjoining marsh and two of the new GPO telegraph poles being washed down, and that repairs to the path, &c., were being carried out, the estimated cost being £40 to £50…That the damage was caused through the negligence of weir keeper W. Campkin, and that this man had been suspended from duty (with loss of pay) and another man placed in charge of the weir.

Undaunted by their experience with William Campkin, the Board appointed his younger brother John to replace him. In 1913 John Campkin was transferred to Hertford Lock where he died in 1924, tragically having lost three of his five sons in the war.

At *Carthagena,* Thomas Andrew Galloway was appointed lock-keeper in 1898 on the death of seventy-six-year-old Charles Charvill, having previously been his assistant. Charles Tween told the Board: 'He [Thomas] is a steady man and I suggest we give him a trial at 16/- per week.' The Board provided for Charvill's widow to stay at Carthagena with an allowance of 5s a week although what Galloway thought of this arrangement is not recorded. She died in 1906 and in 1911 Galloway married his housekeeper, Emma Caple. In 1913 he received a raise of a shilling a week and the Board resolved 'That the Scale of Wages of Collectors, Lock keepers, Weir keepers, Police Constables and Water Bailiffs on the Lee Navigation be not reconsidered by the Board during the next five years', but they reckoned without the war and the consequent inflation. Galloway's wages steadily increased until in 1919 he was getting 27s a week with house, garden and uniform.

Thomas Galloway died in 1920 and C. Lambert was offered the post but 'after his wife had seen the cottage she would not allow him to take it'. The present house was built in 1936.

At *Dobbs Weir* in 1883 a new lock-house was built, alongside the lock but about two hundred yards away from the weir, for which the lock-keeper was also responsible. In 1902 George Halls was appointed to the post but evidently complained that the distance was inconvenient because in the following year Tween reported: 'I am having a new hut built, to be placed at this weir as a shelter for the lock keeper whilst attending to the weir at night'. Halls had been the landlord of the Barge Inn at Ware, and in 1909 took the opportunity to move two hundred yards from the lock-house along the towpath to take over the Fish and Eels, just across the parish boundary in Roydon. His successor was William Lambert, who was given an allowance of £1 6s for coal to be used in the shelter. Lambert resigned in 1915 and was replaced by Thomas Brooks who had worked for Broxbourne Rowing Club, but in 1917 Brooks was dismissed for stealing 2½ tons of coal from His Majesty's Barges when they were passing the lock, probably on war business.

The Lee Conservancy Board rented out houses and land that were surplus to their requirements. The Old Lock House at Dobbs Weir was still in good condition when it was occupied by a merchant's clerk called William Jones. In 1911 he shared it with an insurance clerk, a blouse merchant and a corn merchant, and they probably walked along the towpath to catch the train at Broxbourne.

Horse-drawn barge on the Lea , c1905

Chapter 32

Water and Sanitation

The inhabitants of Nazeing had always been largely dependent on wells and pumps for their supply of water. John William Payne recalled:

> Water was brought to the cottage daily from the well which supplied the house, in buckets used only for this purpose. Tanks were placed near the house to collect soft rain water from the roof and used for washing, baths and other household purposes. A very large galvanised iron vessel was used for bathing and was stored in the shed adjoining the house... My mother had a larger 'copper' for washing and a 'dolly peg' for moving the washing around.

Marjorie Sykes wrote:

> Strangely enough, I have no recollection of the use of wells in Nazeing...Rain water was collected from the eaves in water butts, and the village pump supplied drinking water. Purification of water from the ponds and water butts was done by boiling, or by a system of filtering through many layers of pebbles... [Even when piped water was brought to the village], the tap was placed at the outer gate and was still taken to the house in buckets; and it was hard water and not considered good enough for the washing of clothes or persons.

She added:

> 'Uncle would visit the village pump by the Common Gate, always a centre of village social life. After conversational exchanges, we would return home with two buckets filled with ice cold water.'

Similarly, Enid Brent of the Red House remembered her Uncle
Ernie 'walking half way up Common Hill to get a couple of buckets
of water'. He 'used to have this yoke with two buckets hanging
either side of him on chains'.

In 1894 the newly-established rural district councils were given far-
reaching powers over matters of health and when in 1895 Epping
RDC's sanitary inspector visited the Nazeing Gate area he was
very concerned over the quality of the water there. Complicated
negotiations over the best way to remedy the situation, described
at length in *Five Miles from Everywhere,* dragged on for ten years
and caused great ill feeling on all sides.

In 1905 the South East Essex Water Board put forward ambitious
and expensive new proposals which the parish council opposed in
a letter to the district council:

> The Parish is sparsely populated and very scattered and only in a
> few instances has any inconvenience been felt from deficient water
> supply ... The population is at a standstill and to put in force a general
> water scheme at the present time would cause for many years a very
> heavy expenditure to a district which is a purely agricultural one.

Also in 1905, the powerful Metropolitan Water Board applied for
permission to abstract more water from the Lee and Stort rivers,
and shifted the proposed location for a 150-acre sewage works
from a site in Roydon to one in Nazeing between North Street and
the church. The parish council rapidly convened a public meeting
at which forty-six inhabitants voted unanimously to oppose the
scheme, and Ralph Palmer was the Nazeing delegate in a deputation
from the affected local councils which negotiated with the MWB.
He declared that the parish 'objected to paying for something from
which it received no benefit' and the plan was dropped.

In 1907 the parish council successfully opposed an attempt by the Herts and Essex Waterworks Company to begin operations in Nazeing, but over the next few years the company began to extend its service to various parts of the village, and by 1912 it wanted to lay pipes along Middle Street. The parish council declined to contribute because the houses were too isolated but Joe Pegrum negotiated an arrangement whereby the owners there paid a total of £120 and the installation went ahead.

The *Lloyd George Survey* shows that most public buildings had toilet facilities even if they were rather basic. The two schools and the Chapel had WCs, and the Upper Town Sunday School had a urinal and two earth closets, a basic type of toilet with dry earth used to cover excrement. Nothing is recorded for All Saints'. The Crown Hotel had many toilet blocks, urinals and earth closets to serve its large clientele, and the King Harold's Head had two WCs. Of the three pubs owned by Christies of Hoddesdon, the Crooked Billet and the Red Lion only refer to well water and a cesspool while nothing is mentioned for the Sun - although all three may have had facilities that were not recorded.

Bathrooms were only for the privileged few. St Leonards apparently had them in the four principal bedrooms, and Nazeing Park and Collyers each had two. Only eight other dwellings had a bathroom: Snows, Wheelers, Goats, Church House Farm, the Vicarage, Mamelons and Old House. The majority of properties had a 'substantial built wash house', a separate building that housed a copper for heating water, and perhaps a tin bath. Bernard Pegrum described the arrangements at Curtis Farm:

> The household water was obtained from a pump over the sink in a large, brick-floored room known as the wash-house. (We always pronounced it 'washus'.) Given the opportunity – which was not

often – I would try to work the pump but could never move the handle fast enough to make the water gush forth like my father could.

Some of the larger houses would have had WCs although that is one detail the *Survey* seldom went into. Most dwellings had to make do with an earth closet.

A few passing references give clues to facilities before the coming of mains water and drainage. The Upper Recreation Ground (now the Nazeing Triangle) included 'a large pond from which the villagers used to draw their water'. Nazeing Park lists a 'brick built water tower with horse power pumps (not now used)'. Nazeingbury had a well and pump operated by horse power which was in use up until the 1920s. Laundry Cottage and Mayflower had wells, and Brier Villas at Riverside a cesspool. Tenants at Motts obtained water for washing and cooking from a pond in the back garden. Maplecroft had 'no water only pond'.

Chapter 33

Schools

The village had two schools: the Church School in Upper Town and the Council School at Bumbles Green. The *Lloyd George Survey* states that both were owned by Essex Education Committee, and describes them in some detail.

Upper Town Church School

This school was opened in 1854 and closed in 1878 when the Bumbles Green school opened. It re-opened in 1891 and was extended by public subscription in 1907, at which time it had ninety-seven pupils. The vicar and churchwardens managed the school and much of the cost was borne by the church. The *Lloyd George Survey* states that it was a substantially built, white, brick building with a tiled roof, valued at £500. It had two rooms (30ft x 20ft and 20ft x 18ft) with a lobby and outside WCs.

From 1905 to 1915 the headmaster was Alfred Andrew Gwynne-Phillips, with his wife Jessica Agnes as assistant teacher. Both were from Bristol and John William Payne recalled:

> The new master and his wife had taught in a London school and he had been advised by his doctor to move into the country. We were very fortunate to have them at such a tiny school and they did their very best with a lot of rather countrified material.

There were only two classes: seniors taught by the head and juniors by the assistant.

Bumbles Green School

The Nazeing Board School was opened in 1878 by the Epping School Board. It became the Council School when, under the 1902 Education Act, Essex County Council took over responsibility. The *Survey* found that the school was brick-built, in good condition with a tiled roof. The main building was 58ft x 22ft, consisting of a main school room and an infants' room. There were also two cloakrooms, and an outside coal store. Across the yard were separate boys' and girls' 'offices' - bucket lavatories which caused many problems over the years; they were often referred to as being in need of a 'flushing' and in one case as being 'very offensive'.

The value of £1,619 included the attached schoolmaster's house. It was occupied by Noah William Bevan who was the head teacher from 1906 to 1919, with his wife Clarice Maria as the assistant teacher, both of them from Wales. Her mother was a teacher but he came from a coal-mining family, so his obtaining the post aged only twenty-five was a considerable achievement. Mrs Bevan and Marjorie Sykes' Aunt Amy 'would often be seen in a whispered huddle to laugh at something that had amused them... she was a bit of a tease, but we liked her'. Marjorie's cousin Winnie Perry 'became such a useful friend of the family that when they moved to Romford for better jobs, Winnie went with them'.

When Marjorie was seven her mother had a long period in hospital, so she stayed with her Uncle Alf and attended the village school:

> ...the school was very good, although progress was slower than at the town schools. The school room was large and there were two divisions with no dividing screen or curtain. Though I was in the lower division taken by Mrs Bevan, I could quite well follow what was being done in the top set, which was taken by her husband.
> I was quite often punished for talking or inattention; and the punishment was never the cane, but the enforcement to stand on the narrow bench where we sat. This enabled me to see much of village life which I missed by being in school. Sometimes Uncle would be passing along with the cows, or with buckets for the village pump. He would greet me by raising his stick, but I don't think he ever knew the reason for my exalted position in the school.

In 1911 there were two other teachers, both living in Middle Street. Miss Beatrice Pulham was a member of the family that owned the famous terra cotta firm in Broxbourne. She had been a pupil at Nazeing Board School, becoming a monitress in 1899. Although she never received a formal college education, she was a born teacher and many older Nazeing natives still remember her with great affection.

Mrs Emily Drane lived at The Cottage, next door to the Poplars in Middle Street, with her daughter Christina, who was a pupil at the school, and husband George. He was working at home on his own account as a book repairer, presumably drawing his clientele from a fairly wide area. Ten years earlier he had been a market gardener in the Isle of Ely which is quite a change, so they may have moved as a result of her obtaining the teaching post.

Ralph Bury was chairman of the managers and the headmaster had to get his permission on many matters well into the twentieth century, some seemingly quite trivial. Ralph and his mother Anna played a large part in the life of the school and made regular visits. Until her death in 1933 they continued the practice of Christmas 'treats' that she had started with her husband Charles in the 1880s, and handed out prizes for good attendance.

The school log-books give a detailed picture of school life, which was often tough. However, despite rigorous tuition in overcrowded conditions with a high ratio of pupils to teachers, inspectors recorded that 'teaching is kindly and effective' even if pupils were occasionally caned. By 1908 there were forty-three infants and their class room was not big enough for that number, so it was difficult for one teacher to manage. With so many children in the building, disease was rife: hooping (*sic*) cough, measles, scarlet fever, influenza, ringworm and chilblains are recorded. The inspector, the medical officer, the school nurse and the attendance officer all visited. When an illness reached epidemic proportions, the county Medical Officer of Health or the district sanitary inspector would close the school.

For many years the rooms were heated by coal fires but in very cold weather it was difficult to keep them warm and children were often away with chilblains, suggesting that neither home nor school was heated adequately. Although the school was fairly central, many children had long distances to travel, so getting to school would have been arduous and some brought a midday meal with them. Many had poor footwear; as late as 1910 two children could not attend school since they had no boots.

Holidays were limited. The governors allowed one week at Christmas but for Easter only Good Friday and Easter Monday and Tuesday. The four-week summer holiday was known as 'Harvest Holiday' because some children helped with the harvest. On Empire Day (24 May), after a lesson on the Empire and citizenship, and singing patriotic songs, a half-day was given. A week was allowed for the coronations of Edward VII and George V and another holiday was earned when the National Anthem was sung for the Proclamation of George V, perhaps because Ralph Bury, as High Sheriff of Essex, did the proclaiming.

There was some interchange with the church school. In 1909 seven older girls went to cookery classes there and some children from Betts Lane, accompanied by the vicar's wife and one of their teachers, attended hygiene lessons at Bumbles Green.

Noah Bevan made very few references to the war in the school logbook but the children must have been aware of family and friends who had gone to fight, some of whom did not return. A school garden was established in 1914, possibly as an early *Dig for Victory* campaign, and continued after the war. It produced potatoes, broad beans, runner beans and parsnips, with the children keeping diaries on their activities, which included cleaning and oiling their gardening tools. On 16 April 1915 the military authorities took over the infants' classroom as a guardroom and the children were taught in the playground until the soldiers left at 1pm.

Nance Colman recorded her memories of the Bumbles Green School from 1905 to 1914:

I was only four when I started at the board school at Bumbles Green. There were just two rooms, the big room and the little room. I can remember it before the partition was put in to divide the big room into two.

The teachers were Mr. Bevan, Mrs. Bevan, a big woman, and Mrs. Drane.

I wasn't there when Mr. Webb was there, that was before my time when my older brother Harry was at the school. I also remember Miss Pulham who was wonderful with the little children. She used to cluck to them, she was like a speckled hen with her chicks. I used to love her.

We did a lot of needlework, we made simple things. We had to do darning, making pinafores out of a dress, with special seams, rick rack, all by hand. They used to cut holes in things for us to mend and darn. We thought that was a silly thing to do, we used to say we had plenty of stuff at home wanted mending. It was a pity to cut a hole just to mend it again.

We used to do nature rambles and all that sort of thing, in the summer time. Of course with Mr Bevan being a Welshman, we had lots of songs and poetry. He used to get really cross if we were going too full blast when it should be soft and sweet. We used to learn poetry off by heart. Miss Perry and I used to remember them and recite them when we were older and think who else could do that today. We had good memories.

I wasn't a good child at school. I had a terrible sense of humour, not always in the right place. I always got caught at this sort of thing you see, I don't know why.

We had those long forms, and tables with holes for the ink, they were the length of the room. Mr Bevan was in front of me, leaning over the person in the row in front of me. I could see the funny side. He had such a beautiful bottom, that's the sort of naughty thing I would do... what did I do? I got my ruler. I thought 'wouldn't half like to hit his bottom'. I did and I got caught. It was a naughty thing to do. I actually hit him with the ruler. It was stupid. He turned round and looked and went Grrrrr. I always got caught. I didn't say someone had pushed me because they didn't, I had done it!

Chapter 34

Leisure and Recreation

A section in *Five Miles from Everywhere* describes royal celebrations and sports in Nazeing before the Great War, but notes 'most informal leisure activities in any generation go unrecorded'. We are therefore fortunate that John William Payne's memories contain a section entitled *How did we amuse ourselves?* The detail is so fascinating that we reproduce it in full, with just a few minor editorial changes:

Without radio, television or a free library, we were dependent on our own efforts to amuse ourselves in our free time. We were mainly an agricultural community and the greater part of daylight was, for males, working time. Even on Sundays cows had to be milked! Few enjoyed the privilege (not a right to be claimed) of an annual holiday and even on Bank Holidays certain jobs had to be done.

On Saturday afternoons during the summer, but not at hay or harvest time we managed to scrape together eleven men for a cricket match with a neighbouring village. I played for the Upper Nazeing Team at the age of fifteen and when Mr Archdale Palmer arranged a match between his friends and the village he gave us a supper after the match in a tin hut belonging to the Sun public house. Quite an occasion and I was always called upon to propose the vote of thanks!

I missed so much the lack of books – no travelling library – they were indeed lean years. There was an old man who called once or twice a year with a case of books – mainly religious!

Father received his daily paper *The Morning Leader*, a liberal thinking journal, and weekly *The Gardener's Chronicle*, both delivered by the postman between 8 and 9 am. Grandma received weekly three papers, which I devoured when they arrived on Saturday afternoon.

They were *Home Chat*, *The Sunday Circle* and *The Christian Herald*! Grandpa read the local paper *The Herts and Essex Observer*.

When I was quite young an uncle (who stayed with us for a year or so for training in horticulture) cycled into Hoddesdon on Saturday evening and sometimes bought a comic for me – *Comic Cuts*. I was not allowed to read this until Monday, it being quite unsuitable for Sunday reading!

Forgive me, I am writing too much about myself instead of life in the village. When safe we skated, during the winter, on the small lakes at the entrance to the long drive to Nazeing Park. During the early part of this century Nazeing Common was a golf course and small boys acted as caddies. I was not permitted to earn a few coppers in this way!

There were two buildings – the hall beside the Nazeing Chapel and the School building near the lower Post Office in which an occasional social, a magic lantern show or a bazaar was held. I was very interested in the magic lantern and decided to make one for myself. Father had a large 'bullseye' oil lantern. I blacked over the bullseye with a candle and with a matchstick made a drawing on the bullseye lighted the lamp and projected the picture onto a white background. Further blackings had to be made to produce new pictures!

Children had their marbles and 'conkers' during season and collections were made of wild flowers and, I regret to say, bird's eggs, and I remember collecting buttons. When making such a collection a brass button from a soldier's uniform was highly prized. Hoops for trundling, hopscotch, hide and seek and other games were played and on rare occasions one was invited to a party to celebrate a birthday or a festival.

Evening meetings, usually of a religious nature, were arranged by the Congregational Chapel and we must not forget the Band of Hope! A brass band was formed during those early years by members of Nazeing Congregational Chapel. At Christmas carol singers and a carillon of handbells visited most houses during the evenings.

We did not have a phonograph (as it was then called) or recorded cylinders, but I believe at the beginning of this century these were becoming quite popular. We possessed a piano played by my sister. I also remember the first moving picture I saw, a special showing at the little school by the church, organised by the Schoolmaster. It was not a great success as it broke down a number of times during the evening!

John Payne's family came to Nazeing when he was seven and Nance Colman's brothers went to work in London, so it was a myth that Nazeing people knew nothing of the outside world. But in 1914 their horizons were to be expanded as never before.

Drum and fife band in Betts Lane, c1900.
Inset: Arthur and Harry Mead.

Part V

The Great War (1914-1918)

Chapter 35

Nazeing in War Time

A strange thing, war. With its bloodshed and cruelty, its pain, grief and tears, it ought to fill every civilized person with the utmost and unwavering revulsion. It ought to and often does. And yet there is a strange and timeless fascination...

Frederick Forsyth

The Great War was one of the most tragic events in world history, resulting in the deaths of almost ten million people, yet it began almost by accident. Europe had been largely peaceful for a century but by 1914 it had become divided into two armed camps and the Balkans were known as 'the powder keg of Europe', only awaiting a spark to ignite an explosion. After Archduke Franz Ferdinand was assassinated in Sarajevo, Austria-Hungary declared war on Serbia, Russia supported Serbia, Germany supported Austria-Hungary and France supported Russia. There had been hopes that Britain would stay out but Germany's invasion of Belgium triggered a treaty guaranteeing its neutrality and Britain declared war.

The war dragged on for over four years and more than 150 Nazeing men went away to serve, one in six of all Nazeing people. Probably two in three men of military age enlisted and about a fifth of them died, including three from one family which gives some idea of the great sacrifice made. Twenty died in France and Flanders on the Western Front, three in Egypt and Palestine, one at Salonika in Greece, four at sea and five while on service at home (see Chapter 36).

When war came, it changed Nazeing, as everywhere else. Almost all the men in their twenties and thirties were away at the front so women and old men took on their jobs. Nazeing people would have known of the German threat. There were about forty air raids in Essex, but there is no record of any bombs falling in Nazeing although some dropped at Broxbourne, from where the stationmaster usually warned that planes were flying over.

When Britain entered the war on 4 August 1914, the country had enough wheat in stock to last for just 125 days.[42] Over the preceding decades more and more food had been imported, in particular wheat from the USA. An initial outbreak of panic-buying after war was declared soon slowed down, but a sense of unease continued. Shortages of food and other necessities meant that prices rose. Bread had more than doubled in price by May 1915, and in Epping there were food protests by people who believed that the rich were getting more than their fair share. The German blockade brought a shortage of sugar and several people in west Essex were prosecuted for hoarding it or using it inappropriately although if anyone in Nazeing committed similar misdemeanours, they got away with it. Early in 1918 the Government reluctantly brought in rationing and identity cards for sugar and other food but nobody was satisfied; most people felt that distribution was still unfair and farmers complained that they were not getting a fair return on their work. Wages increased however so, for example, the earnings of Nazeing Common's pindar (shepherd) trebled from 16s per week in 1914 to 48s in 1919, before dropping back to 36s.

---

42 This paragraph based on http://www.essexrecordofficeblog.co.uk/document-of-the-month-september-2017-farming-and-national-survival-in-the-first-world-war. Accessed 5 Sept 2017

By 1915 German U-boats were sinking one in four merchant ships and there was a shortage of male labourers and horses, so the Government wanted three million acres of grass to be ploughed up for arable, including 85,000 acres in Essex. The Board of Agriculture set up county War Agricultural Committees to encourage increased productivity. The Essex 'War Ag' census in 1916 found that there were 3,200 acres of farmland in Nazeing, of which 2,662 acres (83%) were grass. One farmer who made the change and did very well out of it was David Pegrum: village gossip reported by Ted Coleman said that he 'made enough money from a field of oats to buy Greenleaves'. In 1916 he had 170 acres of grass, 36 of spring wheat and 24 of 'other arable' but presumably switched more later.

The case of Arthur Hutchings from Galley Hill Lane shows the kinds of hardship that were being endured during the war. He was a farm labourer aged thirty-five in 1916, when he was summonsed and fined 2s 6d for not sending his child to school. His wife said that he was suffering from heart disease so she had to go to work to keep their six children. She asked if she could keep the child because she wanted to go haymaking but the Chairman of the Bench, E.J. Wythes of Copped Hall, insisted that she must send the child to school. The Clerk, G.J. Creed, seems to have had some sympathy and suggested that the School Managers should be approached but the school attendance officer said they had already refused permission. W.C. Waller said 'it seemed to be an exceptional case' and Creed said he would communicate with the Vicar of Nazeing, who was one of the Managers.

Many farm labourers volunteered early in the war but some younger men stayed because their labour was needed. By 1916 when conscription was introduced, there were only eighty farm workers in Nazeing, compared with 129 before the war[43]. After that, most of the males working on the land were too young or too old to fight. Boys of twelve were allowed to work an eight-hour day for the six weeks of harvest and were to be paid 3s 6d a week. Arable farming is more labour intensive than dairy so the shortage of labour was partly met by women. Very little information about them has survived and the only Nazeing land girl whose name we know is Dorothy Savage, who was born on a Nottinghamshire farm and came to work for David Pegrum at Greenleaves.

Altogether 1,000 men and 1,500 women worked at the Gunpowder Factory in Waltham Abbey, but we know only of a few from Nazeing. Because the factory brought jobs and money, local people may have had rather less hardship than elsewhere in Essex.

Conscription and Exemption

At first volunteers provided all the manpower needed, but the appalling rate of losses was such that in 1916 a reluctant government was forced to bring in conscription. Men aged between eighteen and forty-one were called up but it was clear that the national interest would require some men to be exempt. The government set up a tribunal system based on local-authority districts.

Nazeing men appeared at the Epping tribunal, which was chaired by Roger Campbell Lyall, a retired barrister from Harlow. Three panel members were farmers: William Bird from Great Parndon, Hugh William Hart from North Weald and Robert Cecil Savill from Chigwell. Savill was the son of the founder of the well-known property firm, and in the Great War his brother Edwin was appointed

---

43   1911 census and 1916 Essex War Agricultural Committee census. The figures were not compiled on exactly the same basis but the general trend is unmistakeable.

by the War Office to assess compensation to landowners in Essex and
Suffolk for loss of or damage to property.[44] The other members were
Frederick Thomas Basham, a retired hotel proprietor from Harlow
and W.S. Chisenhale-Marsh, a landed proprietor of Gaynes Park in
Theydon Garnon. The panel was also attended by the Epping Rural
District clerk, R.E. Trotter, and by Major William Henry Goschen
of Sheering, a retired Army officer who was entitled to appeal if
he thought a man had been treated too leniently. The presence of
three farmers on the panel might have made this seem likely but,
in fact, they seem to have been quite strict in refusing exemptions.
Of the panel, only Goschen and Savill were under fifty-five years
old. The proceedings of the Epping tribunals were reported in the
Chelmsford Chronicle and the *Essex Newsman*, and the Nazeing cases
give a good idea of the factors taken into consideration.

Farming was a reserved occupation of national importance, so
farmers were exempt. Joe Pegrum's son David was by then farming
Greenleaves and Darmers in his own right but Thomas Nicholls
of Parvills had to apply for exemption for his son Bert, who was
working as his foreman, and it was granted. Ernest Mansfield lived
at Marshgate Farm and worked on his own account, but mainly as a
hay carter rather than a farmer; in September 1916 he was given a six-
week extension to deal with the harvest but then had to go. Clearly
the skills of a shepherd were also regarded as important because the
Trustees of Nazeing Wood or Park obtained an exemption for their
pindar, Henry Gentry, and Joe Pegrum likewise for his shepherd,
James May.

One of the main bones of contention was the extent to which
landowners and farmers could get exemption for their less skilled men;
one claimed that 'it was more important that they should be retained

---

44 http://www.savills.co.uk/about-savills/history.

here producing food than that they should be sent to the trenches'. However, few labourers gained an exemption. Although Thomas Nicholls obtained one for his son, he was unsuccessful for his carter, James Canning. In June 1916 Henry James Starling and James Sadler were given temporary exemptions until after the harvest but then they had to go; Starling was a steam sawyer on Ralph Palmer's estate, and Sadler, Walter Hargreaves' chauffeur, was described as a horsekeeper. Archdale Palmer held on to Percy Mussell for a while, although Mussell appears on the schedule of enlisted men, so presumably he went later.

The workings of the system are well illustrated by the case of Edward James Fowler, the vet. He appealed on behalf of his managing stockman, William Thomas Turner, who was aged twenty-seven and single. Turner was the only man living at Mamelons Farm where Fowler sent his horses when they wanted rest. There were 41½ acres growing a large quantity of hay. Fowler 'could only get down himself on Sundays, and it was impossible to get another man with veterinary knowledge to fill the place'. A Captain Howard, presumably substituting for Major Goschen, suggested that the hay production was just a side line, but Fowler replied: 'It is more than that now. There is very little veterinary business doing.' The tribunal agreed with Howard and dismissed the appeal, the chairman stating that 'they regarded it as a side line and not a business essential to the national interest'.

Some individuals such as Charles Judd the builder appealed on their own behalf, in his case on personal grounds related to the business. It was stated that his partner, Ted Coleman, would be in a later group, so the case would be adjourned to see whether he appealed. The tribunal stated that one of the pair would have to go and Coleman did, without any recorded appeal.

Conscientious objectors were often the subject of abuse and showed great courage, though of a different type from those in the Forces.

William Frederick Whitton (1885-1949) was a member of the Plymouth Brethren and had been a preacher for eight years so refused to be conscripted. He told the tribunal that, as a follower of the Prince of Peace, he could not act against his conscience by taking part in efforts to take life but would be willing to help his country in any other way. Major Goschen described him as 'the best conscientious objector he had seen and an honest man' and recommended him for ambulance work. It was most unusual for a conscientious objector to be given as much respect as Whitton, so he must have been exceptionally impressive. There is, however, no record that he served with the Friends' Ambulance Service, which included non-Quaker pacifists. The next we know of him is in 1921 when his son was born in Wiltshire, where Whitton lived with his family until his death.

Trenches and Volunteers

When war broke out, men began to offer their services for home duties and the government decided to channel their enthusiasm into county-based volunteer forces. Much as with 'Dad's Army' in the Second World War, they were made up of men too young and too old for the forces and those with 'genuine reason' not to serve.[45] As early as 1859, the government had initiated the London Defence Scheme, which was intended to protect the capital from possible invasion. Work was intermittent but the scheme was resurrected when war actually came. Plans for a stop line in the form of a trench that would originally have ended at Epping were adapted and it was decided to extend it through Nazeing to the River Lea. The Middlesex Volunteer Regiment was deployed to do the work.[46]

---

45 SAINSBURY, J.D. Herts V.R. Welwyn, Hart Books, 2005.
46 https://www.victorianforts.co.uk/redan/lmc.htm

The Volunteer Reserve A Company was formed for the districts of Friern Barnet, Finchley and New Southgate in December 1914. Announcements in the *Hendon & Finchley Times* show that a 'party for instructional camp' left Liverpool Street Station on seven trains on Sunday and Monday, 12 and 13 September 1915, and arrangements were made for luggage to Broxbourne. A special party went to Nazeing on Wednesday 20 October to work on the London Defences, the train leaving Liverpool Street at 8.40am. In 1916 Commandant J. Chandler's battle orders reported that the Southgate Battalion had been detailed to find at least thirty officers and men for the camp at Nazeing, from 10 to 13 February. Names of those who could attend were to be sent to the adjutant at once. The party would proceed on 10 February by the 8.42 from Liverpool Street or by a later train if necessary. Clearly rail travel from Liverpool Street to Broxbourne was essential to the logistics of the exercise.

The government offered compensation to farmers for damage caused by war work, although compensation was 'an Act of Grace' so not automatically given, and farmers had to maintain an officially provided book. We are fortunate to have the book kept by W.J. (Johnny) Hollow of Brewitts Farm. There are entries for four fields, initially made on 29 September 1915, with an update on 1 June 1916. Only four pages of the book are used, one for each field affected, summarised in the table below. Strategic thinking is evident in the choice of a location close to two pubs, the Black Swan at Broadley Common and the Sun (see map on page 333). Parties of volunteers who came to work on the trench were accommodated in a camp at Nine Acres Field. A road was built across Buttfield (opposite the Upper Town School) to the camp and trench.

Name/no. of field	Work done and area of damage	Strength of party	Date
Buttfield no 634	Roadway across field. Roadway not used by carts after Nov 1915 but used as footpath in January 1916 by volunteers		29 Sep [1915] 1 June [1916]
Little Buttfield no 648	Roadway SE corner same as field 634		29 Sep [1915] 1 June [1916]
Ten Acres no 649	Roadway to camp & trench in NE corner	Parties have crossed this field all winter chiefly on Sundays	29 Sep [1915] 1 June [1916]
Nine Acres [No 650]	Road to camp & trench along N& E sides. Road was not used after November 1915	Sundays to Dec 1000. Weekday average 30 to Dec. Parties working on Sundays all winter and work re-constructed in May and June	29 Sep [1915]

By combining information from the compensation book and the newspaper articles, we can deduce that the work began in September 1915, when the 'party for instructional camp' set off for initial training. The work was probably completed in February 1916 with some reconstruction in May and June, perhaps necessitated by the effects of spring weather, but no further work was done. The reference in the compensation book to an average of thirty men working during the week ties in with the requirement in February 1916 of at least thirty men for an additional work party. The fact that the men were volunteers explains why they mostly worked on Sundays, with special arrangements announced through the newspaper. The compensation book's extraordinary figure of a thousand people working every Sunday is not impossible but is not confirmed by any other source and may indicate an attempt to get as much redress as possible for the damage caused. The parish council minutes noted in 1921 that W.J. Hollow eventually received his compensation.

Soon after the Middlesex men left, a new group began coming to Nazeing, this time from the Hertfordshire Volunteer Regiment. The *Hertford Mercury and Reformer* reported that on Sunday 9 July 1916 the Stanstead Abbots Platoon, in company with the Ware and Hoddesdon Platoons, was engaged in trench digging at Nazeing. 'There were 25 men on parade, and they all proved equal to their task, getting through quite a considerable amount of work in the short time they were there.' These three platoons formed No.4 Company of the 1st Battalion (East Herts). On 23 July the Stanstead Abbots Platoon was to parade at 10.15 at St Margaret's Station yard, go by train to Broxbourne, 'and thence march to Nazeing for trench digging'. On 6 October 1916 and 6 January 1917, the *Mercury* printed notices that similar exercises would take place on the following Sundays, 'return by 4.28 train from Broxbourne'. There is something reassuringly British about advertising military activities in the local paper, with a frequent reminder that 'Mid-day rations must be taken'.

No compensation book is known to have survived so we cannot be sure exactly where the trenches were, but there are some clues. The parish council minutes noted that trenches across Tinkers Lane (between Hoe Lane and Roydon Hamlet) were not filled in until three years after the war, when the Government paid £130 for the work to be done. And in 1919 Brigadier-General Sir Hereward Wake claimed '£1,863 out of public funds in respect of loss and damage due to the military occupation of parts of Nazeingbury and Pressfields farms and land'. Pressfields is close to Tinkers Lane and the problem may have been caused by the same trench, but we have no other record of damage at Nazeingbury. The War Office challenged his measurements and offered £1,589, which he accepted. But it was something of a test case on compensation 'in respect of reinstatement of lands excavated and disturbed for defence works purposes' so, despite Sir Hereward's distinguished war record, the Defence of the Realm Losses Commission ruled that he should only have £1,130 plus a less than generous £15 15s costs.

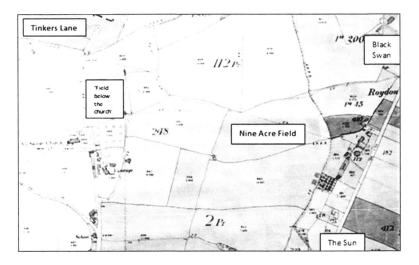

Location of the camp and trenches: map from *Lloyd George Domesday* 1910, based on Ordnance Survey 1896.

At All Saints' Church there is a pair of brass candlesticks, one engraved 'The light shineth in darkness', and the other 'And the darkness comprehended it not – 1917'. The former parish organist Dorothy Wood explained their significance:

> Part of their time was spent practising the digging of trenches in the field below the church. The officer in charge stayed at Church Cottage with Mrs Reynolds, the verger, caretaker, gravedigger etc. being away in France. When the soldiers were posted to the Western Front the officer gave the candlesticks to our church.

Ridges in 'the field below the church' next to Tinkers Lane are still visible but Dorothy was not born until 1926, so she must have been reporting conversation with her parents or their contemporaries. We therefore cannot be sure whether the soldiers were regulars training for the front, or whether in fact the work was being done by the Hertfordshire Volunteers as part of the London Defences.

Marjorie Sykes

Marjorie's reminiscences add a wealth of personal detail to the information from the written sources:

> Country customs and agricultural methods that had been almost unchanged for centuries already before the 1914 war were showing signs of change. The bicycle had arrived and soon became an essential of country life. This proved to be a good thing and just in time, as in the early days of the war, farm horses were commandeered for the Army; most of the young men joined up, and the older men and women, left to fend for themselves, were thankful that they had bikes...

There was, of course, concern about the 'boys' in the front line:

> In every village or town, the chief topic of conversation, the chief interests were the 'boys', the fighting men. It was generally known when each mother or wife heard from them; bad news, and there was plenty of that, spread quickly. Food parcels were sent regularly. Those fighting in France would send pretty postcards with embroideries in silk on finest muslin, but real news was hard to come by. Those home on leave, or recovering from wounds, or trench feet, or gassing, had terrible tales to tell, and many were nervous wrecks, though mostly cheerful before their families.

The absence of so many young men meant that the older ones had to bring in the harvest:

I remember a visit to Nazeing when the war had been on for some time. Hay-making was in its last stages in the back field. Instead of the jolly crowd of hay makers with their hoary old jokes and field picnics, with the beer brought out to them, four old men ... were loading up the final wagon, two on top of the load, two forking it up so that the stack could be made up ready for the winter feed.

They were: her uncle A.J. Pegrum, Jim Pegrum of Curtis Farm, who worked at the gunpowder factory but helped his family with the harvest, Edward Perry of Long Green, A.J's father-in-law, and another. Doubtless the Pegrum cousins seemed old to Marjorie but they were actually in their forties!

The haycart. This photo taken by Marjorie's father
is not the occasion she described, but A.J. is on
the cart and it would have been similar.

Nazeing people suffered hardship as well:

> The war seemed endless. When it began, many said it would be
> over by Christmas, but it actually landed us in a weary drag for
> over four years that seemed like an eternity.
> *Each new morn*
> *New widows howl, new orphans cry, new sorrows*
> *Strike Heaven on the face*[47]
> When it did come to an end in November 1918, we could hardly
> believe that we were no longer at war, without the men folk, with
> constant worry and anxiety. But peace brings problems and the old
> days and scenes were over. Bicycles, cars, even aeroplanes had come,
> and the role of women had changed… The bad old days had gone
> – but so had a whole heap of good customs and personal contacts.

There are more of Marjorie's war reminiscences in *Seventeen Miles
from Town*, pages 79-83.

To and from the Western Front
Bandages and garments for the sick and wounded
Bandages and bedclothes for soldiers in hospital were almost all
hand-made by groups and individuals world-wide, often paying for
the materials out of their own pockets. Their work is an example of
the importance of voluntary effort during the Great War. A Work
Party was formed in Nazeing and was registered by Mrs Elizabeth
Green from Collyers. Many ladies from the village would have been
involved. The group provided their own materials and received regular
information as to immediate hospital requirements. Home Workers
qualified for the Central Work Rooms Certificate and a Volunteer
Worker Badge by sending in 50 approved garments or 100 bandages.

---

47 *Macbeth*, Act IV, scene 3: Macduff to Malcolm, describing death and
    destruction in the land – a very appropriate quotation.

Emily Cook's certificate for her voluntary work.

Silk cards from the soldiers

Marjorie Sykes recalled that 'Those fighting in France would send pretty postcards with embroideries in silk on finest muslin'. Before the Great War, convents in Belgium and Northern France had embroidered church vestments and commercial articles to provide financial support for their ministry. After 1915, they organised refugee workers to embroider war-themed souvenir 'memory' items which were sent to 'finishing factories' for mass cutting and then incorporated into postcards. The cards became enormously popular with British soldiers who wanted a 'souvenir' of their war involvement which would express their strong feelings of love and patriotism and mark special occasions. These postcards were rarely posted in the open mail but sent home to loved ones in 'Blighty' via courier, having been approved by an Official Censor who initialled each card. There were no stamps on the cards because troops were entitled to free postage.

Emily Cook, the postmaster's daughter, received four silk cards which all said *'Fabrication française'* [made in France], including one from her next door neighbour and future brother-in-law Arthur Mead. It was probably sent shortly after the death on 5 June 1916 of the Secretary of State for War, Lord Kitchener, who was one of over 600 people who died when *H.M.S. Hampshire* struck a German mine. It has the following message:

Dear E, Just a P.C. hoping that it will find you & M. & F. in the pink as it leaves me in one. What bad news it is of poor Lord K[itchener]. I met in B[oulogne] here the other day Biles who used to be butler at Bury's. He is in E.F.C. [Expeditionary Force Canteen]. I thought perhaps you would like one of these P. C. for your a[lbum]. How are all the Nazeing people keeping, quite alright I hope. Remember me to all I know. Love Arthur.

Silk postcard from Arthur Mead

James Biles died of wounds on 29 June 1918 (see page 355).

Emily also received an ordinary postcard dated 26 Aug 1915 from Harry Mead, who she later married, showing 'The ruined Chateau VERMELLES Pas de Calais'. The censor has made an ineffectual attempt to cover the name of Vermelles, which was later to become the site of a British war cemetery. Harry wrote:

Dear Emily, just a PC to let you know I'm still in the land of the living & quite well, having a very quiet time at present. The weather is glorious after the rain last week, everyone busy harvesting at home I suppose, you ought to see the French women gathering in the corn hard at it all day. Tell your father I hope to soon be able to split that bottle with him. Kind Regards to all,

    yrs sincerely, H.

War postcard from Harry Mead

Chapter 36

Nazeing Men Who Died in the Great War[48]

The 28 Men Whose Names Appear on
the Memorials and Enlisted Rolls

Name	Unit	Date of death	Age
Alfred Brooks	Hertfordshire Regt	27 September 1917	31
Albert Henry Burton	Royal Fusiliers	23 April 1917	22
Ernest George Coleman	County of London Regt	30 December 1915	24
James Edward Field	Royal Sussex Regt	4 June 1916	33
Frederick John Flack	King's Royal Rifle Corps	16 September 1917	25
James Flack	Manchester Regt	31 July 1917	40
Henry Edwin Green	London Regt	13 October 1916	28
John Hale	Royal Sussex Regt	13 November 1916	30
Alfred Harman	Norfolk Regt	5 April 1917	18
Alan Archibald Johnson	Royal Naval Volunteer Reserve	30 December 1917	22
George William Mansfield	Northamptonshire Regt	2 November 1917	23
Ernest Myson	Bedfordshire Regt	17 November 1915	34

---

48 This chapter is based on research by Doug Ball.

Joseph Nicholls	Middlesex Regt	12 March 1918	35
Harold Parsons	Royal West Kent Regt	22 September 1918	36
Wilfred Pegrum	Machine Gun Corps	1 December 1917	22
Charles Perry	London Regt	30 April 1918	20
David Ernest Pigg	Royal Naval Air Service	4 July 1917	22
Robert David Smith or Turner	Welsh Regt	24 June 1917	24

[*Shown separately on Nazeing Memorials and Rolls of Honour but they are the same person*]

Frederick Snell	Royal Sussex Regt	21 September 1918	20
John Victor Starling	King's Shropshire Light Infantry	9 April 1917	30
Frederick Thurlow	Royal Navy	30 December 1915	24
Charles Arthur Turner	Middlesex Regt	4 October 1917	30
George Turner	East Kent Regt	8 August 1917	23
Sidney Turner	Royal Navy	1 January 1915	22
Frank William Watts	Bedfordshire Regt	16 March 1915	27
Eric George Wellesley	Yorkshire Regt	21 December 1915	18
Ronald Arthur Wellesley	Canadian Expeditionary Force	19 September 1914	19
Joseph Samuel Wright	Bedfordshire Regt	27 July 1916	34

Men with Nazeing Connections Not Listed on Memorials

Cuthbert Frederick Biggs	Rifle Brigade	15 April 1918	22
James Biles	Gloucestershire Regt	29 June 1918	32
Norman Elce Bugg	Royal Engineers	14 July 1916	23
William Charles Norton	Royal Fusiliers	24 November 1915	44
Harold Emerson Rose	Royal Army Medical Corps	7 July 1917	31

Alfred Brooks was born in 1885, son of John Brooks and Lucy née Wheal, of Stanford-le-Hope, Essex. The 1911 census shows that he was a boarder at 20 Rumbold Road, Rye Park. He married Mary Ellis on 22 April 1911 when he was a cab driver and she was a domestic servant aged twenty-two. He enlisted in Hertford, served as Private 266369, Hertfordshire Regiment in France and Flanders and was killed in action on 27 September 1917. His next of kin were recorded as his parents and his wife Mary Ann of 3 Council Houses, Nazeing. His name appears on the Tyne Cot Memorial (Panel 153), Zonnebeke, West-Vlaanderen, Belgium. In the Congregational Church minute book there is only an H. Brookes, which is probably an error. An A. Brooks appears on the Hoddesdon war memorial.

Albert Henry Burton was born 22 April 1895, son of James George, labourer and Annie Elizabeth née Thurgood. In 1901 the family was in Kenners Lane with his father a horse keeper on a farm. The 1911 census shows that he was a cowman on a farm, living in Back Lane, Nazeing, with his parents, eight siblings and grandfather. Albert enlisted in Mill Hill and served initially as Private 39314, Queens West Surrey Regiment and then as Private 62937 7th Battalion, Royal Fusiliers in

France and Flanders. He was killed in action on 23 April 1917, a day after his twenty-second birthday. His death was registered as Henry Albert Burton with his parents as next-of-kin. The Nazeing memorials and enlisted rolls show him as A, A H or Albert H Burton. He is commemorated on Bay 3 of the Arras Memorial, Pas de Calais, France.

Ernest George Coleman

Ernest George Coleman was born in Nazeing in the summer of 1891, the youngest son of Alfred and Sarah (see Chapter 9). In 1911 he was a farm labourer/cowman and living with his parents at Darmers. He enlisted in Bermondsey and served as Serjeant 2054, 1st/22nd Battalion, County of London Regiment (The Queens) in France and Flanders. He was killed in action on 30 December 1915 and family tradition says that he was blown up while tunnelling. His body was not recovered and he is commemorated on Panel 130 of the Loos Memorial, Pas de Calais, France.

James Edward Field was born at Waltham Abbey in 1883, son of Charles Reuben, labourer and Mary Sophia née Cant, and was baptised at All Saints' on 6 April 1884. In 1891 the family lived in Back Lane but by 1901 the parents had moved to Motts (now Walnut Tree Cottages) in Middle Street with James and seven daughters. James and his father were both listed as haybinders on a farm in 1901 and as general farm labourers in 1911. James enlisted in Nazeing and served as Private SD/5531, 14th Battalion, Royal Sussex Regiment and died on 4 June 1916, when his next of kin were his father and late mother. One record states that he died of wounds at home but the death certificate states that he was 'Found dead apparently from drowning in the River Lea... but as to how he came into the said river, and so met his death, there was no evidence to show.' He was buried at All Saints' on 9 June 1916 in the old churchyard (IV/116). The grave has a Commonwealth War Graves Commission headstone with his rank, name, regiment, date of death and age below the badge.

James Flack was born in 1877, in Chrishall, Essex, son of John and Rachel Flack who moved to Nazeing in 1893. He married Lizzie Smith in 1904 and in 1911 they were living at Southside in Back Lane with their two children and his widowed mother. James worked in market gardening and enlisted in Nazeing. He served as Private 41662, 17th Battalion, Manchester Regiment in France and Flanders and was killed in action on 31 July 1917, the first day of the Battle of Passchendaele. Although his name is on enlisted rolls and other Nazeing memorials, it was omitted from the tablet near the lychgate (see page 362), possibly because of confusion with his nephew, Frederick John. It has now been added to the list of names read out at the annual Remembrance Service.

```
┌─────────────────────────────────────────────────────┐
│         Awarded "The Military Medal."                 │
│                                                        │
│   Surname          F lack                              │
│                                                        │
│   Christian Name     F  J                              │
│                                                        │
│   Rank             Pte                                 │
│                                                        │
│   Corps    7ᵗʰ Bn. K.R.R.C                             │
│                                                        │
│   Regimental Number  R/38188                           │
│                                                        │
│   Date of Gazette         2 - NOV 1917                 │
│                                                        │
│   Registered Paper  68/121/295        108633           │
│                                                        │
│   68/Gen. No./2730 (M.S. 3).                           │
└─────────────────────────────────────────────────────┘
```

Frederick John Flack was born in 1892 in Chrishall, Essex, son of Dennis John and Bethia née Player who in 1906 moved to Nazeing via Walthamstow. In 1911 Frederick was living at Profits Hill Cottages in Back Lane with his parents, five sisters and a baby brother. He was the nephew of James Flack and had a similar job – nursery worker (domestic). At All Saints' on 16 January 1915 he married Phoebe May Myson, whose brother Ernest also died in the war. He enlisted in Epping, initially as Rifleman TR/13/1832, 16th Battalion, King's Royal Rifle Corps but later became Rifleman R/38188, 7th Battalion, serving in France and Flanders. He died of wounds on 16 September 1917, six weeks after his uncle, and is buried in the Trois Arbres Cemetery, Steenwerck, Nord, France, Plot I.Y. 29. He received the Military Medal, which is awarded for acts of gallantry and devotion to duty under fire, and is the non-commissioned officers' equivalent of the Military Cross.

Henry Edwin Green   John Hale

Henry Edwin Green was the son of Frederick William and Elizabeth Louisa of Collyers (see Chapter 5). He served as Captain, 22nd Battalion, London Regiment and died of wounds on 13 October 1916, aged twenty-eight. He is buried in the Dernancourt Communal Cemetery Extension, Somme, France, Plot III G.47.

John Hale, son of William and Caroline née Brace, was born in Nazeing in 1886, and lived with them at Riddens View (see Chapter 16). He enlisted in Warley and served as Private G/15442, 12th Battalion, Royal Sussex Regiment, in the British Expeditionary Force. He died of wounds on 13 November 1916 and is buried in the Puchevilliers British Cemetery, Somme, France, Plot VI A.18.

Alfred Harman is included on the enlisted rolls and the memorials in Nazeing, but initially no information was found which would link him to any family in Nazeing. However, he is possibly Alfred Elijah Harman, son of Alfred John and Elizabeth née Skiffington, who married in Hoxton in 1896 and moved to Walthamstow about

1903. The 1911 census shows him living with his parents at 72 Hartington Road. He enlisted at Epping and was recorded as being of 5 Rensburg Road Walthamstow, Private 27791 of the Norfolk Regiment. He died of bronchitis aged eighteen, while on home service at the Herman de Stern Hospital, a convalescent home on the sea front at Felixstowe, which was attached to the London Hospital. Alfred is buried in Plot B1042, Queen's Road Cemetery, Walthamstow. He could have come to Nazeing under the scheme whereby London children were given a taste of the countryside, which may be why he enlisted at Epping.

Alan Archibald Johnson was included on the enlisted roll at All Saints' with the rank of Captain and on the memorials in Nazeing. He was born 5 December 1894 in Australia, son of Mrs Leura J. Johnson, who had married Duncan McIntyre Johnson in Melbourne in 1887 and divorced him in 1908, going on to marry Charles B. D'Arcy at Marylebone in 1920. Leura is the name of a town in New South Wales and is occasionally used as a forename, but by 1919 she seems to have settled for Laura, more familiar to the British. On the 1911 census she was shown as the manageress of a tea-room at 70 Marylebone High Street, while Alan was a boarder at Cranleigh, a public school near Guildford. He was a Temporary Lieutenant with Drake Battalion in the Royal Naval Volunteer Reserve, which was formed from Royal Navy and Royal Marine reservists and volunteers who were not needed for service at sea. He died on 30 December 1917 and is commemorated on the Thiepval Memorial, Pier and Face 1A. Probate was granted to Laura Jean D'Arcy on 11 September 1920 when his address was shown as Elm Cottage [Wheelers], Nazeing, and his estate amounted to £148 16s.

George William Mansfield, son of Charles Thomas Mansfield and Matilda Susan née Burton, was born in 1894 at Broadley Common, so is sometimes listed as born in Nazeing and sometimes in Roydon.

He was the cousin of Herbert Charles Mansfield, who would later marry Nellie Starling. The 1911 census shows him working as a labourer on the golf course and living with his grandparents George and Jane Burton in Betts Lane, though listed as a boarder. He enlisted in Enfield and served as Private 39275, 1st/4th Battalion, Northamptonshire Regiment in Palestine. After home training he sailed for Lemnos and on 15 August 1915 landed at Suvla Bay in the Gallipoli campaign. He went via Egypt to Palestine where he was killed in action on 12 November 1917, probably at night. He was buried in the Gaza War Cemetery, Israel Plot XV C.3. The National Roll of the Great War gives his address as 16 Kemble Road, Tottenham. His name was omitted from the tablet at the Congregational Church but was added in June 1997. In 1911 his parents were living in Hoddesdon and he is also listed on the memorial there.

Ernest Myson was born in Nazeing in 1881. He was the son of Frederick, labourer, and Phoebe Susan née Samuels, who were both born in Great Parndon. In 1880 the family moved to Rose Cottage in Back Lane, where Frederick was a hay carter and later a garden labourer. In 1906 Ernest married Florrie Hardy of Haslemere in Surrey and went to live there. The 1911 census shows him as a coal merchant's foreman, living with Florrie, their two sons and her brother, listed as a boarder. Ernest enlisted in Guildford, Surrey and served as Sergeant 3/8400, 8th Battalion, Bedfordshire Regiment. He was drowned at sea from the hospital ship *H.M.S. Anglia*, sunk by a mine off Dover on 17 November 1915. He is commemorated on the Hollybrook memorial, Southampton, Hampshire.

Joseph Nicholls was born in Nazeing in 1883. He was the son of John William Nicholls and Jane née Withers who lived at King Harold Cottage (see page 96). By 1901 Joseph was a stockman on a farm and in 1911 he was a farm labourer/coachman. He enlisted in

Nazeing and served initially as Private 30972 Essex Regiment and then as Private G/51489, 2nd/10th Battalion, Middlesex Regiment also known as Duke of Cambridge's Own. He was killed in action in Egypt on 12 March 1918 and was buried in the Jerusalem Cemetery, Israel, Plot L.46.

Harold Parsons was born in 1881 at St George, Barton Regis, now part of Bristol. He was the son of John Parsons, a railway plate layer, and Emily née Robertson. They had both died by the time he was seven and in 1891 he was in an orphanage at Yoxall in Staffordshire. Censuses list him in service in Paddington, in 1901 as a footman and in 1911 as a butler. In 1915 he married Gertrude Amelia Horne in her native Hungerford, Berkshire, although she had previously been in service in Hampshire and Somerset. He enlisted in Enfield and was living there while Gertrude was at Windlesham in Surrey. In 1918 they moved to Keysers Lane and are listed on the electoral register. Harold probably knew that their daughter Bertha Winifred was born on 12 July, but he may never have seen her because he was killed in action on 22 September 1918. He served in the Queen's Own Royal Kent Regiment and is buried at Unicorn Cemetery, Vendhuile, Plot I.C.20. His initial is correctly given as 'H' in the Congregational minute book but on the memorial there he is called Walter, an error that was repeated on the Roll of Honour at All Saints'.

Wilfred Pegrum was born in Nazeing in 1895, son of Alfred and Sarah Ann née Curtis (see Chapter 8). He enlisted in Nazeing and served, initially as Private 7666 2nd Dragoon Guards, and then as Private 47675, 25th Company, Machine Gun Corps (Infantry) in France and Flanders. He was killed in action on 1 December 1917 and is commemorated on the Tyne Cot Memorial, Zonnebekke, West-Vlaanderen, Belgium. Panels 154-159 & 163A.

Charles Perry was born in Nazeing in 1898, the son of Walter Charles, labourer, and Eliza née Cordell. By 1901, when they lived in Back Lane, Walter was a labourer at the gunpowder factory. In 1911 Charles was at school, living in Longyard with his widowed grandmother, Emma King Cordell. He enlisted in Camden Town and served as Corporal 610975, 2nd/19th Battalion, London Regiment in the Egyptian Expeditionary Force. He was killed in action on 30 April 1918 and is commemorated on the Jerusalem Memorial, Panels 47–53.

David Ernest Pigg was born in 1894 at Poplar in London, the son of James and Elizabeth Pigg, who came originally from Essex. In 1911 David was assisting in the family dairy business, living with his parents, four siblings and a boarder at 6 Grand Parade, Streatham Lane, Mitcham. They moved in 1914 to take on a small dairy farm at Mulberries, the home address shown on David's death certificate. David served as Air Mechanic 1st Class F/4376, Kite Balloon Section, Royal Naval Air Service. He died on 4 July 1917 in the Royal Naval Hospital, Shotley, Suffolk, after being injured on the foreshore by enemy aircraft. He was buried in Shotley St. Mary Churchyard, R.N. Plot 127.

Robert David Smith or Turner was born in 1892 at Bishops Stortford. He enlisted in Epping and served as Private 54911, 16th Battalion, Welsh Regiment in France and Flanders. He died of wounds on 24 June 1917 and is buried in Bard Cottage Cemetery, Leper, West-Vlaanderen, Belgium, Plot II. H. 13. On the 1911 census, Arthur Smith of St Lawrence Farm listed his nineteen-year-old grandson as Robert Turner then crossed out 'Turner' and substituted 'Smith'. Robert's mother was unmarried when he was born and evidently one of the Smith family was his father, but her surname was Miller, not Turner. Although the Commonwealth War Graves Commission records list Robert as Smith, some Nazeing ones show him as Turner and some as Smith. After the war, Robert was shown on Nazeing war memorials as Robert D Turner then, in the 1990s, Robert D

Smith was added to the memorials - before it was realised that he and Robert D Turner were the same man. To add further confusion, a Robert Smith from Back Lane also served, but survived. The change of surname remains a mystery.[49]

Frederick Snell was born on 13 August 1898, the son of William James, gardener, and Julia née Mead. The 1911 census shows him at school, living at Harknetts Gate with his parents, older brother and grandmother Emma Mead, described as a 'visitor'. He was born in Broadley Common as were his father and older brother William. Frederick enlisted in Epping and served as Private G/16944, 7th Battalion, Royal Sussex Regiment in the British Expeditionary Force. He was killed in action on 21 September 1918. He was buried in Epehy Wood Farm Cemetery, Epehy, Somme, France, Plot III. J. 17 and is also commemorated on the family headstone in All Saints' old churchyard II/157.

---

49   There is a fuller account of Robert's change of name in the Nazeing History Workshop Archive.

John Victor Starling was born in Nazeing in 1887, the son of William Starling and Elizabeth Purkis (see page 117). The 1911 census shows John as a horse keeper on a farm, living at The Rookery with his parents, two brothers and a boarder. He married Elizabeth Tucker in 1912 and their daughter Iris May Starling was born in 1913. He enlisted in Waltham Abbey and served initially in France and Flanders as Private 40002, Suffolk Regiment and then as Private 20835, 5th Battalion, Kings Shropshire Light Infantry. He died of wounds on 9 April 1917 and was buried in Beaurains Road Cemetery, Pas de Calais, France, Plot B. 12. His family were living at Lily Cottage, King's Head Hill, Chingford, Essex.

Frederick Thurlow was born at Motts (now Walnut Tree Cottages) on 18 November 1891, the son of farm labourer George Thurlow and Emily née Armer. The 1911 census shows him as a farm labourer, living with his parents and two brothers at Motts. He was a Stoker 1st Class SS/112179 on *H.M.S. Natal*, an armoured cruiser which was part of the Second Cruiser Squadron. She was lying at Cromarty on 30 December 1915, when a fire caused a huge explosion and she sank with the loss of twenty-five officers and 380 ratings.[50] Frederick is commemorated on the Chatham Naval Memorial, Panel 12.

Charles Arthur Turner was born in Nazeing on 29 November 1886, the son of Arthur, blacksmith and Mary Ann née Dellar. In 1891 the family were at Motts, neighbours of the Thurlows. The 1911 census shows Charles as a labourer at the gunpowder factory, living with his parents and six siblings at Motts. He enlisted in Nazeing, initially as Private 4335, Essex Regiment and then as Private G/34320, 3rd/10th Battalion Middlesex Regiment, also known as the Duke of Cambridge's Own, serving in France and Flanders.

---

50 Information from Keith Langridge of Western Front Association, Essex Branch.

He was killed in action on 4 October 1917, two months after his younger brother George, and is commemorated on the Tyne Cot Memorial, Zonnebeke, West-Vlaanderen, Belgium, Panels 113-115.

George Turner, brother of Charles Arthur Turner, was born in Nazeing in 1894 and in 1911 was a labourer, living with his parents and siblings. He enlisted in Waltham Abbey, initially as Private 30943, 14th Battalion, Essex Regiment and then as Private 18930 6th Battalion the East Kent Regiment, also known as the Buffs, serving in France and Flanders. He died of wounds on 8 August 1917 and was buried at the Niederzwehren Cemetery, Germany, Plot IX. 5.

Sidney Turner was born on 30 May 1893, brother of Charles Arthur and George, and in 1911 he too was a labourer living with his parents and siblings. He served as Stoker First Class SS/112450, Royal Navy and was killed on *H.M.S. Formidable* in an action with an enemy submarine on 1 January 1915. Like his neighbour Frederick Thurlow, he is commemorated on the Chatham Naval Memorial, Panel 12.

Frank William Watts was born in 1887 at Sherington in Buckinghamshire, the son of Thomas and Lucy née Wright, who were both born in the county. By 1901 they were living at Langridge Farm, where Thomas was a horsekeeper. Frank, then a thirteen-year-old farm labourer, was temporarily in Hertford General Infirmary. In 1911 he was a soldier in G Company, 2nd Battalion, Bedfordshire Regiment, serving in Hamilton, Bermuda. He enlisted in Hertford and served as Private 8854, 1st Battalion, Bedfordshire Regiment in France and Flanders. He was killed in action on 16 March 1915 and is commemorated on the Ypres (Menin Gate) Memorial, West-Vlaanderen, Belgium, Panels 31 and 33.

The lives of *Ronald Arthur Wellesley* and *Eric George Wellesley* are described in detail in Chapter 4. Ronald was buried in the

Quebec City (Mount Hermon) Cemetery, Plot S.G.G. 9996. Eric is commemorated on the Ploegsteert Memorial, Comines-Warneton, Hainault, Belgium, Panel 4.

Joseph Samuel Wright was born Samuel Joseph Wright in Elmdon, Essex, in 1882. He probably reversed his forenames because his father was also a Samuel. In 1911 he was a general labourer, living as a boarder with his sister Minnie Wallis at Queens Cottage in Back Lane. He enlisted in Hertford and served as Private Samuel Joseph Wright 44/7253, 1st Battalion, Bedfordshire Regiment in France and Flanders. He was killed in action on 27 July 1916 and is commemorated on the Thiepval Memorial, Somme, France, Pier and Face 2C. The sequence of his first names is as in the village enlisted rolls and memorials, although the 1911 census and military records list him as Samuel Joseph.

Five other men are not included on any memorials or enlisted rolls in Nazeing but have connections with the village, so their names have been added to the roll of honour read out at the annual Service of Remembrance.

Cuthbert Frederick Biggs was born in 1896 at Amport, Hampshire. The 1911 census shows him at Rushes House in Roydon with his stepfather, John Francis Lawrence, a baker and farmer aged forty-four, brother Hubert aged fourteen, and sister Emily aged thirteen. Cuthbert was employed as a baker but his siblings were still at school. Cuthbert's mother, Francis Ellen Biggs, had married John Lawrence in Staines, Middlesex in 1910, and at the time of the 1911 census was staying with her widowed father, Robert Kite at Broadley Common. Cuthbert served as Lance Corporal S/1181, C Company, 4th Battalion, Rifle Brigade and was killed in action on 15 April 1918 aged twenty-two. His name appears on the Doiran Memorial in Greece, and on the Roydon village war memorial opposite St Peter's church.

Army records show Cuthbert's next of kin as his mother and his stepfather John Lawrence of Warwick House, Bumbles Green. The Lawrence/Biggs/Kite family could have been briefly at Warwick House in the war because nobody was listed there on the 1915 electoral register. On the 1918 register John and 'Ellen Francis' Lawrence were again at Rushes House, while Warwick House was occupied by Martha Pegrum but she later moved to the new council houses and Cuthbert's grandfather Robert Kite returned to Warwick House.

James Biles was born in 1885 at Eastleach in Gloucestershire where the 1891 census shows him living with parents Henry, a farm labourer, and Angelina née Barrett. Henry died in 1899 and James went to live with his uncle George Biles, a carter on a farm, in the nearby hamlet of Horcott in the village of Kempsford, Gloucestershire. James was described in 1901 as a 'house boy', so may already have been in service, and in 1911 he was butler to Anna and Ralph Bury at St Leonards. He enlisted at North Finchley and initially served with the Expeditionary Force Canteen, a forerunner of the NAAFI. He transferred to the 12th (Service) (Bristol) Battalion of his native Gloucestershire Regiment and died of wounds on 29 June 1918. He was buried at the Tannay British Cemetery, Tiennes, France, Plot 3, Row F, Grave 8.

Norman Elce Bugg was born in Nazeing in 1894, the son of Robert, a castrator, and Emma Elce née Acres, who married in 1891. Robert was then living with his father Richard at Paynes Farm, but by 1901 he and his family had moved to Stanstead Abbots. On the 1911 census Norman was listed as a stockbroker's clerk, at 113 Victoria Road, Romford as the grandson of Harriett Acres. He enlisted in London and served as Corporal 143078, 4th Battalion, Special Brigade, Royal Engineers in France and Flanders. He may have used his mother's maiden name because his death is registered as Norman E Acres, although other records show his surname as

Bugg. He was killed in action on 14 July 1916 and is buried in the Berles Position Military Cemetery, Plot D.14.

William Charles Norton was born in the City of London in 1870 and married Victoria Adrina Louie Groves at St Matthew Upper Clapton in 1904. In 1911 they were living at 164 Dalston Lane Hackney, and he was a foreman cabinet-maker. In October 1914, aged forty-four, he volunteered for the army and became an officer's servant with the 30th (City of London) Reserve Battalion of the Royal Fusiliers. On 24 November 1915 he took his own life in a hotel room in Leamington where the regiment was posted. He told the man with whom he was billeted that his life 'had been made a hell on earth by bullying on the part of non-commissioned officers'. The NCOs denied the charge and the jury returned a verdict of suicide whilst of unsound mind, exonerating the officers from any blame. He was described as a veterinary surgeon's assistant, so must have been working for Edward Fowler whose Hackney practice was in Dalston Lane. Victoria was Norton's next of kin and her address was given as Mamelons, Fowler's Nazeing home and premises where Norton may well have worked. A week later in Hackney she gave birth to Ruth Winifred Norton, their only child after ten years of marriage.

Harold Emerson Rose was born in Bristol in 1886, son of John Alfred and Clara. The 1911 census shows him as a medical student, living at 110 Chesterfield Road, Bristol, with his parents, two siblings and a servant. Harold served as a Captain in Royal Army Medical Corps attached to 2nd Battalion, Coldstream Guards, and died of wounds on 7 July 1917. He was buried in Canada Farm Cemetery, Ieper, West-Vlaanderen, Belgium, Plot I.B. 5. Harold had lived at The Limes, Wormley, with his wife Patty Elizabeth Rose, née Martha Elizabeth Green. She was the niece of F.W. Green and stayed with her uncle at Collyers for several years.

Chapter 37

Remembrance

Nazeing's Four War Memorials

Commemoration

When the war ended there was a profound desire throughout the nation to commemorate those who sacrificed their lives for the common good. Memorials were erected in towns and villages usually consisting of a Cross of Sacrifice and a list of the men to be commemorated. There was no central government organisation or funding and local arrangements varied widely.

Less than three weeks after the war ended, a special Nazeing Parish Meeting resolved to erect a memorial which should 'take the form of some work of public utility of advantage to the Parish' and a Memorial Committee was formed. The preference was for a scheme to prevent the flooding of Nazeing Brook on the road between Greenleaves and Marshgate, first suggested to celebrate the coronation of King George V in 1911.

The Memorial Committee commissioned a survey estimating the total cost at £2,500 to £2,800. The committee thought this 'in excess of what we might reasonably expect to raise', so a second special meeting voted for a more modest scheme costing £850. Walter Hargreaves told the Annual Parish Meeting in March 1919 that 'the matter was in abeyance for a while in order to obtain the relatives' consent to the placing of fallen men's names on the Memorial Bridge', but no more was heard of the scheme.

The Chapel Memorial

The Welcome Home celebrations were held at the Congregational Church rather than All Saints' but the provision of a suitable village memorial for the fallen was not implemented until 1920. Traditionally, the parish church would be expected to take the initiative but since the Reverend Thomas Goddard was quite elderly at the time, he may not have been well enough to organise things. The Chapel, however, had a membership approaching eighty, many of whom were young and enthusiastic. At a church meeting on 12 August 1918, it was reported that Goddard had written to the Chapel suggesting that something should be done about a memorial and asking if they had any ideas. The meeting agreed that the senior deacons should meet Goddard to discuss it.

Nothing else about the memorial appeared in subsequent minutes until a meeting held on 24 October 1919. Joe Pegrum (Chairman) said 'that since the village scheme had apparently fallen through; the time had arrived for the [Congregational] Church to do something and erect some form of memorial to those who had fallen in the war'. At this same meeting, the members discussed what form the memorial should take. David Pegrum proposed, and William Lawrence seconded, that a tablet be erected outside the entrance to the Church. This was carried and David suggested that 'Mr. Edward (Ted) Coleman visit the relatives of those who had fallen and ascertain if they were willing to have the names inscribed on the tablet'. This was carried and a committee was appointed (Joe Pegrum, Ted Coleman and Charles Judd) to look for designs and estimates for a suitable tablet.

At the next church meeting on 28 November 1919, the members were not impressed with the two designs and estimates submitted, and Mrs Florence Wells proposed that other firms should be approached before a decision was made. Letters were read out from gentlemen in the village, stating that they were willing to contribute to the memorial. It was proposed that when a design and estimate had been chosen, the design should be printed on a circular and distributed to encourage further contributions.

At the next meeting on 4 February 1920, some more designs and estimates were produced and the meeting chose that of Messrs Hanchett of Waltham Abbey at a cost of £52 10s, plus the cost of lettering. A hundred circulars were to be printed for collecting donations which Mrs Wells and Mrs Clara Lawrence volunteered to do. In some places, the bereaved had to pay if they wanted the names of their loved ones to be inscribed on the war memorial but the Chapel's initiative in organising a collection ensured that this was not the case in Nazeing.

At a meeting on 17 February 1920, Joe Pegrum said that he had had an interview with Mr. Hanchett who had informed him that due to the increase in the price of stone etc., he would be unable to erect the memorial at the original estimate and that the price would be at least £60 plus lettering. Joe then said that he had told him to 'get on with it' and asked the church to confirm his action. William Payne proposed and Jim Pegrum seconded, that the additional expenditure of £7 10s be granted: carried. This action was typical of Joe Pegrum but he always had the Chapel's interests at heart.

The next meetings, on 11 and 14 March 1920, were dominated by arrangements for the unveiling ceremony and who was to be asked to officiate. 8 May 1920 was chosen as the date and the Reverend Thomas Goddard was asked to take some part in the ceremony although the reports give no indication that he accepted or was even present. It was resolved that handbills should be printed inviting all parishioners to be present at the unveiling ceremony and George Francis promised to undertake the delivering of handbills to every house in the parish.

The Chapel war memorial

On 1 June 1920, at the first Church meeting after the unveiling, the collector of monies, Mrs Lawrence, presented the report on the Memorial Fund as follows:

Receipts: £119-19-0

Expenditure: £75-6-6

                 (£71-0-0 for the stone and £4-6-6 other expenses)

Balance: £44-13-6

After discussion on how best to use the surplus to benefit the village, it was finally decided 'that a bath chair be purchased for the use of any in the village who may be in need of it'. This was approved and the arrangements were left to Mrs Lawrence. It was then agreed 'that two or more seats be purchased (as funds allowed) and placed at suitable sites in the village'. Judd & Coleman were asked to make arrangements.

The lychgate

The memorial at the Congregational Church had been in place for two years when in 1922 the first Parochial Church Council was elected and a new vicar, William Fossett, arrived.

At a meeting on 13 October 1924 the PCC resolved to erect a lychgate, a roofed gateway to a churchyard under which a corpse is set down to await the clergyman's arrival for the funeral. The lychgate would be a memorial to those who fell in the Great War and their names would appear on it. It would be paid for by public subscription and an appeal letter would go to every householder.

At the next meeting, on 29 November, Major Frederick Green produced plans and drawings which members of the PCC found to be 'most satisfactory'. The architect advised that for reasons of space the names should not be inscribed on the lychgate but on a separate board in the church and thus the inscription carved on the lychgate read as follows: 'Erected to the memory of those of this Parish who gave their lives in the Great War'.

The lychgate shortly after it was erected in 1925

The memorial was unveiled on 30 June 1925 by Brigadier General R.B. Colvin of Monkhams in Waltham Abbey, later the Lord Lieutenant of Essex. The Bishop of Barking, the Right Reverend James Inskip, conducted the service. Leaflets about it were sent to every household in Nazeing, seating was kept for the relatives of those who had died, and special tickets ensured that those who had lost friends in the war could find room.

At its first meeting afterwards the PCC approved the accounts for the construction: 'Expenditure on lychgate £460/5/5d. Receipts from subscriptions £460/5/5d'. That seems very neat - but begs one question: since that sum could have bought one of the small terraced houses being built in Nazeing at the time, why did the work cost so much?

In 1995 the Nazeing Branch of the Royal British Legion marked the fiftieth anniversary of the end of the Second World War. With the support of the PCC, it placed next to the lychgate of All Saints' a Yorkstone memorial plaque with the names of those who died in both world wars. The vicar, Martin Webster, dedicated it as part of the Remembrance Day service on Sunday 12 November 1995.

The return of 'our boys'
The Chapel decided to mark the return of 'our boys' from the front with a 'meat tea', to which they could each bring a guest. On the platform are the village dignitaries (left to right): Joe Pegrum (with beard), unknown, Walter Hargreaves, Mrs Green, Mrs Hargreaves, Ralph Palmer, F.W. Green. The display of flags illustrates the firm belief that the Allies were fighting together to save the world from German oppression. Most eye-catching is the rising sun of Japan, which to British people twenty years later was to mean something very different.

'Meat tea' in the Chapel Hall

Welcome Home celebration outside the Chapel. People were still mourning their losses, so a moment like this of sheer joy was rare. The single lady present is Miss Sophie Pegrum who became the first woman deacon at the Chapel.

In front of the Chapel Hall:
the returning men who attended the 'meat tea'

The names below were provided by Dennis Mead and his cousin Nita Turner. Nicknames were a great feature of village life and in some cases Dennis and Nita did not know the men's real Christian names.

1. William Hampton. 2. Len Smith. 3. Alan Lawrence. 4. Stan Welch. 5. Jack Payne. 6. Ted Coleman. 7. ? Brace. 8. Bonkey Turner. 10. Harry Hutchings. 11. Arthur Dellar. 12. ? Starling. 13. ? Barnard. 14. Alfred Charles 'Bottle' Starling. 15. Will Turner. 16. Harry Mead. 17. Arthur Brett. 18. Jimmy Savage. 20. Ben Starling. 21. Will Crow. 24. Terry Brace. 25. Ernest Brace. 26. Arthur Mead. 27. Harry Starling. 28. George James. 29. Dinky Brace. 30. Fiffy Mansfield. 31. Mrs Ann Head. 33. Billy Johnson. 34. Alf Eldred. 36. Arthur Reynolds. 44. ? Starling. 45. Percy Mussell. 46. James Robertson. 47. John Harvey. 48. Ernie Mansfield. 49. William Henry Hale. 50. George Crow. 51. Frederick Mason Green. 52. George William Banks. 53. George Hampton. 54. James Brent. 58. Fred Burton.

About 125 men returned but only fifty-eight are in the photo. One lady has asked why her father is not among them. Perhaps there were two sittings at the meal or perhaps they simply did not want to be there; we do not know why and would like to find out.

'Names of Men of Nazeing Who Joined His Majesty's Forces During the Great War 1914 to 1918'

As the war progressed, the names of men who served were recorded in the Chapel minute book. We have transcribed the names and put them into a single alphabetical sequence. The list only gave initials, so to find full names we checked censuses, electoral registers, names of men identified in the 1919 Chapel photograph and those on a list of Royal British Legion members, started around 1920. We have occasionally 'corrected' spellings where they are consistently used in official records. Men who died are marked +.

It is puzzling that three men from old Nazeing families cannot be identified – F. King, B. Turner and A. Webb. This may be because widespread use of middle names and nicknames meant that the compiler of the list used an initial that does not show up in more formal records.

The only two we could not trace at all were *J. Peachey* and *J. Robinson*.

Alan Archibald Johnson and *John Victor Starling* were shown on village war memorials but are not on the Chapel list.

Frederick C.	ASHBY		Patrick	CARRIGAN
George William	BANKS		Alexander	CHARGE
Alfred	BARNARD		Alfred John	CHARGE
Horace	BARNARD		Herbert	CHARGE
S.	BARNARD		Alfred	COLEMAN
Percy	BEZER		B.	COLEMAN
Alfred	BRACE		Edward C. (Ted)	COLEMAN
Ernest Edward	BRACE		Ernest G.	COLEMAN +
George J.	BRACE		Alfred G.	CORDELL
John	BRACE		George W.	CORDELL
James	BRENT		James	CORDELL
G.	BRETT		Joseph	CORDELL
Charles	BRIDGEMAN		Ernest E.	CROW
James	BRIDGEMAN		George	CROW
Alfred	BROOKS +		John A.	CROW
Joseph H.	BROOKS		Thomas H.	CROW
L.H.	BURT		William G.	CROW
Albert H.	BURTON +		Alfred R.	DELLAR
Benjamin	BURTON		Alfred E.	ELDRED
Frederick C.	BURTON		James E.	FIELD +
George	BURTON		Frederick J.	FLACK +
James	BURTON		James	FLACK +
William E.	BURTON		Walter	GENTRY
Ralph F.	BURY		John	GLADDEN

Henry G.	GODFREY	Arthur	REYNOLDS
Norman D.	GRAHAM	James	ROBERTSON
Frederick M.	GREEN	J.	ROBINSON
Henry E.	GREEN +	James	SADLER
Bert	HALE	Harry	SAMUEL
Frank	HALE	William A.	SAMUELS
John	HALE +	James	SAVAGE
Joseph jr.	HALE	Allan H.J.	SMITH
William	HALE	Ernest A.	SMITH
George	HAMPTON	Frederick G.	SMITH
William	HAMPTON	Leonard E.	SMITH
Alfred	HARMAN +	Robert	SMITH
John	HARVEY	Robert D.	SMITH/
Walter	HITCHING		TURNER +
Henry J.	HUTCHINGS	Vaughan	SMITH
William	JOHNSON	Wyndham	SMITH
F.	KING	Frederick	SNELL +
Alan	LAWRENCE	Henry	SPENCER
William F.	LAWRENCE	Alfred C.	STARLING
Maurice G.	LIPSON	Ben	STARLING
Charles	LOCKWOOD	Henry J.	STARLING
Eric	MANSFIELD	William	STARLING
Ernest Edward	MANSFIELD	William C.	STARLING
George W.	MANSFIELD +	Ernest	THURLOW
Herbert	MANSFIELD	Frederick	THURLOW +
John	MANSFIELD	George W.	THURLOW
Philip	MANSFIELD	William J.	TILLBROOK
Arthur	MEAD	Harry	TRELEAVEN
Harry	MEAD	Albert	TURNER
William	MEAD	Alfred	TURNER
Col.Harrison	MIDWOOD	B.	TURNER
Frederick.	MONDIN	Charles A.	TURNER +
Ernest G.	MORRIS	George	TURNER +
Percy J.	MUSSELL	Sidney	TURNER +
Ernest	MYSON+	William T.	TURNER
Sidney	MYSON	Frank	WATTS +
Joseph	NICHOLLS +	A.	WEBB
Harold	PARSONS +	Andrew D.	WELCH
John W.	PAYNE	Stanley J.	WELCH
J.	PEACHEY	Eric G.	WELLESLEY +
Ivan E.	PEART	Ronald A.	WELLESLEY +
Harry	PEGRUM	Edward	WHAY
Wilfred	PEGRUM +	David R.	WOOTTON
Charles	PERRY +	Henry	WOOTTON
David	PIGG +	Joseph S.	WRIGHT +
Sidney	PIGG		
Thomas	PRITCHARD		
Francis E.	RAINCOCK		
David	RAITHBY		

Sources

Censuses, electoral registers and the 1939 Register
Original census books from 1841 to 1911 are held at the National Archive. Fully indexed images are available by subscription from the Findmypast, Ancestry and The Genealogist websites. Nazeing electoral registers from 1859 to 1932, and the 1939 Register are available through Findmypast. Some online sources can be seen free in many public libraries.

Valuation Office Survey of 1910 (Lloyd George Domesday)
In the 1970s, the then Public Record Office failed to understand the way in which these documents were compiled, so it kept maps and field books but offered valuation books to county record offices. The book by Brian Short listed below gives a very clear explanation of the Survey and the documents associated with it.

There are four field books for Nazeing, and the National Archive reference numbers are IR 58/37360, 58/37361, 58/37362 and 58/37363. All TNA images in this book are reproduced with their permission. The Essex Record Office reference for the Nazeing valuation book is A/R 2/5/27. Nazeing History Workshop has copies of all these documents for private study.

Other archival sources at Essex Record Office
A13818 Box 1. Nazeing Parish Council minutes, 1894-1939.
D/CT 249. Nazeing Tithe Award, 1847.
D/DJg B30. Palmer v Guadagni court case, 1907.
D/Z 45/6. Essex War Agricultural Committee: Epping Union Census Forms for Nazeing, 1916.

Directories for Essex were published by White's in 1848 and 1863; by the Post Office in 1851, 1855, 1862, 1867, 1874 and 1878; and by Kelly's in 1882, 1886, 1890, 1895, 1899, 1902, 1906, 1908, 1910, 1912, 1914, 1917, 1922, 1926, 1929, 1933 and 1937. They are available for reference at the Essex Record Office and at Chelmsford and Colchester Libraries, and some can be accessed online.

Newspapers are available online through the British Library Newspaper Archive, Findmypast and other websites. Court reports in this book were accessed through Findmypast. Newspaper images on pages 52 and 269 are © Chelmsford Chronicle. All rights reserved. With thanks to The British Newspaper Archive.

Indexes for **birth, marriage and death records** from 1837 are available free of charge through the FreeBMD website, and also through the General Register Office website where you can order original certificates.

The **Commonwealth War Graves Commission** website gives details of men killed in the Great War and other conflicts.

The **Landpages** database and the **reminiscence**s used in this book are held by the Nazeing History Workshop. We have extensive records of the village, too detailed to be recorded in this publication. We are happy to answer enquiries through our website www.nazeinghistorywork.wixsite.com/mysite or Facebook page https://www.facebook.com/nazeinghistoryworkshop, and would request a minimum £10 donation.

Bibliography

Every effort has been made to trace and seek permission from copyright holders, and to acknowledge all contributions to the making of the book. We shall be glad to hear from anyone who has been inadvertently omitted.

This book is based on a wide range of primary and secondary sources. The following are those of which most use has been made:

Haggard, H. Rider. *Rural England: being an account of agricultural and social researches carried out in the years 1901 & 1902.* Longman, 1906, 2 volumes.

Howkins, Alun. *Reshaping rural England: a social history 1850-1925.* Routledge, 1991.

Hunter, John. The Essex landscape: *a study of its form and history.* Essex Record Office, 1998.

Paxman, Jeremy. *Great Britain's Great War.* Viking, 2013.

Rusiecki, Paul. *The impact of catastrophe: the people of Essex and the First World War (1914-1920).* Essex Record Office, 2008.

Searle, G.R. *A New England? Peace and war 1886-1918.* Oxford University Press, 2004.

Short, Brian. *Land and society in Edwardian Britain.* Cambridge University Press, 1997.

Sykes, Marjorie. *Confident morning: memories of dear old Nazeing.* Unpublished typescript, the Author, 1980.

Thompson, E.P. *Customs in common*. Penguin, 1993.

Victoria County History of Essex. Nazeing is covered in volume 5 and is now available online at http://www.british-history.ac.uk/vch/essex/vol5/pp140-150 as well as in the 'red book' originally published in 1966.

Wormell, Peter. *The countryside in the Golden Age*. Abberton Books, 2000.

Publications of Nazeing History Workshop members as listed on the back of the title page.

Acknowledgments

The contributions of the following people were invaluable and have been noted at the appropriate places in the footnotes: Jennifer Andrews, Derek Armes, Doug Ball, Alice Barrigan, John Carr, Brian Coleman, John Coleman, Richard Coleman, Susan Coleman, Jacky Cooper, Colin Dauris, John Garbutt, Paddy Hutchings, Russell Martin, Gertrude Schoen, Samantha Sillitoe, Brian Starling, Richard Thomas, Joy Tizard.

Julie Moore of the University of Hertfordshire read through the whole text and made many useful suggestions that helped put our local research into a broader context.

Bob Fowke of YouCaxton was a terrific publisher who supported us at every stage and ensured that the finished product was far better than we could have managed on our own.

Index

Where houses have been renamed, references to them are shown under both names.

#0020 - 220518 - C0 - 229/152/25 - PB - 9781911175889